The Politics of the Anthropocene

The Politics of the Anthropocene

John S. Dryzek

Jonathan Pickering

OXFORD
UNIVERSITY PRESS

OXFORD

UNIVERSITY PRESS

Great Clarendon Street, Oxford, OX2 6DP,
United Kingdom

Oxford University Press is a department of the University of Oxford.
It furthers the University's objective of excellence in research, scholarship,
and education by publishing worldwide. Oxford is a registered trade mark of
Oxford University Press in the UK and in certain other countries

First Edition published in 2019

Impression: 1

Published in the United States of America by Oxford University Press
198 Madison Avenue, New York, NY 10016, United States of America

British Library Cataloguing in Publication Data

Data available

Library of Congress Control Number: 2018950279

ISBN 978–0–19–880961–6 (hbk)
       978–0–19–880962–3 (pbk)

PREFACE

The Anthropocene is an emerging epoch of human-induced instability in the Earth system. The challenge the Anthropocene presents to humanity is profound, meaning that in future all politics should be first and foremost a politics of the Anthropocene. We are of course a long way from that happening, as the world seems stuck with institutions, practices, and modes of thinking that were appropriate in the Holocene—the epoch of around 12,000 years of unusual stability in the Earth system, toward the end of which modern institutions such as states and capitalist markets arose. The purpose of this book is to move us a bit closer to making all politics a politics of the Anthropocene. At issue are not just particular institutions, values, and practices, but how we think of a modern world in which we are no longer estranged from the processes of the Earth system, and in which systems once categorized as non-human can be joined in a more productive relationship.

Ours is not the first book on the Anthropocene, or indeed on its specifically political implications. However, we offer here something that we believe earlier treatments miss. Some of them are still a bit stuck in modes of thought, and menus of options, developed under Holocene conditions. Others are quick to rush to prescriptions without really coming to grips with the depth of the challenge. Others still have a sophisticated understanding of the Anthropocene that is not matched by a sophisticated understanding of how governance does and can work. And yet others do not truly come to grips with the dynamic conditions of the Anthropocene that render any institutional proposal unstable, no matter how attractive it might seem. We will try to do better. We have tried to make the treatment accessible (and if there are places where we have not altogether succeeded, that may be explained by the complexity of the issues we are dealing with).

Preliminary versions of parts of this book or its whole were presented at the Workshop "On the Scale of Worlds: Technoscience and Global Governance" in the Program on Science, Technology and Society, Harvard University, 2014; the Democracy Fellows Seminar in the Ash Center, Harvard University, 2014; the 2015 and 2017 annual conferences of the Earth System Governance Project, in Canberra and Lund respectively; the Arne Naess Symposium at the University of Oslo, 2016; the International Ethics Research Seminar organized by Toni Erskine in Canberra, 2017; the Ecological Democracy workshop held at the University of Sydney, 2017; the conference of the European International Studies Association in Barcelona, 2017; the conference of the Australian Political Studies Association in Melbourne, 2017; the

Environmental Politics, Policy and Learning seminar in the Department of Political Science at Stockholm University, 2017; the Sydney Conference on Environmental Justice at the University of Sydney, 2017; the Australasian Aid Conference at the Australian National University, 2018; the convention of the International Studies Association in San Francisco, 2018; and in seminars of our own Centre for Deliberative Democracy and Global Governance at the University of Canberra.

For advice and comments on draft chapters or precursor papers, we thank Karin Bäckstrand, Christian Barry, Robert Bartlett, Andrew Dobson, Christian Downie, Sonya Duus, Victor Galaz, Peter Haas, Clive Hamilton, Marit Hammond, Stephen Hobden, Sigrid Hohle, Sheila Jasanoff, Jonathan Kuyper, Michael Mackenzie, James Meadowcroft, Richard Norgaard, Odin Lysaker, Åsa Persson, Stuart Pickering, Dominic Roser, David Schlosberg, Will Steffen, Hayley Stevenson, Dina Townsend, and Steve Vanderheiden. Annika Hernandez helped with formatting figures. We would also like to thank all our colleagues in the Earth System Governance Project. Jonathan would like to thank John for his advice, inspiration and patience in what proved to be a highly enjoyable collaboration and an ideal introduction to the craft of book-writing. Jonathan would like to thank his family for their wonderful support and encouragement along the way. The need to write clearly about changes in the Earth system that will increasingly affect generations to come was never clearer than when having to explain the idea of Anthropocene to two primary-school-aged boys over breakfast. John thanks his family (which he sometimes forgets to do), and thanks Jonathan for the pleasure of the co-authorship.

This research was supported by Australian Research Council Laureate Fellowship FL140100154. Most of the work was done in the Centre for Deliberative Democracy and Global Governance in the Institute for Governance and Policy Analysis at the University of Canberra. We are lucky to have such an excellent working environment, and such a fine group of colleagues and PhD students. Chapter 5 benefited considerably from background research undertaken by Sonya Duus on the process of negotiating the Sustainable Development Goals. John Dryzek did some of the early work while he was a Senior Democracy Fellow in the Ash Center for Democratic Governance and Innovation at Harvard University in 2014, and he thanks Archon Fung for being a great host.

We have used most of the text from John S. Dryzek, "Institutions for the Anthropocene: Governance in a Changing Earth System," *British Journal of Political Science* 46 (4) (2016): 937–56, mostly in chapters 2 and 3, though it is heavily modified, reorganized, and occasionally redacted. In chapter 7 we have used a smaller amount of text from John S. Dryzek and Jonathan Pickering, "Deliberation as a Catalyst for Reflexive Environmental Governance," *Ecological Economics* 131 (2017): 353–60.

▨ CONTENTS

LIST OF FIGURES

ABBREVIATIONS

CBD	Convention on Biological Diversity
CBDR&RC	common but differentiated responsibilities and respective capabilities
CCS	carbon capture and storage (or carbon capture and sequestration)
G20	Group of 20
HFCs	hydrofluorocarbons
ICLEI	International Council for Local Environmental Initiatives
IPBES	Intergovernmental Science-Policy Platform on Biodiversity and Ecosystem Services
IPCC	Intergovernmental Panel on Climate Change
IUCN	International Union for the Conservation of Nature
MDGs	Millennium Development Goals
NGO	non-government organization
OECD	Organization for Economic Co-operation and Development
ppm	parts per million
SDGs	Sustainable Development Goals
UNFCCC	United Nations Framework Convention on Climate Change

1 Anthropocene: the good, the bad, and the inescapable

For up to two billion years the dominant form of life on Earth consisted of anaerobic bacteria—microscopic organisms that survived without oxygen. Eventually (by about two billion years ago) one particular kind of bacteria—cyanobacteria that get their energy from photosynthesis and release oxygen as waste—had evolved and become so successful that they had managed to produce an oxygen-rich environment that was fatal to most of the existing anaerobic life on the planet.[1] This new environment pushed cyanobacteria themselves to the edge of extinction, for the Earth's climate proved much cooler than in the past. The rest is history. Particular life forms can, then, transform the Earth system in ultimately self-destructive ways, and that now holds for human life forms.

Compared to the scale of what cyanobacteria did to the Earth system to their own eventual detriment, human impacts to date have been relatively minor. The main difference is that for cyanobacteria, it took millions of years to change the character of the Earth system to the point where their existence was imperiled. For humans, the transformations have come in a matter of decades. Cyanobacteria also had plenty of time to evolve into oxygen-tolerant forms, and eventually into what today we recognize as plants (and forms of the bacteria themselves that can tolerate oxygen are still with us). Humans don't have any time at all on a geological timescale to evolve biologically. Our responses are limited to social change, which can involve culture, technology, economic systems, and governance (though there are those who have contemplated re-engineering humans; see Liao, Sandberg, and Roache 2012). The good news is that unlike cyanobacteria we have a capacity to reason through responses to planetary risks. The bad news is that so far we show few signs of exercising that capacity at all effectively.

In this book we will focus on the politics and governance of an emerging epoch of potentially catastrophic impact on the character of the Earth system that is coming to be known as the Anthropocene. Our point in starting with cyanobacteria rather than people is to highlight the sheer novelty of thinking about politics in geological time, and in Earth system terms. The Earth system

---

[1] The name "cyanobacteria" comes from their blue-green color; previously they were known colloquially as blue-green algae.

consists of the interrelated physical, chemical, and biological processes of the planet as a whole. It therefore encompasses all life, including human life, as well as planetary cycles involving carbon, nitrogen, phosphorus, water, and sulfur.

For nearly all of human history, the presence of the Earth system has not been recognized by political actors and thinkers, even if a few of them have thought about the importance of maintaining the environmental basis of human societies. It is still routinely ignored by most of them. And even those who do think something is amiss can be sidetracked by more immediate concerns: the next election, economic crashes, wars...

This will not do.

The Anthropocene

This lack of recognition of the Earth system is perhaps understandable given the unusually benign conditions under which recorded human history has taken place. Dominant forms of social organization (including political institutions) and the ideas that underpin, justify, and even criticize them were developed in Holocene conditions that are now fast disappearing. The Holocene is the recent epoch of around 12,000 years of unusual stability in the Earth system. The Pleistocene that preceded it was much more unstable, featuring occasional rapid global warmings and coolings.

The Anthropocene is an emerging epoch in which human influences become decisive in affecting the parameters of the Earth system, accompanied by the potential to generate instability and even catastrophic shifts in the character of the whole system ("state shifts") of the sort that are common in the planet's deeper history, but unknown in recorded human history. Catastrophic tipping points might stem from melting of the Greenland ice cap, or thoroughgoing tropical deforestation (Lenton et al. 2008). While climate change is the most prominent harbinger of the Anthropocene, other aspects of global environmental change may turn out to matter just as much, such as changes in the phosphorus and nitrogen cycles. For example, when waterways become excessively enriched with nutrients through run-off of phosphate-based fertilizers (a phenomenon referred to as eutrophication), oceans may lose the oxygen that marine organisms need to survive. The Anthropocene entails "an unintended experiment of humankind on its own life support system" (Steffen, Crutzen, and McNeill 2007: 614) as human activity changes the way the Earth system works.

The idea of the Anthropocene has in the past decade become increasingly accepted and disseminated by environmental scientists. The idea now has two of its own journals, *Anthropocene* and the *Anthropocene Review*, and has made its way into the mass media (beginning with *The Economist* in 2011) and global conferences, including the United Nations Rio+20 summit in 2012 (for which a group of prominent scientists prepared a short video on *Welcome to the Anthropocene*). There is some debate about when the Anthropocene began. Candidates include the invention of agriculture, the Industrial Revolution (because it led to discernible increases in the concentration of carbon dioxide in the atmosphere), the European colonization of the Americas (because this changed species distribution on a vast scale), the first atomic bomb test (because it left an enduring radioactive signature). But pinning an exact date on the commencement of the Anthropocene does not really matter that much when it comes to thinking about how to respond to it. There is much to learn from past successes and failures in responding to environmental risks,[2] but it is not as though the challenge of the Anthropocene was ever conceptualized previously, nor has it received anything like an effective global response. What matters most is that we recognize we are now in it, and need to respond.

The Anthropocene only began to press itself on collective human attention in the 1950s, with what leading climate scientist Will Steffen and his co-authors call the "Great Acceleration" in human economic activity and environmental impact (Steffen, Broadgate, et al. 2015; see Figure 1.1). Aspectsof this acceleration include the size of the global economy, investment flows, water and fertilizer use, and the number of motor vehicles. In 1945, the level of carbon dioxide in the atmosphere was just 310 ppm (parts per million), or 11 percent higher than its pre-industrial concentration of around 280 ppm. By 2016 it had increased to 401 ppm, or 43 percent higher than the pre-industrial level (Scripps CO2 Program 2018). Other indicators of ecological damage such as levels of nitrous oxide and methane in the atmosphere, ozone layer depletion, land conversion, and loss of forest cover and biodiversity reveal similar kinds of trends. In 2016 the Anthropocene Working Group of the International Commission on Stratigraphy emphasized the mid-twentieth century as the key transition point. Even though human influence can be traced back as far as the late Pleistocene (the epoch that preceded the Holocene) when hunters wiped out megafauna such as mammoths, the Working Group argued that "human activities only came to have an effect that was both large and synchronous, and thus leave a clear (chrono-) stratigraphic signal, in the mid-20th century" (Zalasiewicz et al. 2017: 57).[3]

---

[2] Bonneuil and Fressoz's (2016) account of the Anthropocene is informative in this regard, although they date the beginning of the Anthropocene to the early industrial era.

[3] The Working Group was unable to reach a majority opinion on the most suitable global stratigraphic signal to mark the beginning of the Anthropocene; the most commonly preferred option was plutonium fallout from nuclear testing (which is not itself an aspect of the Great Acceleration, even though it occurred at the same time as its onset), while other options include plastics and persistent organic pollutants found in geological deposits.

Socio-economic trends

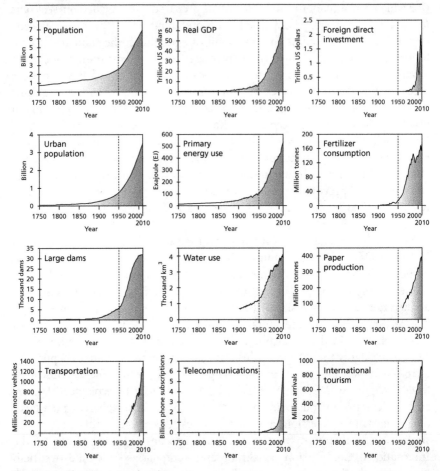

Figure 1.1. The Great Acceleration

Source: Steffen, Broadgate, et al. (2015: 4, 6, 7).

It is only in the past few years that these sorts of developments have been conceptualized in an Anthropocene frame (starting with Crutzen and Stoermer 2000). But even within this frame many thinkers (some of whom we will encounter in this book) view the Anthropocene as just a multiplication of environmental challenges. If that is all it is, then it requires simply an intensification of the existing repertoire of responses, be they tighter curbs on greenhouse gas emissions, strengthening of national and global institutions for environmental protection and resource management, or more effective incentives for people to behave in environmentally benign fashion. The challenge is

Earth system trends

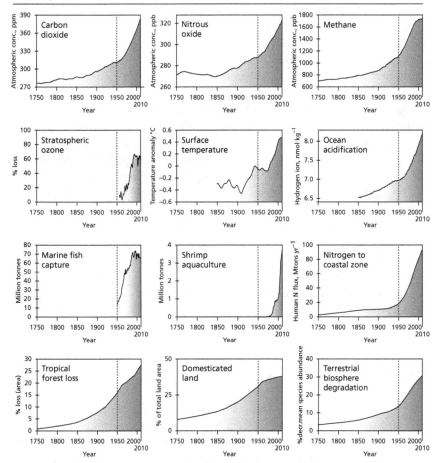

Figure 1.1. Continued

actually greater than that: the Anthropocene requires a "state shift" in the way we think about the place of the political economy in relation to the Earth system. So while it is the magnitude of human effects on the Earth system that drives the transition to the Anthropocene, it is not *just* their magnitude which is important. The transition is categorical, in the sense that what we now have is an Earth system whose core workings are affected by human activity. The Earth system and its non-human components have a much greater claim upon human institutions and practices than before—because that system is so thoroughly inflected with human forces inducing potentially catastrophic instability. The Anthropocene does, then, change the *content* of ecological concerns by putting humans at the heart of causal processes in the Earth system. In highlighting the fact that the character of the system on which we depend is so vulnerable to human action, the idea of the Anthropocene also confirms that this system is not something out there demanding limited and occasional attention. Rather, the Earth system becomes a key player in how planetary history will unfold.

Some scientists upon encountering the Anthropocene view it through restricted disciplinary lenses. But, as Clive Hamilton (2016) points out, seeing the Anthropocene through lenses such as landscape ecology (which ignores oceans) or the geography of species distribution can lead to underestimation of the profundity of the challenge it presents. The Anthropocene ought to be apprehended in more comprehensive Earth system terms; it is possible to think of the Earth system as more than just "a collection of ecosystems" (Hamilton 2016: 94). Of course, what happens in particular ecosystems as illuminated by particular disciplinary studies is still important (Oldfield 2016); it just needs to be seen against the backdrop of the larger Earth system. Moreover, Earth system science must now involve social science in a serious way: the human social processes that social scientists study take on causal primacy in the Earth system of the Anthropocene, as it is those processes that drive changes in the parameters of the Earth system. And this is where we enter in this book.

Bad Anthropocene

Dalby (2016), echoing Sergio Leone's classic Western, distinguishes good, bad, and ugly framings of the Anthropocene. If the Anthropocene were not attended by some actually and potentially bad consequences for both humanity and the Earth system, its arrival would deserve much less attention. It is possible to recognize its arrival but at the same time fight its implications. As Jamieson and Di Paola (2016: 267) put it, "one of the central tasks of politics in the Anthropocene is to restore stability to the Earth's natural systems." Yet the idea of restoring stability to natural systems is now misleading as a guide to action. To see why this is so, let us address the prominent concept of "planetary boundaries" that has been advanced by some of the same scientists who have disseminated the Anthropocene idea (Rockström et al. 2009). As we shall see, the implications of the two concepts may actually stand in some tension.

Planetary boundaries define what Rockström et al. call a "safe operating space" for humanity (see Figure 1.2). In their original formulation, there are nine boundaries that concern climate change, ocean acidification, stratospheric ozone, phosphorus and nitrogen cycles, atmospheric aerosol loading, freshwater, land use, biodiversity, and chemical pollution. The precise location of the boundary for each of these concerns is a judgment call. Thus for climate

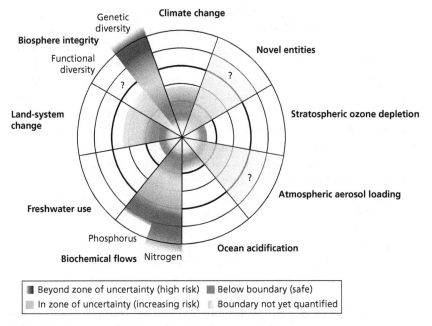

Figure 1.2. Planetary boundaries

Source: Steffen, Richardson, et al. (2015: 736).

change the original planetary boundaries statement specified that the boundary value is a concentration of 350 ppm of carbon dioxide in the atmosphere.
For stratospheric ozone, it is a 5 percent loss of ozone concentration from the
pre-industrial level. For freshwater use, it is 4,000 cubic kilometers per year. As
of 2009, when the concept was first published, three boundaries had already
been exceeded: those for climate change, biodiversity loss, and the nitrogen
cycle. In a 2015 update (Steffen, Richardson, et al. 2015), biodiversity loss was
reconceptualized as biosphere integrity, and along with climate change identified as one of the two core boundaries meriting special attention. "Novel
entities" (artificial substances and modified life forms) replaced "chemical
pollution." The boundary for land system use now appeared to have been
exceeded.

It is possible to think of planetary boundaries in three ways. First, they can
be seen as dramatizing the hazards of environmental destruction: when
approached or transgressed they show that something is seriously amiss and
that the well-being of the Earth system is threatened. In this light, they can
complement the Anthropocene concept and its implications—notably, when
it comes to the need to anticipate and prevent catastrophic state shifts in the
Earth system. But in a second sense they suggest that if we stay within them
(or, in the case of the four that have been violated, return to the safe level) all

will be well—or at least reasonably well. As such, they can be interpreted as a guide for how to avoid the more profound undesirable implications of the Anthropocene (Dryzek, Norgaard, and Schlosberg 2013: 117). In this light, the Anthropocene does not look like a thoroughly different and inescapable new epoch in the Earth system—rather it appears as a scenario that can be negated by intelligent collective action. Rockström et al. (2009) want planetary boundaries to be set at levels that would maintain Holocene conditions. This understanding of planetary boundaries shows how to resist the onset of the Anthropocene, but does not tell us much about what to do once we are in the Anthropocene in a major way. Indeed, as Lövbrand et al. (2015) note, this understanding implicitly treats nature as though it were something external to human society, rather than something in which humans are now the driving force. At one level, proponents of a Holocene-based view of planetary boundaries recognize integrated social-ecological systems, and indeed insist that their analysis is grounded in complex systems thinking. But at another level their understanding of what might constitute stability remains inflected by understandings that pre-date recognition of such integration and interconnection.

If we are already in the Anthropocene, there is no turning back to stable Holocene conditions. So this second way of thinking about planetary boundaries is possibly misleading. For one hallmark of the Anthropocene is continual change, as existing human impacts on the Earth system play out—for example, even if greenhouse gas emissions were to cease completely today, inertia in the climate system means that the consequences of past emissions would still take decades to make themselves felt—and are joined by new ones. Moreover, as the proponents of the concept recognize, different boundaries interact. So for example catastrophic loss of biosphere integrity may suggest that other boundaries need to be tightened as well.

Accompanying continual change is uncertainty and the possibility of surprise. In the dynamic and unstable Earth system that the Anthropocene heralds, boundaries may lose their precision. If the imagery of planetary boundaries is used as a guide to avoiding the Anthropocene, it is too static in the fixed guideposts it provides. As we outline in chapter 5, if the idea of planetary boundaries is to play a constructive role in informing humanity's future, it would need to be recast in a third, dynamic way that is untethered from a Holocene baseline, where boundaries can be rethought and redrawn in response to advances in scientific knowledge and to changes in the Earth system and in societal perceptions of risk. It may be the case that with time societal tolerance of particular risks can change in different directions. Thus people may become more averse to risking climate change, or less averse when it comes to risking ozone layer depletion. Here it is not unreflective public opinion that should matter, but rather considered and informed social judgments. This position stands in contrast to those in the planetary boundaries community who think that boundaries should be non-negotiable—though we recognize that these sorts of questions are debated within that community (Galaz 2014), and only some of its members take the "non-negotiable" position in which boundaries should be specified based solely on the best available science, rather than informed by considered public judgment.

The idea of avoidance and return to some historical baseline (be it valued for reasons of safety, aesthetics, or intrinsic worth) is embedded in the long-standing vocabulary of environmental concern. The words "preservation," "conservation," and "restoration," now recognizable as Holocene concepts, all suggest there is some baseline condition of environments or natural systems that can be preserved, conserved, or restored. In the Anthropocene, the condition of the system is continually moving. We cannot rewind ecosystems back to a state untouched by humans. There are some regions of the planet—notably the oceans, Antarctica, Central Greenland, and the central Sahara desert—that remain barely inhabited by humans (Caro et al. 2012). Yet the accumulating impacts of climate change mean that no corner of Earth is spared from some degree of human influence. Given the long-term effects of greenhouse gas emissions on the Earth's climate, this would remain true even if humans were to disappear overnight. Idealizations of unspoiled nature also can overlook the possibility that completely isolating wilderness from humans may not be beneficial either for humans, other species, or for wilderness itself (Cronon 1996; see also Wapner 2014). It is possible to reach deep into the pre-industrial past to find traditional ways of living that adopted a more integrated approach to humans and nature (Schmidt et al. 2016: 189). Thus for thousands of years before European occupation, Indigenous Australian peoples actively cultivated landscapes through fire and other strategies in order to maintain abundant wildlife and food (Gammage 2011). Some of these traditional practices have found new life in contemporary fire management while sequestering carbon in Australian landscapes and thereby mitigating climate change (Russell-Smith et al. 2017).

Recognition that we cannot turn the clock back to untouched ecosystems need not imply, as some would have it, the "end of nature" (for example, Vogel 2015). Nor does it mean that society should give up on setting aspirations, goals, or targets for environmental protection. Instead, it requires a capacity to rethink what nature means, embodying that capacity in institutions, and using that capacity to shape environmental policies that cultivate conditions for flourishing into the future rather than returning to the past.

Good Anthropocene

The idea of a "good Anthropocene" has gained some currency among commentators with substantial if not unbounded faith in the ability of humans collectively to assert control over social-ecological systems to good effect. The idea is especially associated with the US-based Breakthrough Institute, and encapsulated in their *Ecomodernist Manifesto* (Breakthrough Institute 2015). This manifesto positions itself in contrast to an alleged environmental mainstream that fixates on gloom and impending catastrophe. Proponents of a good Anthropocene advance specific policy prescriptions in favor of high-density city living and efficient agriculture (in order to take as many people as possible out of ecosystems still styled as "natural"), genetically modified foods, and nuclear power. If necessary, geoengineering can be called upon to rectify or prevent damage to the Earth system—for example, by injecting sulfate aerosols into the upper atmosphere to block sunlight and so reduce global warming. Advocates of a good Anthropocene are mainly concerned to celebrate and advance the idea of benign human control over the natural world. They are certainly alive to the potential of human-induced environmental catastrophes involving climate change, ocean acidification, ozone layer depletion, and the like, but they believe the catastrophes can be averted and a bright future assured. The rhetoric emphasizes hope, optimism, and opportunity—not dire warnings.

Some of the specific policy proposals advanced by advocates of the good Anthropocene, such as expanding nuclear power and genetically modified agriculture, might be controversial in environmental circles—though a defensible case could also be made for them. What sets the idea of the good Anthropocene apart is perhaps the rhetoric—and the sense of reassurance it seeks to provide that all can be well, provided we craft the proper developmental path. What this kind of rhetoric downplays is the possibility of surprise, which is one of the hallmarks of the Anthropocene—crystallized in the idea of potentially catastrophic state shifts. We will argue in chapter 3 that a primary requirement of political institutions in the Anthropocene is the capacity to anticipate and prevent potentially catastrophic shifts in the Earth system. In addition, technological optimism can cloud the need to think in terms of social, political, and economic structures that have their own logic and momentum that will shape (for example) which technologies get adopted, and to what end. For example, genetically modified agriculture could mean feeding people more efficiently and reducing pressure to clear forests for farmland—or it could mean concentration of economic power in the hands of a few companies, the subordination of farmers in developing countries, and an environment thoroughly degraded by agrochemicals. Above all, in reasserting human domination—even if it is in the interests of leaving some of nature alone—the proponents of a good Anthropocene do not recognize the active role of "nature" itself, and the need to think in terms of social-ecological systems, rather than human systems and ecological systems separately. There is a need to listen to those systems more effectively—rather than either to engineer them or to leave them alone (which is the combination the

Breakthrough Institute seems to favor). If it was human arrogance that created the manifold problems accompanying the Anthropocene, it is far from clear that the solution should involve still more hubris.

Inescapable Anthropocene

The Anthropocene is not just something bad to be lamented and avoided as far as possible. Nor is it something good to be embraced, mastered, and celebrated. Rather, it is inescapable, and must be negotiated. The challenge extends well beyond areas of governance and policy traditionally classified as environmental. The Anthropocene is something that humanity must continually learn and relearn to live with, for the Anthropocene admits no response that is permanently adequate. Its hallmark is the generation of novel challenges and crises in the Earth system, even if and as we learn to remake connections with social-ecological systems in more productive fashion. Our understandings of how to negotiate the relationship between human and non-human nature need to change accordingly. The Anthropocene is now for better or worse humanity's chronic condition, a constant presence.

We have already argued that the Anthropocene, understood in biophysical terms, involves a categorical shift resulting from the impact of the "Great Acceleration" of material production and consumption and consequent environmental degradation in recent decades. It also entails a categorical shift in the way we think about the place of humanity within the Earth system. In subsequent chapters we will show how this shift requires a thoroughgoing reappraisal of concepts of rationality, democracy, sustainability, and justice.

To illustrate the challenges posed by an inescapable Anthropocene, let us contrast our picture with that of Naomi Klein (2014) in her bestselling book about climate change, *This Changes Everything*. Klein thinks that the contemporary international capitalist economy will have to be discarded, along with its institutions, because it is incapable of controlling itself in the way climate change demands. Such discarding—and replacement by something better—is the kind of once-and-for-all change that the idea of an inescapable Anthropocene reveals as inadequate. In the Anthropocene, no institutional solution may be stable for very long—and that includes Klein's own proposed stress on democratic planning, collectivism, and human development.

While Klein's view is radical, it is also prosaic. That is, she sees the world in terms of the options set in industrial society, even if she wants to overthrow its currently dominant system (liberal democratic capitalism). The Anthropocene involves thinking about social-ecological systems in novel terms in which the non-human is an active participant, and not just in terms of options developed in industrial society well before recognition of the profound, whole Earth system character of ecological challenges.

We should also stress the distinction between *changing* everything (which Klein stresses) and *rethinking* everything (which we stress). Calls for change are not necessarily preceded by a rigorous process of rethinking, let alone recognition of the necessity for continual rethinking. Conversely, it is possible to rethink everything but conclude that not everything needs to change, if the maintenance of some existing institutions proves conducive to the ability to contemplate systemic change that we prize. We will argue that some (but not all) aspects of existing democratic institutions can have such value.

In short, the Anthropocene requires deep, thoroughgoing, and imaginative response on a scale beyond that envisaged by Klein in response to climate change. The problem of climate change is enormous, but it is not the full story. If climate change does indeed change everything in the way Klein suggests, it would seem that an effective response to the Anthropocene requires more than just changing everything. Instead, it needs to involve a permanent capacity to rethink everything: institutions, practices, social structures, worldviews, principles, and systems. Especially, given the lack of fixed reference points in ever-unfolding social-ecological systems, institutions for the Anthropocene are better analyzed not in light of static criteria (referring perhaps to their efficiency in solving problems, their capacity to coordinate actions across different facets of responses to complex problems, or even the degree to which they can respect global ecological limits), but rather in these sorts of dynamic terms.

The broad-ranging requirement to be able to rethink everything means that, although environmental concerns are prominent, the Anthropocene has implications well beyond what has traditionally been classified as environmental affairs. Accordingly, this book is not confined to environmental politics, but is about politics in general in the Anthropocene. While we will explain why current political institutions struggle to deal with the implications of the Anthropocene, our ultimate aim is to specify how political institutions and practices should respond to the challenges posed by the Anthropocene.

The social disciplines respond, questionably

As we have already noted, the Anthropocene ought to presage enhanced roles for thinking about the place of human action and social systems in both causing and responding to ecological change. There has recently been an explosion of such thinking in academic and public debate. To date the contributions have not always been salutary; obviously we hope to do better! At the same time, we have sought to learn from insights that this thinking has produced so far.

The Anthropocene for Show. Environmental concerns have been around for a long time. The Anthropocene concept means seeing them in a new way—or at least adding a new title. So for example the landmark statement published in *Science* in 2012 by thirty-two leading environmental social scientists is entitled "Navigating the Anthropocene: Improving Earth System Governance" (Biermann et al. 2012). The word "Anthropocene" does, then, figure prominently in the title of the article—but does not appear in its text. The article sets out an approach to better global environmental governance—but it could have been written without the onset of the Anthropocene having been recognized. In a subsequent book by Biermann (2014), with Anthropocene in the subtitle, the word achieves greater prominence in the text, though most of the analysis would stand without reference to the idea. Jedediah Purdy's (2015) book *After Nature: A Politics for the Anthropocene* is mostly a history of American environmental law and policy over several centuries (although he does begin to explore what the Anthropocene might mean for legal and political institutions in the final chapter).

The Anthropocene for show is also on display whenever contemporary developments are treated as necessarily helping to define the epoch. Jamieson and Di Paola (2016) do this in their treatment of "new kinds of agents"—such as transnational corporations, non-governmental organizations, international organizations, and criminal syndicates. Such agents have of course long been recognized and analyzed by those both without and with an interest in global ecological affairs. What can happen here is that the Anthropocene just provides a new heading for established analyses of and prescriptions for ecological issues—without changing anything when it comes to their content. "In the Anthropocene,..." can be used to add rhetorical force to a point without affecting its substance.

It's the Economy, Stupid. The Anthropocene presses itself on us with the "Great Acceleration" that begins around 1950. Central to that acceleration is economic growth—more so than human population growth. While the human population has tripled since 1950, the size of the global economy has increased by a factor of 15 or so. For this reason, Norgaard (2013) suggests we should refer to the "Econocene" rather than Anthropocene. Most (though not all) of that growth has involved capitalist economies, so Jason Moore and Donna Haraway are more specific still in referring to a "Capitalocene" (Moore 2016; Haraway 2015). While it is possible to recognize the logic, humans will always need economic organization, but in that case there is no real difference between invoking the Econocene and invoking the Anthropocene. For Norgaard it is economic *growth* rather than the economy per se that justifies his terminology, but then what happens should growth cease but human impacts continue? The Capitalocene for its part ties itself too closely to what may prove to be an ephemeral aspect of human social organization. The Soviet Union left behind a legacy of widespread environmental destruction (McNeill and

Engelke 2016), and it is entirely possible that capitalism as we know it will be superseded by a different economic system—but human impacts on the Earth system will continue unabated.

Complicating the Definition. In a comment in the leading scientific journal *Nature*, Ellis, Maslin, Boivin, and Bauer (2016) argue that social scientists should play a greater role in ongoing debates about when to date the beginning of the Anthropocene. Their reasoning is in some ways the opposite of that of Norgaard and Haraway, in that they stress the importance of recognizing the long history of human environmental impacts in many different sorts of societies (not just recent capitalist ones). In emphasizing the geographically variable nature of these impacts, they also question the centrality of thinking in terms of the Earth system as a whole. Again, it is possible to see the logic, given the primacy that human social processes have assumed in affecting the character of ecological systems—including the Earth system. However, participation by social scientists here would come at some cost. It is not just that the social sciences are riven by internal disagreements that could be manifested in defin-itional disputes. We suspect that the formal characteristics of the Anthropocene as a geological epoch are primarily a matter for natural scientists. Social scientists can still illuminate the causes of the Anthropocene, and of course the implications for social, political, and economic institutions and practices.

Deconstructing the Concept. Words can come with plenty of implicit baggage, and the Anthropocene is no exception. In stark contrast to its initiators and developers, for whom the Anthropocene is a scientific concept, some social thinkers treat it as a primarily political construct that serves some interests and represses others. In this sense (not the one we use in this book), "the politics of the Anthropocene" would mean political controversy around what the word means and the political effects of its use. For example, the concept may appear to invoke an undifferentiated humanity as being to blame for the dire condi-tion of the Earth system (Di Chiro 2016)—as opposed to wealthy consumers and producers, mainly in developed countries, who should more rightfully be blamed (we will pursue this question further in our chapter 4 on justice). Some feminists argue that the epoch should more properly be styled the Manthropo-cene, reflecting the responsibility of male domination in ecologically destructive societies (Di Chiro 2017). From a different perspective, Crist (2013) thinks that the concept of the Anthropocene necessarily celebrates rather than simply describes human domination of what was the natural world. As we have seen, advocates of a "good Anthropocene" may be celebrating but certainly not those who see the emerging epoch as either bad or inescapable.

Lövbrand et al. (2015) want to "unsettle the Anthropocene" with "inter-pretive multiplicity," to show how the concept can and should mean so many different things to different sorts of people. They celebrate the variety of ways that people can and do interact with each other and with non-humans, and in this light treat the Anthropocene as a cultural rather than a scientific object. They criticize Earth system science, which they believe sees the Anthropocene as presenting a managerial problem requiring expert administrative solution and consequently involving thorough depoliticization. They want to shed light on the values and beliefs that may be taken for granted by experts who think about the Earth system and the Anthropocene. However, seeking to revoke the special status of expert knowledge here is risky. We will argue (beginning in chapter 2) that it is possible to recognize scientific knowledge while seeing the politics in very different—and very democratic and non-managerial—terms.

The view held by some postmodern theorists that scientific concepts can be assessed in political terms has been appropriated most effectively by climate change deniers—for whom climate science is simply "warmist" ideology. Such an approach resonates with the kind of post-truth politics for which opinions are much more important than facts—including facts as revealed by scientists—and facts are subordinated to ideology. We find in contemporary populism a contempt for experts and scientific knowledge. There is an unfortunate continuity from the more extreme kind of deconstruction to demagogues such as Donald Trump (even though most deconstructionists might oppose the substance of Trump's politics).

Addressing the Anthropocene

Keeping in mind the pitfalls we have identified, our own analysis will attempt to interrogate exactly what is novel about the depth of the challenge to institutions and practices presented by the Anthropocene. We shall not venture to rename the new epoch, or worry about when it begins. We are receptive to interpretive multiplicity (indeed, one of us has written a book that sets out the variety of environmental discourses that interpret the world in very different ways; see Dryzek 2013b). However, it is possible for something to be socially interpreted *and* real. The Anthropocene may be open to interpretation in different ways, but at the same time it captures some real developments in the Earth system. In the same way, people can make very different things of climate change, or loss of biological diversity; yet climate change *is* happening, and it *is* due primarily to greenhouse gas emissions; biological diversity *is* being lost worldwide.

Systems Thinking for the Anthropocene. Thinking in terms of systems is necessary for understanding the Anthropocene and its implications for human institutions and practices. First and foremost, the very idea of the

Anthropocene turns on recognition of the way human influence affects how the Earth system works. The Earth system now exemplifies how coupled or integrated social-ecological systems—in which social institutions and ecosystems operate not in isolation but as interacting wholes—may exist at a global scale, in addition to regional and local scales. Feedback loops in the Earth system play a critical role in producing the unstable conditions of the Anthropocene, for example when human-induced climate change melts polar ice, thereby reducing the Earth's ability to reflect solar radiation and triggering further warming. In chapter 2 we will encounter other kinds of feedback loops that serve to entrench Holocene institutions.[4]

Thinking in terms of whole systems is, then, essential. However, it can be hazardous if it obscures what is going on in particular elements of systems—particularly the human elements. In the words of the Brundtland report (which we will encounter again in chapter 5), "The Earth is one but the world is not" (World Commission on Environment and Development 1987: 27). We have already addressed the concern that an Earth system perspective could come at the cost of recognizing differences in responsibility among social and economic groups for damaging the Earth system, and for correcting that damage. Another concern (raised by Lövbrand et al. 2015) is that lumping social and ecological systems together can make it too easy to assume that social systems function like ecosystems. Thus, properties such as self-organization and decentralization may be accorded greater value in social systems simply because they are observed as properties of ecosystems. There is a long history of justifying human social arrangements on the grounds that they are consistent with nature (Dryzek and Schlosberg 1995; Purdy 2015). In the past century and a half, these sorts of arguments have been used to justify everything from free market capitalism to liberal democracy to anarchism to fascism to socialism.

This dubious history suggests that straightforward analogies between social and ecological systems should be treated with caution. Yet the quest to link social and ecological systems perspectives is not futile. Rather, a sounder foundation for social-ecological systems analysis may be established through recognizing first that social and political systems function in distinctive ways, then identifying and remedying the ecological blind spots of existing perspectives on those systems. There are plenty of ecological blind spots in social systems perspectives—particularly those that ignore the Earth system, or treat it as (for example) simply a pathway for the transmission of economic "externalities" from some human actors to others. But there are also blind spots in ecological systems perspectives that do not recognize the capacity of human systems to reflect upon their own structure and process, and intentionally reorganize themselves.

---

[4] For an accessible introduction to key concepts in systems thinking, see Meadows (2008).

Democratic Thinking for the Anthropocene. One promising way to overcome these sorts of blind spots, which we will revisit later in this book, involves rethinking the institutions of democracy. The anthropocentric (human-centered) bias of traditional conceptions of liberal democracy and corresponding subordination of the non-human world are well established (see Eckersley 2004). We will argue that a deliberative understanding of democracy—with meaningful communication at its heart—can help render democratic institutions more responsive to signals from the natural world. But equally a systems perspective on deliberative democracy is vital for appreciating how signals from human and non-human nature are represented and transmitted through political institutions, and how those institutions may rethink their core aims and values in light of Anthropocene conditions and modify their practices accordingly. Building the capacity of deliberative systems requires more than ticking off a checklist of required institutions (such as periodic elections or an independent judiciary). Deliberative capacity depends on the quality of relationships among different parts of the system (Dryzek 2009). The parts in question are not restricted to the formal institutions of government (such as legislatures, executives, and international organizations), but can also cover civil society, the media, experts, citizens—and non-human nature. The relationships can involve both the transmission of information about conditions, preferences, principles, practices, and values and also the accountability of power-holders to others in the system.

Preview

When it comes to confronting the implications of the Anthropocene, it is essential to contemplate how in the late Holocene humans and their social institutions managed to endanger their planetary comfort zone. In chapter 2 we take a close look at how governance has evolved under Holocene conditions. Further evolution that could enable governance to grapple with Anthropocene conditions proves to be blocked where it is most needed, as dominant institutions such as states and markets have found ways to organize feedback that confirms their own necessity, but fails to take signals from a changing Earth system seriously enough—let alone anticipate future crises in that system. As a result they block institutional and policy innovation, and dysfunctional institutions and practices help constitute highly problematic—even pathological—path dependency.

The opposite of path dependency is reflexivity, which can be defined as the capacity of structures, systems, and sets of ideas to question their own core commitments, and if necessary change themselves; to be something different, rather than just do different things. Chapter 3 develops the idea of a specifically ecological reflexivity—one that listens and responds to signals from the Earth system, and has the foresight to anticipate potentially catastrophic changes in the system. We apply this idea to governance, and show exactly how ecological reflexivity struggles with problematic path dependencies, and how more effectively deliberative practices and institutions can help. We do not offer any new model of governance (because no fixed model is appropriate in an ever-changing Earth system)—but we do show how to think about building the capacity of governance to change, which is much more important than any particular model.

Reflexivity means the capacity to reconsider core values. In chapter 4 we make our own contribution to this rethinking about the core value of justice, which many people think is the most important social value (we do not necessarily agree). Against those who think invoking an Anthropocene emergency threatens to obliterate justice, we show how justice itself can be productively reimagined to make sense of the Anthropocene. The resultant planetary justice can incorporate traditional concerns about distribution across rich and poor and the need to alleviate poverty. But planetary justice is much more imaginative in how it integrates justice toward future generations, non-humans, and the Earth system itself.

The concept of sustainability has been around longer than that of the Anthropocene, and indeed its discourse has dominated global environmental affairs for several decades, though sustainable development has nowhere been achieved in practice. Recognition of the Anthropocene means that sustainability too needs to be rethought under more challenging circumstances, and this is what we do in chapter 5. Sustainability needs to become more reflexive: more open to a range of understandings about its own essence (within limits), more ecologically grounded, more dynamic in its responsiveness to changing conditions in society and the Earth system, more far-sighted in its ability to anticipate future problems (such as state shifts in the Earth system), and more effectively integrated with other social values (such as justice and democracy).

The first five chapters suggest that substantial rethinking is necessary when it comes to governance, justice, sustainability, and related concepts. But who exactly is capable of this kind of rethinking, disrupting path dependencies in ideas, and so giving shape to the Anthropocene? In chapter 6 we look at the agents who might step up: notably, discourse entrepreneurs (who can advance the standing of particular discourses such as that of the Anthropocene itself, or shift the balance within or across discourses—for example in bending moral or religious discourses in an ecological direction), scientists and other experts, cities and sub-national governments, and those most vulnerable to a damaged Earth system. We also show how non-human nature has some of the attributes of agents, and can play a role in the necessary rethinking. We pay less attention to more conventional agents such as states, international organizations, and corporations, whose actions are of course vitally important—but who are not well placed to be the motive force of change in ideas.

All of the agents discussed in chapter 6 have their problems and limitations. Many of these limitations can be overcome in interactions between these agents—provided these interactions are in good deliberative and democratic order. In chapter 7 we develop the idea of a "formative sphere" of such interactions, which gives form or shape to the meaning of the Anthropocene and how its implications will be taken on board in collective decision-making. An effective formative sphere will operate according to principles of a deliberative and ecological democracy that is capable of questioning its own foundations; we show what this can look like in practice. Chapter 8 concludes with reflections on the possibility of a practical politics that can create pathways toward the transformations needed to face the Anthropocene.

Conclusion

The Anthropocene now represents an inescapable condition with dramatic consequences for human institutions, values, principles, and practices. If that condition is not recognized or (even worse) if it is explicitly denied, humanity will continue to stumble into a succession of catastrophes. If it is recognized, then there remains much work to be done to figure out how to respond most effectively, for it is not at all obvious how to do so. In this book we aim to contribute to that effort. We begin in the next chapter by examining dominant political institutions and exactly why they appear so poorly equipped to respond to the challenges of the Anthropocene.

2 Governance in the Holocene

As befits a book about the politics of the Anthropocene, we mostly look forward in trying to develop principles and practices for this emerging epoch. But appropriate to a politics that we can now recognize as properly located in deep geological time, before looking forward we need to look back. We need to see exactly why governance institutions (including markets as well as states and international organizations) got to be the way they are—and what this can tell us about how they might change in future. In this chapter we therefore examine how and why dominant institutions that developed under seemingly benign Holocene conditions have come to be bogged down in some pathological path dependencies that severely limit their capacity to respond to the challenges of the Anthropocene. Those institutions have occasionally tried to respond—and their attempts are instructive in thinking about how better to move forward. To date these attempts have been insufficient in overcoming the complicity of entrenched institutions in further destabilizing the Earth system, suggesting something more thoroughgoing is required when it comes to building capacity for institutional transformation. That capacity will be the topic of the next chapter.

History lessons

A glance at human history suggests we have done quite well collectively in solving some major problems—a few of which once looked like permanent conditions. Take for example war. War between countries, once a chronic feature of the international system, now rarely happens Pinker (2011). Even though a number of serious interstate conflicts have flared up in recent decades—and a growing share of organized violence worldwide takes the form of civil wars or terrorism—global death rates from war have fallen considerably since the end of World War II and especially since the end of the Cold War. Global cooperation on public health has also yielded notable successes in eradicating diseases that have stalked humanity for much of its history, including smallpox and polio (Deaton 2013). Of course we cannot be sure past successes will persist. There is no guarantee war between states will not return; after all, ninety-nine years of relative peace in Europe ended in 1914.[1] Despite success in controlling many (although by no means all) infectious diseases, national and global institutions have struggled to deal with growing rates of non-communicable diseases associated with the diffusion of unhealthy lifestyles beyond Western countries.

The cases of interstate war and infectious disease control do though suggest that things can change for the better; but some things do not change, even when it is apparent that they should. Countries can collapse into chaos rather than craft effective responses to the challenges that beset them; think of China in the early twentieth century. Looking into the deeper past, Jared Diamond (2005) shows how societies such as the Greenland Norse, Anasazi, Maya, and Easter Islanders failed to adapt to environmental change, and perished as a result.[2] When it comes to confronting existential challenges, the lessons of history turn out to be quite ambiguous—or perhaps just very subtle.

Human institutions are quite well adapted to confronting some kinds of challenges—but much less well adapted when it comes to other sorts. Existing institutions such as national governments, international organizations, and capitalist markets must have done something well, otherwise they would not have persisted for such a long time (in human historical time, that is; in geological time, they have not been around very long at all). So what is it that they have done well, and what are the implications for confronting the challenges of the Anthropocene?

Aside from the decline of war between countries and controlling infectious diseases, dominant institutions in today's world are especially good when it comes to producing and maintaining economic growth. The institutions in question are the capitalist market economy and states. The latter are so well adapted to the task that they can mostly be described as capitalist states.

But states were not always capitalist states, so it is instructive to see how they got to be that way. Early modern states—operating from the seventeenth to the nineteenth century—had to perform three main tasks: keep order internally, respond to threats from potentially hostile states, and raise the money necessary for both keeping internal order (mostly by coercive means) and for external competition (Skocpol 1979). It was only with the rise of capitalist market economies that states realized they could raise more money not just by squeezing taxpayers ever more tightly, but also, and more effectively, by

---

[1] This period still included a number of interstate wars (among them the Crimean War and the Franco-Prussian War) but the scale was considerably smaller than in the periods before or after (Pinker 2011: 52–3; Gat 2013: 152).

[2] While some of Diamond's cases are controversial (see Hunt 2006 and Rull et al. 2013), his general point that—societies *can* collapse rather than effectively confront environmental change—holds.

encouraging the conditions for economic growth, while keeping tax rates constant (or even reducing them). Thus economic growth became the main priority of states, reinforced by a new mutually beneficial relationship between government and business elites.

The capitalist state was not the end of the story: capitalism created an organized working class, whose threat in many countries to the state's internal order was eventually neutralized by creation of the welfare state, beginning at the end of the nineteenth century. Workers whose standards of living were secured by the welfare state had less incentive to support radical movements that would try to overthrow that state. The demise of the organized working class associated with falling union membership in established industrialized countries a century later enabled a return to a purer capitalist state.

This potted history of governance suggests that dominant institutions such as states can adapt to new challenges and opportunities—but only if the challenge strikes at one of their existing core priorities, or the opportunity reinforces one of those priorities. In addition, the threat of political instability can receive a significant response, as shown by the creation of the welfare state in response to the threat posed by an organized working class. A much smaller-scale manifestation of this sort of effect—though very significant in light of our ecological concerns—can be found around 1970, when the United States government under President Richard Nixon adopted a range of environmental institutions and policies in a successful effort to draw the environmental movement away from a potentially destabilizing counterculture and into mainstream politics (Gottlieb 1993: 109).

If these circumstances involving danger to core state priorities do not hold, then a very different dynamic comes into play, one that can obstruct innovation and adaptation in governance rather than facilitate them. In the absence of clear threats to their core established priorities, dominant institutions are free to organize feedback that reinforces their own necessity. And this they do with alacrity. Dominant financial institutions such as banks become so central to the economy that, even if they fail, governments have to come to their rescue. Financial markets establish mechanisms (such as capital flight across borders) to ensure that national and sub-national governments do not adopt policies that will hurt the interests of business. Governments fear above all the reactions of financial markets, and so do everything they can to accommodate them and maintain the conditions for economic growth. National governments have joined in establishing global institutions such as the World Trade Organization that reinforce market imperatives and punish states that step out of line.

This different dynamic in which dominant Holocene institutions perpetuate themselves and obstruct alternatives can be thought of and analyzed in terms of path dependency, and that is what we will do in the rest of this chapter. Now, not all path dependency is bad; if an institution, practice, or set of ideas has manifestly and permanently benign consequences, then its path dependency should be welcomed. Examples might include government departments with an explicitly environmental mandate, or the solidification into a constitution of the precautionary principle and the "polluter pays" principle (for damage caused by pollution), or the entrenchment of a system of environmental rights in a legal system. Conversely, not all disruption of path dependency should be applauded; the administration of Donald Trump successfully disrupted continuity in the mission of the US Environmental Protection Agency by undermining its capacity to enforce regulations, through budget and staffing cuts and discretionary executive actions to relax environmental standards for many pollutants.

Thus it is only a particular kind of path dependency that needs to be condemned and countered in the Anthropocene. Our concern is not with path dependency as such, but only with path dependency that ignores feedbacks from a changing Earth system. What we will refer to as pathological path dependency decouples human institutions from the Earth system by embodying feedback mechanisms that systematically repress information about the condition of the Earth system, and systematically prioritize narrowly economic concerns.[3] As a result, such institutions undermine the conditions for the flourishing of human and ecological systems alike. For ease of exposition we will sometimes omit the "pathological" adjective; but it should always be read as present, except when we refer explicitly to "benign path dependency."[4]

In chapter 1 we argued that the Anthropocene demands an enduring ability to rethink institutions, practices, worldviews, principles, and systems that is clearly the opposite of path dependency. In chapter 3 we elaborate on the idea of reflexivity to capture such a capacity. There is a contest between pathological path dependency and reflexivity, which reflexivity needs to win. But to do so, reflexivity needs to interrupt path dependency, to become itself a core priority of dominant institutions, in a way without precedent in human history. This is the most profound challenge that the Anthropocene now presents.

In order to meet the challenge we need a thorough understanding of how Holocene institutions are stuck in pathological path dependencies—and why existing dominant economic and political institutions have mostly failed to respond effectively to the Anthropocene. We look at how environmental concern has fared in institutions that developed under Holocene conditions, and set out their path dependencies, explaining why dysfunctional institutions persist. Path dependency in dominant institutions is complicit in destabilizing

---

[3] It would be possible to speak of "ecologically decoupled path dependency" as the core problem but that is a bit of a mouthful, so we will use "pathological path dependency" instead.

[4] An emphasis on path dependency is evident in theories of ecology and evolutionary biology as well as in political science and economics. Despite this, analyses of political path dependency are often at pains to emphasize the disanalogy between the social and the ecological realms (see for example Pierson 2000: 253).

the Earth system, and constrains what these institutions can do and how they can be changed in response to the emerging epoch of the Anthropocene.

Holocene institutions

It was during the Holocene that large-scale civilization—and its political institutions—arose, and so this epoch represents "the only state of the Earth system that we know for sure can support contemporary society" (Steffen et al. 2011: 739). This unusual stability meant that political and economic institutions could generally take for granted the presence of the non-human world and the ecological systems in which human societies are embedded—though, as we have already noted, local ecological collapses did spell the end of some societies. Of course, the non-human world and ecological systems have always been vital for human existence, even when they were not noticed.

Some ecologically successful institutions took shape in the Holocene. Notably, resource-dependent communities often created rules to prevent the abuse of commons resources such as forests, fisheries, and water supply (Ostrom 1990). Some of these rules have persisted for centuries—suggesting benign path dependency. Those rules were a matter of necessity, for abuse of these resources could otherwise lead to their destruction and so to the end of the communities that depended on them. But even in the case of commons resources, institutional success came most straightforwardly in the form of rules or informal arrangements to control access (such as limiting the catch an individual could take, or the season in which the resource could be used) rather than in adaptation to ecological dynamism of the sort that could be expected were stable Holocene conditions to change. In addition, most of the success stories highlighted by Ostrom and colleagues involved local, small-scale communities. Once we move beyond the local level, success is less easily identified. Indeed, Holocene institutions eventually proved adept at simply ignoring ecological constraints, because they were detached from local resource and environmental limitations. If it is possible to secure food and other resources through trade with distant others (or through colonial exploitation), there is much less incentive to conserve what can be found locally, and to take care of the local ecosystems that sustain these resources.

Above the local level, the main political institution of the modern (late Holocene) era is the state. As states took on more functions—notably for ensuring economic growth and providing social welfare—the non-human world was still generally ignored or suppressed. At most it was treated as potentially productive land and resources, to which property rights could be attached so that the land could become economically useful.

Liberal democracies eventually came to do a better job of recognizing ecological concerns than earlier forms of states. They did so in response to social and political mobilization on behalf of environmental values, be they wilderness preservation, recreational opportunities, or opposition to pollution and its evident damage to human health. Arguably these movements were boosted by a "post-material" consciousness under which material security enables people to begin thinking about other values—such as wilderness, or clean and safe environment (Inglehart 1977). The rise of environmental activism beginning in the 1960s could even be seen as a benign aspect of path dependency to the degree it is generated by growing prosperity attending economic growth. However, as we will see in chapter 4, activism on the part of those calling for environmental justice and emphasizing the degree to which environmental damage falls most heavily on the poor and marginalized also came to play an important role.

By the 1960s the idea of environmental policy crystallized (though particular anti-pollution and resource conservation policies have a longer history). Broad recognition of the global nature of the ecological challenge to human societies arrived in the 1970s. This recognition peaked with the publication in 1972 of *The Limits to Growth* report, whose analysis found that if existing global trends in population and economic growth continued, the world faced a future of economic and social collapse once global carrying capacity was exceeded (Meadows et al. 1972). The concept of carrying capacity comes from the idea that in any ecosystem there is an upper boundary on the numbers of any one species that the ecosystem can support. For example, just as a grassland ecosystem can support a relatively large number of deer, and a much smaller number of wolves, so there may be an upper limit to the number of people the global ecosystem can support. However, when it comes to people, carrying capacity depends crucially on the amount of resources each person consumes. The ability of each person to consume large quantities of resources is far greater than that of a single deer or wolf because humans are able to create complex systems to extract, transform, exchange, accumulate, and destroy raw materials, so the size of the global economy is more relevant than population. The *Limits to Growth* did contain some policy prescriptions—notably, an endorsement of the idea put forward by political philosopher John Stuart Mill in the nineteenth century of a "stationary state" in which there is no economic growth (Meadows et al. 1972: 175)—but said little about how political institutions would need to change.

The concept of limits to growth has fluctuated in its prominence in global environmental affairs since the 1970s, but it has never quite gone away. While the Club of Rome, which sponsored the *Limits to Growth* report, was composed largely of prominent business people, the concept of limits also finds a place in more radical sorts of Green politics, where it helps give a sense of urgency to what Greens want to do (Dobson 1990: 3). In the 1980s the concept took a back seat to the idea of sustainable development, which became the dominant way of thinking about global environmental affairs. The 1987 Brundtland Report to the United Nations, *Our Common Future*, sought the simultaneous pursuit of economic growth, environmental conservation, and social justice. But the concept of limits lingered in the background of the Brundtland Report (World Commission on Environment and Development 1987: 45) and sustainable development more generally. However, the limits concept was often treated in ambiguous fashion, as making sustainability necessary but at the same time putting few restrictions on economic growth—provided that growth is pursued the right way. Unfortunately, since 1987 economic growth has generally not embodied sustainability of the kind that Brundtland and her successors sought.

The 1970s did see an expansion in the scope of environmental concerns and responses by many governments, and that expansion has continued incrementally since then—along with setbacks when anti-environmental governments came to power, or global negotiations on issues such as climate change featured prolonged impasse. However, for all national governments, ecological concerns have remained subordinate to the core economic, security, and welfare priorities of states that we described earlier (for more detail, see Dryzek et al. 2003).

Turning to the global level, states have engaged with each other in attempts to negotiate global environmental agreements, but to date they fall far short of the sort of action that *The Limits to Growth*—and its more recent successor, planetary boundaries, as discussed in chapter 1—imply is necessary.[5] The 1987 Montreal Protocol for protection of the ozone layer remains the only unambiguously successful collective response to a potentially catastrophic problem (which can be interpreted as an effort to stay within one planetary boundary, that for stratospheric ozone). For a long time, climate change has proved a much tougher issue to confront. The Conference of the Parties to the United Nations Framework Convention on Climate Change (UNFCCC) held in Paris in 2015 did produce a landmark agreement, and an aspiration to keep the average global temperature rise to within 1.5 degrees Celsius above pre-industrial averages. But the sum of commitments that countries have made under the Paris Agreement to reduce emissions of greenhouse gases does not yet come close to making this aspiration possible (UNEP 2016a). And in the past, different countries have proved very good at negotiating the terms of their compliance with international environmental agreements in ways which

---

[5] Planetary boundaries dispense with the idea of global carrying capacity that was central to *Limits*, and say much less about the dynamics of overshoot and collapse. Planetary boundaries are more carefully framed in terms of complex systems, but are silent on the dynamics of human systems (concerning, for example, the trajectory of economic growth). We will have more to say in chapter 5 about how planetary boundaries can be rethought.

meet the letter of their commitment—but which in practice let them get around the commitment and keep polluting at high levels (Stevenson 2013). So for example industrialized states can appear to meet greenhouse gas emission reduction targets by purchasing offsets in other countries, without making the necessary changes to their domestic energy systems. Such activities further entrench an unsustainable, high-emission economic model.

In short, Holocene institutions at the levels of the state and global governance have yet to demonstrate much capacity to respond to profound ecological challenges. Their problems as we encounter the Anthropocene run very deep, as we will now explain.

Pathological path dependency in Holocene institutions

To see why dominant Holocene institutions are so inappropriate to the Anthropocene we need to take a step back and think about what we mean by an institution to begin with. Most definitions of "institution" specify a high degree of continuity over time. So in his definition based on a comprehensive survey of thinking about institutions, Robert Goodin refers to "the stable, recurring, repetitive, patterned nature of the behavior that occurs within institutions, and because of them" (Goodin 1996a: 22). At one level, this sort of continuity is unremarkable, and indeed helpful to the degree it provides a predictable context in which people can make decisions and act upon them. But continuity can also cause problems when institutions begin to fail on a systematic basis but do not change in response to that failure. As we recognize that we have entered the Anthropocene, strong continuity looks problematic.

Excessively strong continuity is associated with pathological path dependency.

The classic illustration here is not exactly an institution, but rather a widespread design feature: the inefficient QWERTY keyboard, which was originally designed to inhibit typewriter keys jamming. Now that electronic keyboards have become universal, there would be benefit in adopting a more efficient alternative—but hardly anybody does, because of the high learning costs for users. The QWERTY example shows that path dependency arises when the costs of changing course are high, though other dynamics can produce path dependency. In a broad sense, path dependency (or path dependence) means that early decisions or outcomes constrain later ones (North 1990; Kay 2005). Path dependency may arise when institutions generate feedback that reinforces their own necessity (Pierson 2000). To illustrate such feedback, consider what happens when governments in market systems defy market orthodoxy—for example, by introducing stringent environmental regulations or taxes on business. Businesses will threaten to disinvest and move to more lenient jurisdictions, and governments will often give in (Lindblom 1982).

Path dependency may also arise when actors develop material stakes in existing institutions (Kay 2005). So, for example, many cities—particularly in North America and Australia—have grown in a sprawling, low-density form that encourages reliance on cars rather than lower-polluting forms of public transport. Not only is overhauling transport infrastructure highly costly and often slow, but constituencies develop (e.g. drivers' and car industry associations as well as suburban real estate developers) that call on governments to invest in more roads, which may alleviate traffic congestion in the short term but will ultimately starve public transport of the investment needed to yield a longer-term solution. The ideas and norms generated by an institution's operation can further solidify the path; market institutions are reinforced by the widely accepted idea that economic growth is essential, and that markets are the best way to achieve it. Similarly, individuals may come to see their cars as a symbol of personal freedom, and view measures to make driving more costly as an attack on their autonomy (Paterson 2007).

The case of transport infrastructure is part of a broader "carbon lock-in," where societies remain wedded to structures that involve high levels of greenhouse gas emissions—such as energy grids that rely on fossil fuels, and energy-intensive buildings. Many of the decisions that helped yield lock-in were pursued in the name of increased social welfare (Seto et al. 2016: 437). The fact that governments in Australia, India, the United States, and elsewhere maintain plans to open new coal mines and build coal-fired power plants (with government subsidy if need be) shows the power of entrenched interests and patterns of thinking, despite growing evidence that most of the world's coal and oil reserves needs to stay in the ground to avoid dangerous climate change (Meinshausen et al. 2009).

Cronon (2013: xii) encapsulates well the range of entanglements between institutions and culture that may inhibit change:

The scale of our [...] dependence on the automobile is so vast—ranging fractally from the largest public works project in history (the interstate highway system) all the way to what we do when we feel the impulse to drink a well-made cup of coffee—that unwinding these dependencies is hard even to imagine. And yet we may have no choice in the matter, since some of the elements on which the system depends—cheap liquid fuel most of all—may prove less sustainable in the twenty-first century than they appeared to be in the twentieth.

Paradoxically, as this quotation by Cronon suggests, the Anthropocene may constrain not only the options that societies have for future institutional change but also the opportunities societies have to keep flourishing *in the absence* of such change. Just as the Anthropocene itself is now inescapable, equally the world cannot escape the choice of how to address the problems that Holocene institutions have engendered.

Path dependency means that an established institution may pose a barrier to the creation of alternative institutions that would work better. So even institutions that clearly fail in the face of changing conditions may persist (Young 2010). Truly powerful institutions may be able to change their social environment in order to perpetuate themselves and drive out alternatives. Think for example of the institutions of global finance which, despite their failure as revealed by the global financial crisis of 2008, positioned themselves as essential—"too big to fail"—and so foreclosed alternatives, meaning that after a few bailouts the post-2008 financial system looked very much like the pre-2008 one. Eventually global financial institutions managed to eat away at the regulations governments introduced in 2008–9 to curb their wilder activities. To take another example, the UNFCCC established in 1992 failed for twenty-three years to produce a comprehensive global treaty on greenhouse gas emission limitation—but nevertheless that aspiration remained the focus for efforts by governments, civil society, and corporations concerned with climate change. A comprehensive agreement was achieved at Paris in 2015—but a huge amount of effort in the intervening twenty-three years could perhaps have been usefully targeted elsewhere (for example, at alternative "polycentric" approaches to dealing with climate change, which we will discuss in chapter 3).

Path dependency in human institutions works in part through impersonal structural forces, when institutions such as capitalist markets become part of the basic structure of society. But the ideas that underwrite institutions can also contribute to path dependency, especially when powerful actors in those institutions have a material stake in the persistence of the ideas in question (Hay 2006: 65). So the main reason for the persistence of problematic financial institutions after the 2008 crisis was the widely shared belief that they were too big to fail, and that there was essentially no alternative to them. We will show in chapter 6 that the importance of ideas can be turned to good use when it comes to tackling pathological path dependency, because it opens the door to argument, rhetoric, and deliberation in which established ideas can be challenged, with practical effect.

Analysts of path dependency generally confine themselves to explaining "the construction, maintenance, and adaptation of institutions" (Sanders 2006: 42). They often have little interest in institutional evaluation and prescription.[6] However, their insights can be drawn upon to illuminate common institutional characteristics that became pervasive in the Holocene but become problematic in the Anthropocene. As we have already noted, path dependency can

---

[6] For an argument that they should, see Kuyper 2013.

sometimes be benign. But many of the institutions that developed in the Holocene, such as sovereign states and capitalist markets, were complicit in generating the unstable Earth system that now characterizes the Anthropocene, such that their path dependencies become pathological.

States typically have a priority for economic growth that subordinates ecological concerns, and a preoccupation with sovereignty that impedes global collective action. Capitalist markets for their part are equally addicted to material growth, and generally recognize ecological constraints only when forced to do so by non-market forces such as government regulators—who for reasons we have just explained are reluctant to do anything that would significantly hurt economic growth. Sometimes "pollution prevention pays," meaning that firms will reduce their environmental damage to improve their bottom line—as where manufacturers install more energy-efficient machinery or lighting. However, such changes often yield at best marginal improvements at a systemic level. Consumer demand may also encourage markets to take account of ecological concerns, but this role should not be overstated. Since consumers are generally less interested in making environmentally virtuous purchases than in paying less for a given good, typically only a limited segment of the market is likely to cater to environmental concerns in the absence of industry-wide regulation. Green consumerism may even be counterproductive if it diverts attention away from thinking about the underlying system of production (Akenji 2014).

Even when it comes to established institutions with a record of environmental success, path dependency can cause problems in Anthropocene conditions. Consider for example a wildlife protection agency, committed to the preservation or conservation of species and ecosystems. In the Anthropocene, co-evolution may often be a more appropriate way of thinking than preservation or conservation. Co-evolution implies a dynamic relationship in which human influences on the character of a social-ecological system are unavoidable, but one in which humans should strive to respect non-human interests (Norgaard 1988). As we pointed out in chapter 1, preservation and conservation tend to imply that there is a fixed target ecological state that is determined by non-human nature, a state that is independent of human intervention.

Adaptive institutions: better but not good enough

If Holocene institutions are now problematic to the degree they feature pathological path dependency, how might we think of arrangements in human society that are more appropriate to the Anthropocene? We might begin by noting that institutions can vary in their degree of path dependency. Path dependency, as Pierson (2000: 252) points out, is not simply a generic claim that "history matters." Nor does it imply that past choices *determine* present ones (as opposed to constraining them: see Marsh 2010). Certain conditions may be more or less likely to generate path dependency, and path dependency may be stronger or weaker depending on how far the range of possible institutional choices is constrained. Accordingly, if the range of future choices becomes less constrained, we can envisage institutions for the Anthropocene that are able to adapt to a rapidly changing (and potentially catastrophic) social-ecological context. For example, markets could adapt to constitute what Newell and Paterson (2010) call "climate capitalism." This kind of stretched capitalism could involve setting up markets in emissions permits (under a cap on the total number of permits to limit environmental damage), which would mean there is money to be made by brokers in the permits—and by companies that buy and sell them intelligently. Climate capitalism could also involve markets in offsets, under which individuals and organizations compensate for their bad environmental behavior by paying for something apparently benign—like planting trees. There is also money to be made in markets for clean technologies, such as solar and wind energy.

This capacity to adapt may not however go far enough, for even institutions that do adapt can remain significant sources of instability in the Earth system. For example, the (limited) adaptation of markets to climate change has been accompanied by a host of problems. The dirtiest polluters may also be those with the power to secure exemption from emissions trading schemes (Spash 2010). Offsets may simply enable high-polluting activities to continue, while proving ecologically destructive to (say) the tropical ecosystems where fast-growing tree species are introduced and paid for by offsets. Even without such problems of implementation, "climate capitalism" schemes may simply render more secure the ultimately destructive material growth imperative of the political economy (encompassing governments as well as markets). And in a market economy greater energy efficiency may itself lead to further stress on ecological systems, if the resulting drop in energy prices enables people to boost their energy consumption[7] or to use the extra income to purchase environmentally damaging goods.

In this light, the fact that institutions can adapt does not necessarily mean that they have freed themselves from path dependency, and have become able to perform adequately from the point of view of concerns larger than their own survival. They may still respond effectively to imperatives generated in social systems—such as the capitalist market economy, and governments beholden to it—that continue to push ecological concerns to the margins. In so doing, they will continue to help solidify the imperatives of dominant institutions, such as continued material economic growth. Adaptation here

---

[7] This dynamic is known as the "rebound effect" or the "Jevons paradox" after the economist William Stanley Jevons, who identified the effect in the nineteenth century.

may simply mean that institutions can perpetuate themselves in a more unstable social-ecological context—yet in the end do little to reduce that instability, and indeed continue to contribute to the production of instability.

The idea of adaptation can be pushed a bit further (but, as we shall see, still not far enough) in the form of adaptive management and adaptive governance. Adaptive management is a popular doctrine widely advocated as a response to uncertainty, and widely practiced in resource management. Adaptive management stresses learning from success and failure (National Research Council 2010), and so is essentially an experimental approach to public policy, treating each new policy innovation as almost like a scientific experiment. Adaptive governance has still larger ambitions for the reorientation of the way government as a whole operates. However, both take the structure of government and the goals of policy as given, which limits their ability to counteract pathological path dependency. So for example Folke et al.'s (2005: 457) exemplary case of adaptive governance is a new system for wetlands management in Sweden, which "took place within the existing institutional framework." Camacho looks at some promising cases from US environmental policy, involving respectively the Climate Ready Estuaries and the Interagency Climate Change Science programs. Both proved limited by their inability to find a way to engender the required learning capacity in the governments that initiated the programs (Camacho 2009: 59–64).

At the global level, perhaps the most successful example of adaptive or experimental governance may be found under the 1987 Montreal Protocol for the protection of the ozone layer, involving "broad stakeholder participation, revisability of goals, and continuous learning from the monitoring of performance" (de Búrca, Keohane, and Sabel 2013: 268). The Protocol led to the establishment of new funding mechanisms to enable developing countries to transition away from ozone-destroying chlorofluorocarbons, and transnational panels to review progress and revise rules if necessary. Even though it will take some decades until the ozone layer is fully repaired, ozone presents a relatively easy case where the benefits of action massively exceed the costs, and only a few non-essential chemicals need regulating. Thus the case could be easily resolved within the dominant institutional order. More substantial capacity for institutional self-transformation may be necessary when it comes to more complex cases (such as climate change and biodiversity) of the sort that constitute the most profound challenges in the Anthropocene.

Requiem for Holocene governance

If governance institutions in the late Holocene still have an air of inevitability about them, that is because they represent what we have become so strongly socialized into: states, international organizations, and markets.

These institutions are solidified by their successes in restricting violent conflict, securing economic growth, and achieving a measure of social justice, as well as enabling an expanding sphere of human rights and democracy. (Of course, there have been plenty of failures in these terms too.) But their very successes have come to help these institutions secure themselves in the face of the very different kind of challenges that the Anthropocene presents. Post-materialist developments notwithstanding, the dominant axis of political conflict remains left versus right, reflecting a fossilized stand-off that fails to capture the challenge that the Anthropocene presents. It is particularly unfortunate when environmental issues are caricatured as disputes between left and right—as has happened in the United States, where concern about climate change is associated with a left-wing position, and denial with the right. The left–right cleavage has been disrupted to a degree by a division between those prospering from, and those left behind by, economic globalization. US President Trump, for example, gained office championing the cause of workers affected by the decline of US manufacturing, even while pursuing cherished Republican aims such as tax cuts for the wealthy. But this disruption is of no help in facilitating an effective response to the Anthropocene, and even makes matters worse, when leaders empowered by the rejection of globalization pursue willful denial and deliberate environmental destruction.

However, not all is gloom. There have been attempts to change governance institutions to make them better able to adapt to a more unstable Earth system. But adaptive governance does not go far enough: a more thoroughgoing capacity to question established institutions, practices, policies, and ideas is necessary. This capacity can be captured in the idea of reflexivity. In the next chapter we will show how ecological reflexivity can be a practical and effective antidote to pathological path dependency, and so provide the foundations for thinking about governance in the Anthropocene.

3 Governance in the Anthropocene

We began the last chapter with some history lessons that showed how human institutions can be well adapted to respond to some kinds of challenges (such as war, disease, and threats to economic growth)—but we went on to show how institutional path dependencies restrict the capacity for effective response to the challenges now facing us in the Anthropocene. In this chapter, we are going to be more positive in trying to determine what effective governance in the Anthropocene should look like. It would be nice if there were some exemplary positive history lessons that we could draw on, so we could say with confidence "*This* is what we need!" Unfortunately, there are no such cases, which means the profound challenge of the Anthropocene is to develop some capacities that have never been fully demonstrated before. Still, we will do our best to squeeze positive lessons out of some ambiguous case histories—especially recent changes in the global regime for climate governance.

Pathological path dependency hobbles the capacity of Holocene institutions to cope with the challenges posed by the Anthropocene. We will explore how governance institutions can perform better, by thinking in terms of reflexivity: the capacity of structures, systems, and sets of ideas to question their own core commitments, and if necessary change themselves in response. We stress system-wide processes, and the need to think of reflexivity as a property of whole systems of governance. Reflexivity is the antidote to pathological path dependency. A specifically ecological reflexivity recognizes the active influence of the Earth system itself, and so involves listening more effectively to ecological systems (see the appendix to this chapter on how the concept navigates the tension between its specifically ecological substance and its more open-ended reflexive procedure). We explain why it is better to think in terms of ecological reflexivity rather than the fashionable idea of resilience.

Ecological reflexivity proves to be the primary requirement for institutions in the Anthropocene.[1] The consequences of thinking in terms of ecological

---

[1] Dryzek (2016b), on which this chapter draws, mainly uses the term "ecosystemic reflexivity." But this is a bit of a mouthful and raised queries from some commentators about whether the term applied only to ecosystems in a narrower sense, so we now use the term "ecological reflexivity." They mean the same thing. In both cases, reflexivity applies not to ecosystems in isolation but to linked social and ecological systems.

reflexivity for key institutions such as states, markets, and global governance in all areas, not just those traditionally classified as environmental, are profound.

To contextualize our discussion, we present a case study of the tug-of-war between reflexivity and path dependency in global climate governance. We then address two debates on how to engender reflexivity. First, do catastrophic ecological state shifts give rise to "critical junctures" that provide opportunities to interrupt pathological path dependency? We argue that relying on this kind of reactive response is a mistake. Ecological reflexivity requires cultivating the capacity of institutions to anticipate and prevent ecological state shifts. Second, are some institutions more conducive to ecological reflexivity than others? We scrutinize three prominent proposals for global governance responses to the Anthropocene, generated by the Earth System Governance Project, the Resilience Alliance, and less well-organized proponents of poly-centrism. We argue that thinking in terms of choice across alternative institutional models or architectures is not sufficient. It is far better to think dynamically, in terms of processes of change beginning from where we are now. We look at how ecological reflexivity can begin to gain a foothold in existing institutions, and in doing so weave together some of the preceding theoretical threads.

Ecological reflexivity

Reflexivity in a social context means the self-critical capacity of a structure or process or set of ideas to change itself after scrutiny of its own failures, or indeed successes (Beck, Giddens, and Lash 1994). Reflexivity entails a capacity to *be* something different when necessary, rather than just *do* something different, which distinguishes it from adaptive management and adaptive governance as described in chapter 2.

Humans may well be the only agents capable of activating the cognitive processes necessary for reflexivity. But in the Anthropocene, consistent with the idea that the Earth system itself becomes recognized as a key player, the crucial entities whose well-being is the target of reflexivity are social-ecological systems, rather than social systems per se (Young 2017: 96). The human components of social-ecological systems can then respond not just to human voices, but also to the non-human components that cannot speak like humans do—but to whose signals we can try to listen better (Dryzek 1995; Schlosberg 2007: 190–2; Dobson 2010). Unfortunately, contemporary human institutions have become very bad at listening to the non-human world. These institutions can often ignore the screams that come from species extinctions, crashes in biological diversity, drastic disruptions of the nitrogen cycle,

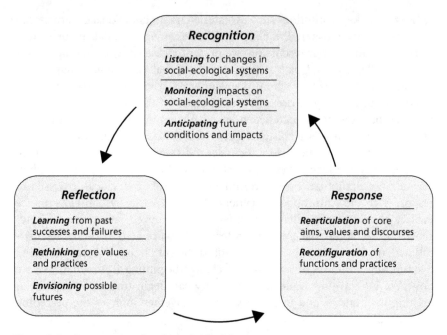

Figure 3.1. Components of ecological reflexivity

climbing concentrations of greenhouse gases in the atmosphere, increasingly acidic oceans, the bleaching of coral reefs, or the death of once healthy waters.

Listening is necessary for reflexivity, but it is not sufficient by itself to ensure reflexivity. Listening, along with monitoring one's own impacts on social-ecological systems and anticipation of possible future state shifts (which we discuss further below), forms part of a broader need for the *recognition* of ecological conditions and changes. Two further components of reflexivity are required. The next is *reflection* that combines learning from past experience (including institutional successes and failures), rethinking core values in the light of lessons learnt as well as feedback from social-ecological systems, and envisioning possible futures.[2] Finally, reflexivity requires *response*, understood as changes to institutional goals, policies, structures, and practices following listening and reflection. These three components—recognition, reflection, and response—join in an ongoing, iterative process where successive phases of recognition and reflection are informed by the results of previous phases of response (see Figure 3.1).

---

[2] Young (2017: 98) argues that reflexivity may be part of the problem when people's reactions to the behavior of others trigger positive feedback loops (e.g. a run on the banks or an arms race) that spiral into crises. However, if those reactions lack critical reflection, they may be adaptive but (on our account) not reflexive. Reflexivity may nevertheless have other limitations, as we point out in the appendix to this chapter.

WHAT ABOUT RESILIENCE?

We will now pause to explain why we emphasize the idea of reflexivity, and not the seemingly related idea of resilience. Resilience rooted in the science of ecology has become popular in recent years—though mostly it is natural scientists who are keen on applying it to social-ecological systems. Social scientists are less enthusiastic about the idea (Olsson et al. 2015), for reasons we will go into shortly.

The idea has been promoted by the Resilience Alliance, a large global network of natural scientists and a few social scientists. The Resilience Alliance (2018) defines resilience as "the ability to absorb disturbances, to be changed and then to re-organize and still have the same identity (retain the same basic structure and ways of functioning)." This definition would seem to rest on some core structure that provides fixed reference points: the idea of resilience is to return to these reference points from a situation of disequilibrium caused by shocks to the system. That is why, for social scientists, resilience is one of the *causes* of path dependency in human institutions such as governments or markets (Pierson 2004), rather than a solution to any problems created by path dependency. So in the Anthropocene we might want social-ecological systems to be resilient, but not want other institutions (such as financial markets) to be resilient if they generate feedback that ignores ecological systems.

We can find examples of long-lived social-ecological systems that are resilient (in the terms of the Resilience Alliance definition) existing in humanity's past. An example might be the kind of agro-ecosystems that have flourished for hundreds of years in many parts of the world, in which farming has been practiced on a sustainable basis. It is much harder to find examples of resilient social-ecological systems in contemporary industrial or post-industrial societies—and that applies to the way agriculture is increasingly practiced in those societies too.

Resilience was originally conceptualized in terms of the capacity of a system to return to equilibrium after disturbance (Folke 2006: 256)—for example, if a forest can regenerate itself after logging, fire, or a destructive insect infestation. The old idea that resilience is essentially the capacity to bounce back from punishment to restore the status quo can fuel the idea that it is essentially conservative, standing in the way of efforts to improve society, and requiring vulnerable people in particular to absorb the punishment (Catney and Doyle 2011: 190). This understanding of resilience is vulnerable to criticisms similar to those we made in relation to adaptive governance, because it seeks to preserve existing institutions (see chapter 2). However, as we have already argued, in the Anthropocene there are no clear equilibrium states of the Earth system. Instead, we see evolving dynamism, as the way the system works keeps changing under human influences. In such a situation, resilience needs to involve action that is constructive and dynamic, not merely preservative.

Resilience thinkers have gone some way toward recognizing this situation, and so claim to be interested in transformation—not just restoring the status quo in response to disturbance. Thus while much resilience thinking is closely associated with ideas of adaptation and adaptive governance (discussed in chapter 2), Folke et al. (2010) treat "transformability" as an aspect of resilience. The idea of "transformative resilience" even finds a place in a report by the World Economic Forum (WEF 2018: 54), a body that hosts a famous annual meeting where the world's wealthiest individuals (who have a sizeable stake in the status quo) mix with global leaders in Davos, Switzerland. However, this really stretches the concept of resilience, and introduces a tension with the basic Resilience Alliance definition quoted earlier because it is not clear whether "basic structure" is to be preserved or can be transformed. As Olsson et al. (2015) point out, there is something paradoxical about the idea of "transformation for the sake of persistence of the system."

One way to solve this paradox might be to see resilience in terms of preserving some core values (such as basic human needs, or biodiversity) while accepting that the structure of social-ecological systems can change. However, holding on to core values can itself cause social collapse if these values do not adjust to changes in the world. In his bestselling book *Collapse*, Jared Diamond (2005) argues that societies can cling to core values that eventually contribute to their demise. For example, the Greenland Norse clung to European values and ways of life while resisting Inuit sensibilities and practices that would have facilitated survival. Thus core values should not be immune to transformation, though in Diamond's analysis the key core value of societal survival appears non-negotiable.[3] In many contemporary societies, ideals such as social justice, sustainability, and democracy are treated as core values. We will show in chapters 4, 5, and 7 how these values need to be rethought for the Anthropocene.

In light of its multiple, ambiguous, and stretched definitions, associated with reasonable disagreement over its meaning, it is best to treat resilience as a discourse rather than a concept that can be defined with any precision. By a discourse we mean a shared way of looking at the world with some common understandings but also some internal disputes. Resilience is a lot like "sustainable development" and "democracy," both of which have numerous contested meanings across which no definitive resolution is possible. Resilience as a discourse has some undeniable uses, but also undeniable limitations. Resilience discourse is useful because it drives home the point that the Earth system can be an active participant in how history unfolds. Institutional reflexivity therefore needs to encompass the idea that humans can live in a relationship of

[3] Whether humanity should continue to exist at all can be questioned in philosophical terms (see Sanklecha 2017), but we proceed on the basis that humans, along with other species, have at least some claims to existence and flourishing.

productive co-evolution with the non-human elements of the Earth system, under which change occurs to their mutual advantage (Norgaard 1988). Resilience discourse is limited because it is grounded in the science of ecology, and so has a hard time when it comes to human systems (or the human aspects of social-ecological systems) in which the exercise of power and the capacity to think and reflect before acting are crucial (Olsson et al. 2015). Reflection before action is central to the idea of reflexivity, not to the idea of resilience.

This detour into resilience discourse sharpens the way we need to conceptualize a specifically ecological reflexivity. Ecological reflexivity differs from simple reflexivity in at least two ways: the incorporation into human institutions of better ways to listen to ecological systems that have a different kind of voice; and an ability to rethink what core values such as justice, sustainability, and democracy mean in the context of an active and unstable Earth system.

Reflexivity versus path dependency in global climate governance: did Paris make a difference?

To illustrate reflexivity's fight with pathological path dependency, consider the global governance of climate change, which, as noted in chapter 2, long featured strong path dependency—accompanied by very little in the way of positive results. The central institution in that governance is the United Nations Framework Convention on Climate Change (UNFCCC). The UNFCCC makes institutional sense in the context of an international system whose dominant actors are sovereign states, and where legitimate collective global action must rest on agreement among sovereign states. In organizing negotiations among almost all the world's states under the auspices of the United Nations, the UNFCCC has the hallmarks of a legitimate institution. But for over twenty years after its establishment in 1992, that legitimacy did not translate into much success. Everything about the UNFCCC was geared toward producing a comprehensive global treaty for the reduction of greenhouse gas emissions. Many actors devoted themselves to their roles in this pursuit, and became strongly socialized into those roles. This devotion applied to the thousands of civil society activists and organizations that targeted the negotiations (showing up every year for the two weeks of the Conference of the Parties) as much as to the United Nations officials and national negotiating teams, and continued irrespective of the success or failure of the negotiations.

For over twenty years the UNFCCC looked like a case study in pathological path dependency, so much so that during one of its darker periods Depledge (2006) characterized the UNFCCC as an "ossified" regime that exemplified "the opposite of learning" due to its inability to overcome entrenched divides between developing and developed countries. By 2015 matters began to look less problematic with the adoption of a comprehensive agreement, to much acclaim, at the Paris Conference of the Parties. But did this mean that all was well, and that pathological path dependency had been broken? Not really.

Two aspects of the Paris Agreement show in greater depth the ways in which the drafting process could secure only modest reflexivity: the changing roles of states and other actors in what has long been a state-centric regime; and the nature of differentiation between developed and developing countries.

To begin with the first aspect, the idea of "Nationally Determined Contributions" (NDCs) was central to the Paris Agreement: each country should decide for itself what policies, targets, and timetables for emissions reduction to adopt, and then be required to report on progress against these promised contributions. Beyond loss of face, there is no formal mechanism to punish states that fail to achieve the targets set out in their NDCs. Much, then, depends on the willingness and ability of states to make effective promises and keep to them.[4] The adoption of this new form of governance can be interpreted as a response to the failure of previous attempts to impose legally binding targets on countries. For this new form to work, priorities must be different at the national level. All those states that have in the past proved adept at negotiating the terms of compliance with global climate agreements in ways that meet the letter of the agreement but undermine the intent (Stevenson 2013) must now become more honest and public-spirited participants in the international climate order.

The Paris Agreement envisages new roles for non-governmental organizations (NGOs) and businesses (collectively referred to as "non-state actors") as well as sub-national governments, now enlisted in what international relations scholars call "orchestration" (Abbott 2017). Orchestration refers to a distinctive form of relationship between governing bodies (e.g. international organizations or states) and other actors. Rather than formally delegating authority to those actors, the governing body enlists the voluntary support of "intermediaries" to advance shared goals. Here, the orchestrator is the UNFCCC; non-state and sub-state actors then play the crucial roles of leading by example through pledging to act on climate change, building mutual assurance that a groundswell of action is taking place irrespective of what national governments are doing, and lobbying national governments to do better. However, the Paris Agreement incorporates few *formal* mechanisms for non-state actors to hold governments to account for their commitments (van Asselt 2016).

In terms of the deliberative systems framework we introduced in chapter 1, the agreement therefore falls short on *accountability*. It is crucial that actors are held accountable for more than their progress against commitments they

[4] Evidence from the UN human rights regime shows that shaming recalcitrant governments can have some salutary effects in inducing compliance (Terman and Voeten 2018).

have already made. After all, existing commitments may fall well short of what is required to avert major risks to the Earth system. Instead, accountability mechanisms should further require states and others to answer for the adequacy of their commitments when set against the best available knowledge about Earth system risks and informed public preferences about acceptable levels of risk. In the context of global climate governance, this means calling on states to justify whether their pledges are sufficient to avoid dangerous climate change. The Paris Agreement's provision for a periodic "global stocktake" of progress on combating climate change holds some promise (UNFCCC 2016, Article 14). However, it remains to be seen how effective the process will be and whether it will prompt countries to rethink their existing commitments.

In the light of the developments we have described around the Paris Agreement, Bäckstrand et al. (2017) refer to an emerging "hybrid multilateralism" that mixes the traditional top-down approach of the UNFCCC negotiations with the proliferating bottom-up initiatives in climate governance, involving for example transnational emissions trading schemes, networks to share information on low-emission planning practices and technologies, clean technology transfer, and offset schemes. These latter initiatives are described under headings of polycentric governance (Ostrom 2009) or experimental governance (Hoffmann 2011). They can involve many different configurations of actors, be they national, regional, or local governments, international organizations, corporations, or civil society activists and organizations. The bottom-up initiatives were long seen as a response to the failure of the multilateral UNFCCC process and so separate from it but, as Bäckstrand et al. point out, that separation no longer holds.

To date hybrid multilateralism is a somewhat disjointed work in progress, and it remains to be seen how it will work out. It is possible to imagine more thoroughgoing innovation that would also strengthen the accountability of diverse polycentric (bottom-up) governance initiatives to the UNFCCC, which in turn would become more clearly accountable to global civil society for both its overall performance and for the way it coordinates these initiatives (Stevenson and Dryzek 2014: 194–5). However, we can see signs of reflexivity in existing developments. The UNFCCC has changed itself in response to its previous failures, in terms of the new roles for itself, its component states, and non-state actors. We do not yet know if these new roles will significantly boost collective performance—and begin to move the world away from its trajectory toward catastrophic climate change.[5] But there are signs that the UNFCCC's

---

[5] A study of international cooperative initiatives outside the UNFCCC (including non-state and intergovernmental partnerships) found that, once overlaps with national targets were taken into account, the expected contribution to global reductions in greenhouse gas emissions was discernible but modest (PBL 2015).

orchestration practices may help to unsettle prevailing norms about the state-centric focus of national commitments. So, for example, the UNFCCC listed on its Non-State Actor Zone for Climate Action a pledge by US business leaders and state and local governments to stand by their country's commitment under the Paris Agreement, despite US President Trump's announcement that the US was withdrawing from the Agreement (UNFCCC 2017).

One limit to reflexivity in existing hybrid multilateralism arises from the fact that orchestration treats non-state actors as assistants to the orchestrator: their task is to ensure that the goals of the orchestrator are met. Acting as assistants, rather than as equals in shaping the terms of the partnership, risks suppressing their more critical side, which might involve holding the orchestrator to account, assessing the adequacy of the goals in whose service non-state actors have been enlisted, and raising questions about the performance of existing institutional arrangements. As the costs of exiting orchestration arrangements are relatively low (compared to a state formally withdrawing from a treaty), it remains open to non-state actors to sever their relationship with the orchestrator if their goals diverge. Thus while the turn to hybrid multilateralism in general and to orchestration in particular indicates reflexivity in the UNFCCC, if this turn depletes the critical capacities of non-state actors or the impact of their critiques on state practice, it might impair reflexivity in the larger climate governance system (Dryzek 2017). Moreover, without stronger mechanisms for holding participants to account in the implementation of their own pledges, orchestration may erode reflexivity by enabling non-state actors to reap the reputational benefits of having their good intentions recognized by the UNFCCC, while failing to follow through on their promised actions (Bäckstrand and Kuyper 2017).

The second aspect of the Paris Agreement that exhibits signs of reflexivity concerns the changing way the roles of developed and developing countries are differentiated. The issue of differentiation has been a longstanding flashpoint in the global climate regime (which incidentally underscores our point in chapter 1 that Anthropocene thinking need not entail the notion of an undifferentiated humanity). A key structural element of the UNFCCC as originally adopted is the division of member states into two major groups: Annex I countries (comprising countries that were members of the Organization for Economic Co-operation and Development [OECD] in 1992, as well as "Economies in Transition," mainly countries that were formerly part of the Soviet Union) and non-Annex I (or developing) countries. The distinction between the two groups had major implications for the subsequent evolution of the UNFCCC, particularly as Annex I countries were expected to "take the lead" in protecting the climate system (UNFCCC 1992, Article 3.1). This provision was invoked to justify the bifurcated approach of the 1997 Kyoto Protocol, whereby developed countries had legally binding emissions targets but developing countries did not.

Differentiation enshrined an important moral concern that those countries that had contributed more to the problem of climate change—and with greater economic capacity to address the problem—should have the main responsibility for fixing it (Moellendorf 2012). But over time the rigidity of the Annex I/non-Annex I distinction (or "firewall" as it came to be called) became increasingly problematic, particularly as the developing world's share of global greenhouse gas emissions rose. By the mid-2000s, advances in scientific knowledge had confirmed that rapid cuts to global emissions were essential if the world was to avoid dangerous climate change, and that the involvement of developing countries would be crucial. Yet for years the UNFCCC struggled to find a way of expanding participation in mitigation without erasing the idea of differentiation. While the Convention always allowed for movement between Annexes, very few countries—even high-income countries such as Singapore, Israel, South Korea and Qatar—took up the opportunity to do so, thus supporting Depledge's (2006) view that the climate regime had ossified.

The Paris Agreement achieved a more nuanced approach to differentiation, but without explicitly breaching the firewall (Rajamani 2016). An important feature of the Agreement is that many key obligations—including those to maintain and report on NDCs—are universal in application and legal character. The Agreement still contained elements of differentiation (in relation to reporting standards and financial obligations, for example), but the Annex structure became less central. The move towards "national" differentiation (Pickering, Vanderheiden, and Millerty 2012) or "self-differentiation" (Voigt and Ferreira 2016) heralded by the Agreement played an important role in securing the participation of major developing economies. At the same time, the UNFCCC has not yet demonstrated that it can adequately address the injustices that still endure, such as shortfalls in funding for those countries most vulnerable to the impacts of climate change (Ciplet, Roberts, and Khan 2015).

In short, after long years of impasse, the global climate regime eventually began to demonstrate a limited degree of reflexivity—but there is a long way to go before that capacity measures up to the magnitude of the challenge, when it comes to climate change in particular and the Anthropocene in general. What then might spur more profound change?

Can reflexivity be triggered by ecological crisis or must it be cultivated?

With a clearer conception of ecological reflexivity in place, and an appreciation that limited advances are possible in global governance, we can now ask what sorts of factors are necessary to bring about more thoroughgoing reflexivity. We begin with those who think moments of crisis are necessary or sufficient to do so.

ARE STATE SHIFTS AND CRITICAL JUNCTURES IN THE EARTH SYSTEM SUFFICIENT TO TRIGGER REFLEXIVITY?

The instability of the Anthropocene is revealed most dramatically in the renewed possibility of state shifts in the Earth system, where apparent stability yields suddenly to a qualitatively different system, with a different distribution of ecosystems across the globe, and (for example) sea levels much higher than they are today. The Holocene was a period of unusual stability in which ecological state shifts were relatively rare and did not occur at the global level (despite minor, regionally uneven fluctuations such as the Medieval Climate Anomaly and subsequent Little Ice Age: Masson-Delmotte et al. 2013: 409–11). In contrast, the preceding Pleistocene featured frequent phases of rapid global warming (Steffen et al. 2011: 752). Global state shifts have occurred in Earth's deeper history, each one attended by mass extinctions of species (Barnosky et al. 2012).

Might such a state shift provide the occasion for a reworking of institutional orders to good effect? Gunderson and Holling (2002) suggest that social and ecological systems alike generally feature slow change with occasional bursts of reorganization, so could we imagine an ecological state shift receiving immediate positive response in human institutions? After all, in purely human affairs, the extreme pressure of critical junctures can constitute an opportunity for institutional transformation. For example, the basic institutions of the international system have several times transformed themselves in the wake of total war. The Peace of Westphalia in 1648 responded to wars of religion in Europe by setting up the contemporary system of sovereign states. At the conclusion of the Napoleonic wars in 1815, the Congress of Vienna set up a new European system that yielded almost a century of relative peace. After World War I, the Treaty of Versailles in 1919 remodeled Europe. World War II produced even greater global institutional change after 1945, with the Bretton Woods system for governance of the global economy followed by the establishment of the United Nations system. World War II also demonstrated how quickly states could transform their economies from consumer-oriented markets to centrally-planned systems with broad provisions for social welfare to serve war-making.

These sorts of precedents lead Biermann et al. (2012) and Biermann (2014: 210) to call for a similar sort of "constitutional moment" in global environmental governance as we enter the Anthropocene. Constitutional conventions might seem to offer opportunities for reflexivity inasmuch as they involve deliberation about the qualities of the political system itself—"meta-deliberation." However, they are too infrequent to provide a standing capacity to monitor how well processes are functioning. We may see some intimations of constitutional moments in high-level environmental summits, or successive efforts to formulate global development goals (such as the Sustainable Development Goals). Such initiatives have some potential to engage in reflexive rethinking of both core values such as sustainability (a process we will discuss in chapter 5) as well as the deliberative processes required to achieve a more sustainable world. Yet existing initiatives of this kind prove highly constrained in the scope of rethinking they encompass, not least because of the extent to which they are molded by the priorities of the states that negotiate them, which are in turn conditioned by pathological path dependencies of the sort we have criticized.

Referring more explicitly to state shifts, Young (2010: 384) concludes by recommending "that well-crafted options are available when crises open up windows of opportunity for the introduction of substantial institutional changes." Unfortunately, there are several issues here that may frustrate these kinds of hopes.

First, there is no guarantee that a state shift will receive any response at all—think again of Diamond's (2005) argument about societies that have collapsed in the face of local or regional state shifts. The possibility that there will be no effective response is increased by the fact that, while some ecological state shifts may look sudden in geological time, in human time they will seem prolonged, and so not yield the same sort of immediacy as (for example) reconstruction after total war. Climate change exemplifies this problem, as many impacts unfold over decades (more local cases such as collapse of a fishery can be sudden in human time). Even the onset of disasters whose risks are heightened by climate change—ranging from Hurricane Katrina in the United States to Typhoon Haiyan in the Philippines—has so far failed to trigger systemic change.

A second problem is that reconfiguring institutions in the context of crisis may be inadequate if the product is stable institutions that embody renewed path dependency, thereby contributing to further social-ecological instability. Consider, in this light, the raft of environmental laws and agencies established around 1970 in the United States, which included the establishment of the Environmental Protection Agency, the passing of the National Environmental Policy Act, and strengthening of clean air and water pollution control legislation. As mentioned briefly in chapter 1, the United States at that time faced a political crisis in which anti-war, civil rights, and other social movements associated with a growing counterculture seemed to threaten social stability. Responding to this political crisis—rather than to ecological crisis—the Nixon administration successfully pulled environmentalists out of the counterculture and into the political mainstream through its actions. This burst of institutional innovation made the United States an environmental leader among the countries of the world (Dryzek et al. 2003: 59–60). However, this moment of seemingly positive and thoroughgoing institutional reconstruction also established the terms of a stand-off between environmental and development interests that continues to this day, preventing any profound subsequent reforms.

Stuck in this stand-off, the US found it hard even to explore, let alone institutionalize, ideas about sustainable development and ecological modernization that gained currency and influenced policy practice elsewhere in the world (Bryner 2000: 277). Sustainable development and ecological modernization seek ways of synthesizing environmental and economic concerns— rather than seeing them as necessarily opposed. In the United States, in contrast, gain on one side generally has to mean loss on the other side. The United States turned from leader to laggard in environmental affairs, and old-fashioned economic development interests could flex their muscles sufficiently to ensure that the US eventually became one of the primary impediments to effective global action. The US did manage to make an exemplary global contribution to the 1987 Montreal Protocol for the protection of the ozone layer, and the US administration under President Obama invested considerable diplomatic effort to secure the Paris Agreement on climate change in 2015. Beyond this, however, the recent history of US involvement in global environmental affairs is a sorry one.

Critical junctures of the sort an ecological state shift connotes do not, then, guarantee a positive response. Moreover, even if institutions do respond, that does not necessarily mean impetus for continuing positive transformation, as opposed to renewed and pathological path dependency. Thus recognition of the opportunities provided by state shifts and critical junctures does not remove the need for ongoing reflexivity.

THE NEED FOR FORESIGHT AND THE ANTICIPATION OF STATE SHIFTS

A further reason why institutional transformation needs to be more than just a response to crisis—such as an ecological state shift—stems from the possibility that bad institutions may themselves be complicit in the production of catastrophic state shifts. That is, those shifts do not just arrive from outside. Relying on institutions to transform themselves in response to such shifts when they arrive is therefore not enough, because that means living too long with institutions that are producing disaster. An ecological state shift is one thing institutions should be trying to avoid, given that historically such state shifts have often been accompanied by catastrophe (such as mass extinctions).

What is therefore required is for institutions to embody *foresight*. Foresight here must be much more than a concern for the future effects of current actions and a recognition that what worked in the past will not necessarily work in the future. Foresight must also involve a capacity to anticipate human-caused state shifts and act before the shift occurs. This is a demanding criterion. It means embodying responsiveness to early warnings of the sort that only science seems capable of providing.[6] Ecological reflexivity requires a capacity to seek, receive, interpret, and act upon early warnings as provided by science. Unfortunately, we see today that early warnings of the sort given by climate science can meet with a storm of political opposition, as those who believe their material interests will be hurt by anticipatory action mobilize not just against the action but also against the science that shows action to be necessary. In Canada, the United States, and Australia, governments have closed down scientific advisory bodies, banned government departments from talking about science, and de-funded research that might yield unwelcome conclusions about environmental damage. In a "post-truth" world, the knowledge yielded by science no longer seems to matter in political debate, and the foresight that science can enable is obstructed.

A substantial body of work in communicating climate change can be drawn upon here to inform institutional design that would receive—and possibly respond to—such early warnings more effectively. In summary, this work finds that most people (including politicians) accord low priority to climate change. There are additional challenges in the Anglo-American countries (but much less so elsewhere) where those who do attend to climate change process scientific claims through ideological filters, and certainly not through dispassionate assessment of the science (McCright and Dunlap 2011). This means that communicators such as Al Gore, who shared the 2007 Nobel Peace Prize for his efforts, can reach those ideologically disposed to act upon climate change, but not those ideologically opposed.

We also know that more knowledge does not necessarily lead to change in behavior or political action, that frightening people with disastrous scenarios is generally counterproductive, and that asserting the authority of science has no effect on the willingness of most people to do anything (Moser and Dilling 2011: 164–5). Based on studies that show what does not work in communicating climate change, and what does work in the area of public health, Moser and Dilling (2011: 169) conclude that "people in a democratic society are best served by actively engaging with an issue, making their voices and values heard, and contributing to the formulation of societal responses" as opposed to being seen as the target of mass media messages. Of course the science as

---

[6] Traditional knowledge held by Indigenous peoples and local communities may play valuable roles in anticipating shorter-term and responding to more localized changes (such as droughts or heavy rains) and informing understandings of historical environmental change (Tengö et al. 2014). However, anticipation of global state shifts requires complex system modeling that in turn necessitates scientific input.

such will continue to be produced by the scientists, but broader participation involving ordinary people in face-to-face communication about climate change with experts and advocates could help establish the agenda of questions for scientists that need answering, prioritize problems that need to be addressed, interpret the importance of scientific findings, and reconcile scientific findings with lay knowledge. These findings point to the importance of integrating climate science with meaningful democratic processes, about which we will have much more to say in chapter 7. Many scientists now recognize the need to engage more effectively about the science with citizens (Dietz 2013).

Ecological reflexivity does, then, necessitate foresight to anticipate and prevent catastrophes such as state shifts, as well as the ability to listen more effectively to ecological systems and rethink core values and institutional structures. These qualities are permanent reflexive virtues that institutions need to cultivate.

Building reflexive governance: models versus processes

Any call to cultivate reflexive virtues will lack political traction unless it is clear how it can translate into institutional change. One common approach to reform in general (not just in the interests of reflexivity) is to specify desirable institutional models or "architectures." We now argue that a model-based approach is insufficient for grappling with the challenges posed by the Anthropocene. Instead of designing institutional blueprints, it is more productive to think about changing fundamental institutional dynamics, starting from where we are now.

WHY INSTITUTIONAL MODELS WON'T SUFFICE

The ideas about path dependency and reflexivity that we have developed in chapter 2 and this chapter can be used to shed light on what others have said about the question of institutional reform. We will now examine what two particularly prominent research groups have had to say about models—the Resilience Alliance and the Earth System Governance Project—as well as a more diffuse group of scholars associated with polycentric or decentralized models.

Folke et al., key figures in the Resilience Alliance, suggest that "the attributes of transformability have much in common with those of general resilience, including high levels of all forms of capital, diversity in landscapes and seascapes and of institutions, actor groups, and networks, learning platforms, collective action, and support from higher scales in the governance structure" (Folke et al. 2010). Yet such vague generalities tell us very little. Exactly what kinds of "diverse institutions" should enter into the mix? If it is a diversity of (say) capitalist markets, low-visibility financial networks, and sovereign states, all subject to pathological path dependencies, the mix may well be worse than any of its components. "All forms of capital" require scrutiny rather than endorsement. One prominent kind of "capital" is social capital, widely extolled as having positive effects because it refers to the degree to which people in a society associate productively with each other and so strengthen their community (Putnam 1993). Its importance to resilience is stressed by Folke et al. (2005: 449–52). However, social capital may impede reflexivity if it induces people to avoid thinking about controversial issues that threaten social cohesion (as suggested by Eliasoph 1998 in her studies of political culture in the United States).

A more precise governance prescription for the Anthropocene was published as a manifesto in the leading scientific journal *Science* by Biermann et al. (2012), members of the Earth System Governance Project. This project was established in 2008, and constitutes the world's biggest network of environmental social scientists concerned with governance; we have been involved in it ourselves for a number of years.[7] Essentially Biermann et al. recommend stronger and more coordinated institutions of global governance, linked to a reinvigorated United Nations system. But there is no real argument in this piece that this is what the Anthropocene truly requires; indeed, though "Navigating the Anthropocene" is the title of the article, the word "Anthropocene" does not appear in its text (thus exemplifying what we called "The Anthropocene for show" in chapter 1). We might for example ask why something with a modest record—central management of environmental affairs—should be picked out from the repertoire of available collective human responses and given a task far harder than it has shown itself capable of accomplishing so far.[8] The real significance of the article by Biermann et al. lies perhaps not in the content of its argument, but in the fact of its publication by thirty-two social scientists in one of the world's highest-profile scientific journals (this short article does not encompass the richness of the work undertaken by members of the Earth System Governance project). Biermann (2014) elsewhere argues in more nuanced terms but maintains that "there is no way around strong and effective international institutions" (p. 207) as

---

[7] Our roles have involved convening its annual conference (JD), serving on its Scientific Steering Committee (JD), co-chairing a working group on ecological democracy (JP), and contributing to its science plan (JD/JP).

[8] On the shortcomings of environmental management and administration, see Ostrom and Janssen 2004, 243–5; Paehlke and Torgerson 2005.

an alternative to "conflictive" fragmentation and its associated limited and ineffective solutions.[9]

If conflictive fragmentation is the problem then more integration and institutional centralization are indeed obvious answers. But Keohane and Victor (2011) argue that the devolution of the global climate regime into a more fragmented regime complex (with multiple, only loosely connected organizations, practices, and initiatives) is positive because at least it moved the world beyond impasse in the multilateral UN negotiations. Keohane and Victor stress the importance of multiple governance arrangements that exist outside the UNFCCC. These include bilateral agreements between large countries such as the US and China or blocs such as the European Union; unilateral national initiatives to curb emissions; programs sponsored by the World Bank; and actions taken in "clubs" of countries such as the G20 group of major economies. Using a different language, Ostrom (2009) points to the virtues of a complex polycentric approach to global environmental governance that would include a mix of many different kinds of institutions and practices at different levels of government, from the local to the global. Hoffmann (2011) criticizes "mega-multilateralism" of the sort Biermann seems to favor, for its failure to yield tangible results, and applauds instead the variety of experimental initiatives that involve (for example) networks of cities and voluntary technology transfer and emission trading schemes. For Biermann, all these sorts of decentralization constitute only "fragmentation" and weak, ineffective responses that do not really make enough of a global difference.

So which side is right, the multilateralists like Biermann or the decentralists? Perhaps both are right in their criticism of the other side, while both are overconfident in what they advocate. Though multilateralism received a welcome boost with the signing of the Paris Agreement in 2015, its effectiveness remains to be demonstrated. And existing polycentric and decentralized approaches are clearly insufficient in sum when it comes to responding to climate change and the multi-faceted challenges of the Anthropocene in general.

Biermann (2014) would reply that the problem with existing multilateralism is that it does not go far enough: that what he proposes is a "realistic utopia" featuring much stronger global institutions such as a World Environment Organization (as a counterpart to the World Trade Organization), a Global Environmental Assessment Commission, and a United Nations Sustainable Development Council to integrate sustainability with other domains of global governance. Biermann would say the "realism" comes

---

[9] Biermann et al. (2009) employ a conception of fragmentation that is intended to be neutral from an evaluative standpoint: "a patchwork of international institutions that are different in their character (organizations, regimes, and implicit norms), their constituencies (public and private), their spatial scope (from bilateral to global), and their subject matter (from specific policy fields to universal concerns)." While they observe that fragmentation may be synergistic, cooperative or conflictive, they devote considerable attention to the negative consequences of conflictive fragmentation.

from the fact that similar institutions already exist for global economic governance. The problem is however that economic governance got there first and, along with the market-oriented free trade regime that it reinforces, imposes severe constraints on environmental governance at any level. Proponents of polycentrism and decentralization could perhaps come up with their own "realistic utopia" that would improve upon current inadequate efforts, so even if we compare realistic utopias it is not clear which would be better.

Thus we have three sets of sweeping institutional prescriptions for the Anthropocene. Folke et al. and Biermann et al. illustrate views commonly found in the two most prominent scholarly networks that have contemplated governance in the Anthropocene, respectively the Resilience Alliance and Earth System Governance Project. The decentralists advocating the third set of prescriptions (variously regime complexes, polycentrism, and experimental governance) are less well organized but still influential. The three sets of prescriptions are quite different. But all three are happy to rush to conclusions about appropriate institutional architecture before thoroughly engaging in the prior task: to establish more secure foundations for institutional analysis, design, and experimentation.

THINKING IN TERMS OF PROCESSES OF CHANGE, NOT MODELS

We do not believe it is possible to reach satisfactory conclusions based on any comparison of governance models of the sort the three schools propose, or for that matter any comparison of markets versus hierarchies versus networks versus cooperative arrangements, or consensual versus adversarial politics. So while (for example) the debate between decentralists such as Ostrom and Hoffmann, critics of fragmentation such as Biermann et al., and those such as Abbott (2012) who stake out some middle ground can be instructive, it does not yet operate in quite the right territory, because it still compares institutional models. Instead, it is more productive to start from where we are now and think in terms of processes of institutional change and available opportunities for overcoming pathological path dependency and enhancing reflexivity. This in turn requires careful analysis and evaluation of existing institutions and practices before thinking about prescription—not in the interests of preserving these institutions, but in the interests of changing them effectively. Commitments to periodic review of institutional arrangements may help to embed phases of reflexive rethinking, but there is much more to the story.

Chapter 2 and the preceding sections of this chapter offer some examples of what is possible in these terms. We have argued that the adaptive capacity of capitalist markets in unstable social-ecological contexts such as that presented by climate change may actually reinforce pathological path dependency and inhibit reflexivity, that there are ways to think about particular multilateral institutions (such as the UNFCCC) responding to their own failure through reflexive contemplation of a different kind of role, that we should be wary of particular transformational opportunities (such as that which occurred in US environmental affairs around 1970) yielding strong and undesirable renewed path dependency, and that foresight could be enhanced through more effective engagement of scientists and citizens. These examples suggest what it is possible to do productively without being tempted by advocacy of some comprehensive, all-purpose model of governance.

This reflexivity framework can shed further light on institutional proposals, including the three competitors we just highlighted. For example, if indeed a "constitutional moment" as envisaged by Biermann did come to pass in global environmental affairs, we might ask of any multilateral program to produce stronger global institutions whether it would embody strong path dependency of the sort we see in the Bretton Woods system for economic governance (involving the International Monetary Fund and the World Bank) and United Nations institutions established after 1945. Or we could ask of the components of the polycentric approach to global climate governance advocated by Ostrom whether they contributed, either individually or jointly, to global reflexivity beyond local contributions to (say) reduction of greenhouse gas emissions in cities or states such as California which have taken the lead in this area.

A partial answer to this last question can be gleaned from Hoffmann (2011). In treating multiple new forms of climate governance (such as voluntary emissions trading schemes, or networks of global cities) as an "experimental system," Hoffmann hopes that new material interests (for example, carbon traders) will become increasingly powerful constituencies, and people such as government officials and consumers will be socialized by their experience in the new forms. These new material interests would act as counterweights to currently dominant fossil fuel corporations, and that would surely be beneficial. At the same time, we should be wary of renewed path dependency based on either material interest or ideas impeding future transformative capacity, however much this new path might seem to solidify a more effective response to climate change in the short term.

The idea of an experimental system raises the question of whether the concept of "experimentalist governance" proposed by de Búrca et al. (2013; 2014) could provide a reflexive alternative to the models we have surveyed. Global experimentalist governance refers to "an institutionalized process of participatory and multilevel collective problem solving, in which the problems (and the means of addressing them) are framed in an open-ended way, and subjected to periodic revision by various forms of peer review in the light of locally generated knowledge" (de Búrca et al. 2014: 477). The open-ended, iterative nature of experimentalist governance makes clear its close affinities with the idea of reflexivity. At the same time, proponents of experimentalist governance acknowledge that—as with orchestration—their approach is most likely to thrive "in the 'Goldilocks Zone'—where the balance between too much and too little agreement is, like the temperature of Goldilocks' porridge, 'just right'" (de Búrca et al. 2014: 484). Thus, while the experimentalist approach is capable within limits of revising goals, it is less suited to situations where participants fundamentally disagree about core values. Yet such disagreement is precisely the kind of situation obstructing action on core problems of the Anthropocene, illustrated most strikingly by political polarization on climate change in the US, Australia, and Canada. And it is in circumstances of deep disagreement where reflexivity remains essential, but achieving it may require reaching beyond experimentation to other modes of interaction, such as deliberation (Dryzek and Pickering 2017). Deliberation is, among other things, a mode of conflict resolution that is capable of yielding mutually acceptable outcomes in situations of deep difference.

There are other ways in which our reflexivity framework can be deployed, notably in technology assessment. The failure of the world to curb greenhouse gas emissions has led to serious exploration of geoengineering technologies (see for example Lomborg 2010). Among the many possibilities, the most popular proposal currently involves injecting sulfate aerosols or fine titanium dioxide particles into the upper atmosphere to help block solar radiation. Once this technology has been chosen, there is no going back: given the aerosols or particles eventually return to earth, the machines to pump them into the upper atmosphere must keep running in perpetuity. If they were ever switched off, that would mean catastrophic rapid global temperature increase. The required institutions of geoengineering governance would need to be global, paramount, and permanent: meaning the efficacy of the institutions and so of the technology rests on establishing a path dependency of a scope and strength unprecedented in human history, foreclosing other institutional options, and shutting down reflexivity. For this reason alone, geoengineering on this scale should be abandoned.

WHERE TO START REBUILDING INSTITUTIONS FOR THE ANTHROPOCENE

Contemplation of the draconian politics that would have to accompany geoengineering drives home the intensity of the political challenge of the Anthropocene. The bitter politics of climate change that we see in the Anglo-American countries (capable of holding back global progress) offers but a foretaste. Getting the requisite qualities embedded in existing dominant institutions (such as states and international organizations) is going to be a struggle. So the proponents of polycentric, pluralistic, and experimental governance may be right about at least one thing: it is easier to start with governance initiatives at some distance from these established centers of power (and their associated pathological path dependencies).

We have argued that existing dominant institutions, be they states, international organizations, or markets, are not suited to governing in the Anthropocene in their current form. Their inappropriateness is confirmed by their pathological path dependencies. Yet haste to the prescription of alternatives is also problematic, threatening to short-circuit the kind of learning process necessary in the novel and complex conditions accompanying the challenge of the Anthropocene. One solution to this conundrum lies in the experimental exploration of structures and processes embodying the listening, learning, and anticipation that help constitute ecological reflexivity. We can begin by locating a few promising signs.

We have already located some hints of reflexivity in our earlier discussion of developments in the global governance of climate change, related notably to the move to orchestration. Further promise can be found in the experimental governance associated with ozone layer protection that we also mentioned.

Institutional experimentation need not of course be confined to the global level. There are many local initiatives such as the Transition Towns (or Transition Initiative) movement, which describes itself as a response to the failure of higher levels of government to confront resource constraints and climate change (Felicetti 2016). Networks across localities—such as the International Council for Local Environmental Initiatives cities network—also provide sites for sharing ideas for new practices (Bulkeley et al. 2010). While such sharing is not necessarily about restructuring of component cities, the network form itself can be a target of experimentation. Networked environmental governance (of the sort we can see in decentralized and polycentric initiatives) is however often in practice a low-visibility affair. Often it is dominated by moderate viewpoints that seek an easy accommodation between the existing economic system and ecological values—even if it is labeled "green growth" or "ecological modernization."

Reflexivity in networks could benefit from more contestatory and critical voices, be they from science, citizens' forums, or social movements. In this regard, the rapid worldwide expansion of the fossil fuel divestment movement is encouraging. The movement, whose origins are often traced to the advocacy group 350.org and its founder Bill McKibben, has adopted a more radical, confrontational strategy to encourage investors to scale back their exposure to fossil fuels (Ayling and Gunningham 2017). While both proponents and critics of the movement recognize that divestment alone is unlikely to make a major difference to global greenhouse gas emissions—not least because less scrupulous investors could step into the shoes of those who divest—it nevertheless has considerable potential to catalyze further policy change by calling into question fossil fuel companies' "social license to operate." In networks and elsewhere, the institutional challenge can be captured in terms of the need for more productive combinations of moments of decision and moments of contestation, which in turn ought to contribute to the capacity of such systems to transform themselves when necessary. In short, while there are no easy recipes for institutional innovators, there are plenty of instructive initiatives from which to learn and ways to think about their connection.

Instructive though they may be, these sorts of initiatives and experiments face significant obstacles. In the previous chapter we examined two dynamics that both involved the core priorities of dominant institutions. The first involved changing imperatives of states as a result of either a threat (such as that of the organized working class to capitalism inducing the rise of the welfare state) or an opportunity (such as that provided by the rise of capitalism for states to increase their revenues by promoting economic growth, rather than by squeezing taxpayers further). The second was pathological path dependency, which means both crisis and opportunity go suppressed or unrecognized.

These two dynamics both feature thoroughgoing institutional change only in response to infrequent crisis or still more infrequent opportunity—critical junctures, in the language we later used. We have tried to establish that the novelty of the Anthropocene means that this sort of reflexivity being forced into play at moments of crisis (or critical juncture) will not do. Rather, if catastrophes such as state shifts are to be averted, reflexivity is required as a permanent capacity of institutions—as *itself* a core priority. The institutional requirements of the Anthropocene really are unprecedented. We will have much more to say about who might step up to the task and how their actions and interactions might move the world forward in these terms in chapters 6 and 7.

Conclusion

Recognition of the Anthropocene entails a powerful challenge to human institutions, as the non-human world becomes impossible to ignore as a central player in human history. This challenge merits a response whose scope is broader than either environmental governance—conceived as a niche area to be consigned to a government department or an academic sub-discipline—or even the "mainstreaming" of ecological concerns into all areas of government. By confirming the causal force of human social processes in driving the character of the Earth system, whose instability in turn becomes a larger force, the Anthropocene compels a rethink of social-ecological systems and the place of political institutions in them (along with deep commitments about what constitutes rationality in these institutions and beyond). The depth, novelty, dynamism, and complexity of the challenge call into question the rush to prescription of the (few) existing institutional analyses of the Anthropocene, which tend to miss the mark by thinking in terms of models to be adopted or avoided, rather than in terms of processes of reconstruction that always move from where we are now.

We have identified ecological reflexivity as the primary requirement for political institutions in the Anthropocene. The ecological dimension of reflexivity involves listening more effectively to an active Earth system, a stronger capacity to reconsider core values such as justice and sustainability in this light, and an ability to seek, receive, and respond to early warnings about potential ecological state shifts. We have shown how this framework can be applied in institutional analysis, evaluation, and design in a way that is true to the dynamic nature of the Anthropocene, and so avoids the temptation to think in terms of static institutional models. Taking the Anthropocene seriously suggests an evolving thinking about institutions that joins inquiry and practice, in the face of existing dominant institutions that fall so far short of the requirements of this emerging epoch.

Rethinking governance for a changing Earth system will require rethinking core values such as justice and sustainability that (sometimes) motivate collective action, and it is to this task that we turn in the next two chapters.

▧ APPENDIX: PROCEDURE AND SUBSTANCE IN ECOLOGICAL REFLEXIVITY

A critical question facing the concept of ecological reflexivity is whether it should be understood as a substantive or a procedural value, or a mix of both.[10] A purely substantive understanding of ecological reflexivity would stress the priority of protecting ecosystems relative to other values (such as human development). On this understanding, institutions could still be condemned as non-reflexive if they reflect upon their values and operations but continue to pursue environmentally destructive practices. However, such a substantive view could be criticized for prejudging the very questions of priority among values that reflexive institutions should be scrutinizing.

In contrast, a highly procedural understanding of ecological reflexivity would be neutral about substantive values (ecological or otherwise). An institution could be judged reflexive so long as it scrutinized its practices and was open to changing core values—regardless of whether those values became more or less ecologically harmful as a result. Conceptions of reflexive governance are often highly procedural (see for example Smith and Stirling 2007), prizing contestation over substantive values. So, for example, procedural reflexivity could apply to fossil fuel companies, despite the ecological harms they produce, if they are capable of restructuring themselves. Procedural reflexivity comes at a high price, becoming detached from the social-ecological values that reflexivity is supposed to serve.

---

[10] This question is explored in greater detail in Pickering (2018).

Reflexivity is impossible without procedures of critical reflection, but substantive values must also come into play. Starting with where we are now, reflexive inquiry begins with core values that societies already hold—such as democracy, justice, and sustainability—and interrogates them in the light of changing ecological conditions. Evolving scientific understanding about the dependence of human societies on the Earth system means that Earth system values must be accorded high priority. Exactly how high should remain the subject of reflexive debate.

In this light, reflexivity might not guarantee democratically legitimate, just, or sustainable outcomes in practice. So, for example, the highly successful international effort to reverse ozone layer depletion had one unfortunate side effect, for one of the substitutes for ozone-depleting substances (hydrofluorocarbons or HFCs) turned out to be a potent greenhouse gas. But a reflexive institution should be self-correcting, such that negative effects of policy responses become the subject of further scrutiny. The UN ozone regime eventually passed an amendment to phase out HFCs, thereby helping to minimize the adverse climate change effects of those substances (UNEP 2016b).[11]

The idea of ecological reflexivity—like that of ecological democracy—reflects a mix of procedural and substantive values. These two aspects can come into tension, just as democratic processes may not inevitably yield ideal environmental outcomes. However, the tension does not undermine the validity of the concept; rather the tension is constructive in that it opens up space for contestation and rethinking within broad ecological parameters.

---

[11] The ozone regime has delivered important benefits for climate change mitigation in other ways, because most ozone-depleting substances targeted by the Montreal Protocol are also greenhouse gases. In a comment that the drafters of the UNFCCC would envy, Molina et al. (2009: 20617) describe the Montreal Protocol as "the most successful climate treaty to date."

4 Planetary justice

Almost everyone thinks justice is a good thing. Some people think it is the very best thing to pursue, at least when it comes to a society's collective decisions. Yet injustice looms large in a disrupted Earth system. Climate change reveals stark differences between those who are most responsible for destabilizing the Earth system and those who suffer most from the consequences. The very existence of some low-lying Pacific island states is threatened by sea level rise, yet it is overwhelmingly emissions produced in industrialized states that have caused the problem. The Anthropocene not only reveals new sorts of injustice but also intensifies pre-existing injustices. Archbishop Desmond Tutu has warned of "climate apartheid" if measures to adapt to climate change insulate the wealthy from heatwaves and rising sea levels while leaving the poor still more exposed to risks (Tutu 2007; see also Lukacs 2014).

But who exactly should be held responsible for remedying these injustices? Is it the governments of the heaviest-polluting nations, individual citizens within them, the companies that have extracted and exported fossil fuels, or all of the above? And what about wealthy consumers in poor countries? Should poor people in rich countries be exempt? Problems in assigning responsibilities surround injustices that arise in the Anthropocene, because of the complex links among humans and non-humans through their interactions with the Earth system. For example, demand for food or biofuels in one country could accelerate deforestation in another country, not only hastening biodiversity loss but also depriving forest-dependent communities of their means of subsistence.

The Anthropocene not only complicates the task of assigning responsibility to promote justice, but also calls into question prevailing assumptions about the meaning and scope of justice itself. Principles of justice, Rawls argues, "provide a way of assigning rights and duties in the basic institutions of society and they define the appropriate distribution of the benefits and burdens of social cooperation" (Rawls 1999b: 4). Recognizing the Anthropocene calls into question what constitutes a society to begin with, because interactions involving an active Earth system do not respect national boundaries—or species boundaries. As the intensity and duration of humanity's influence over the Earth continues to grow, it becomes increasingly urgent to rethink what humans owe to their fellow humans living today and also to future generations and non-humans.

This chapter explores why and how justice needs to be rethought under Anthropocene conditions. We are less concerned with how the word "justice" should be defined than with what kinds of duties, rights, and institutions justice requires in the Anthropocene, and what this means for political practice.[1] We begin by replying to three arguments that dispense with Anthropocene justice. The first is that the very idea of the Anthropocene suppresses questions of justice, so there is no point in thinking about it. The second is that the Anthropocene is too complex a place for *social* justice, such that individual virtues should be cultivated instead. The third is that old ideas about justice can still be applied. We then discuss expansion of the scope of justice to a planetary level by attending to the global, intergenerational, and non-human dimensions of justice. We address two kinds of risk that could attend the pursuit of planetary justice. The first is that expanding the scope of responsibilities for promoting justice could result paradoxically in a sense of powerlessness and evasion of moral responsibility. The second risk is that efforts to distribute responsibilities for remedying injustice across the web of actors involved in disrupting the Earth system could result in either too many or too few actors being held responsible. We show how a multifaceted approach to thinking about justice, and a better understanding of political strategies for pursuing planetary justice, can overcome these risks.

Can justice survive the Anthropocene?

Calls to rethink justice in the Anthropocene immediately face three different criticisms. Some critics are concerned that the very notion of the Anthropocene means turning a blind eye to justice. Others accept the idea of the Anthropocene but believe that social justice becomes unattainable, and should yield to individual virtue. Others still believe that existing notions of justice do not need to change much. We take issue with each view, before identifying a deeper concern with Holocene understandings of justice: that they are complicit in path dependencies that obstruct effective response to the Anthropocene.

DOES THE IDEA OF THE ANTHROPOCENE SUPPRESS JUSTICE?

One important line of criticism (flagged briefly in chapter 1) is that the Anthropocene concept obscures important differences of wealth and power across and within societies. First, critics argue, it means blaming humanity as a whole for the biggest risks facing the Earth system, while disguising the unjust disproportion between the responsibility of some—mainly industrialized

---

[1] For a related distinction between the concept of justice itself and different conceptions of justice, see Rawls (1999b: 3).

countries—and the suffering of others (Malm and Hornborg 2014; Baskin 2015). Some of these critics suggest alternative terms to the Anthropocene (such as the Capitalocene) which more clearly blame certain groups (e.g. capitalists) for global environmental change and its associated injustices. Second, it is argued that the Anthropocene concept is largely promulgated by those (read: natural scientists) who favor technocratic strategies for fixing environmental problems which ignore justice and inequalities of power (Malm and Hornborg 2014). Technocratic responses might aim to overhaul energy systems while showing little regard for workers who lose their jobs when fossil fuel industries shut down; or they may seek to protect large swathes of tropical forest without considering how to safeguard the livelihoods of communities who depend on forest resources for food and fuel. Third, and relatedly, Baskin (2015: 22) argues that in invoking planetary crisis Anthropocene discourse embodies "deeply authoritarian and de-politicizing tendencies" which suppress justice in the interests of averting disaster.

Concerning the first criticism, the Anthropocene concept is capable of recognizing differentiated responsibilities and sufferings. While earlier accounts of the Anthropocene often maintained a broad-brush global focus, subsequent accounts are considerably more attuned to societal differences and the need to consider inequality and injustice (see for example Biermann et al. 2016: 342). Indeed, as we argue later, current patterns of global injustice will persist if the implications of the Anthropocene's emergence are *not* recognized. The concept of climate justice shows how to integrate universal and differentiated perspectives on a single problem. The global character of climate change—and its widely accepted description as human-induced or anthropogenic—has not impeded the emergence of the idea of climate justice that emphasizes global inequalities accompanying a warming world (Schlosberg and Collins 2014).

In response to the second concern about technocracy, while the Anthropocene concept originated in the natural sciences, debate over the term has since broadened considerably to encompass the social sciences, humanities, media, and even science fiction (Lorimer 2017). Admittedly not all of this debate has been illuminating or constructive, and there remains scope for more effective engagement across the voices represented. As we argue later in this chapter, debate about justice in the Anthropocene needs to attend to multiple understandings held by different social groups—particularly those most affected by injustice—as to what justice and injustice should mean (Dryzek 2015). But the Anthropocene concept is not inherently blinded to justice by a technocratic fixation.

The third concern taps into a genuine worry that invocations of planetary crisis may drown out calls for justice, if the need to avert disaster is so overwhelming that we simply do not have the luxury of attending to justice (Gardiner 2011b: 309). This worry reflects (mostly discredited) arguments from the 1970s for an authoritarian response to global ecological crisis. But eco-authoritarianism is unconvincing, not least because there is little guarantee that authoritarian rulers will be more inclined than democratic governments to protect the Earth system rather than endanger it further (Niemeyer 2014a).

Now, there may indeed be circumstances in which the time available to respond to an emergency is so limited that justice cannot attract attention; think, for example, of the minutes or hours following an earthquake or a terrorist attack. But if the Anthropocene has the character of a planetary emergency, it is more akin to the chronic, complex humanitarian emergencies generated by long-standing conflict or political instability rather than the immediate aftermath of a natural disaster (Keen 2008). The changes necessary to respond to risks to the Earth system cannot be mobilized at a moment's notice but will require far-reaching responses over years and decades.

Even if an unstable Earth system makes acute disasters such as cyclones and floods more frequent or intense, the periods before and after catastrophic events still present opportunities to take concerns of justice into account through equitable disaster risk reduction and recovery (Berke, Kartez, and Wenger 1993). Hurricane Katrina, which devastated New Orleans in 2005, generated a political storm as environmental injustice was so clearly evident in the race and class disparities in both suffering and the capacity to recover (Bullard and Wright 2009). Thus, even if the Anthropocene does involve a planetary emergency, lack of time is a bad reason to sideline justice. Moreover, major reforms to confront planetary risks are likely to founder in the face of political resistance if those reforms generate new kinds of injustice. If anyone does nevertheless invoke the Anthropocene emergency to suspend justice, the solution is not to abandon the concept. Instead, it becomes all the more important to explore how the Anthropocene might require us to think about justice in a new light.

SHOULD WE RETREAT FROM SOCIAL JUSTICE TO INDIVIDUAL VIRTUE?

A very different view accepts the idea of the Anthropocene but argues that the pursuit of justice becomes chimerical in an increasingly complex world. Traditional conceptions of personal morality emerged from situations where an individual's actions produced clear short-term effects upon a small and well-defined number of other individuals (Lichtenberg 2010: 558–9; Jamieson 2014: 148–50).[2] But these conditions do not hold at a planetary scale, not only

[2] Philosophers often see personal ethics as distinct from social justice. Individual people may have ethical obligations (e.g. not to harm others) independently of societal requirements of justice, but questions of social justice may intersect with personal ethics where duties of justice devolve from collectives to individuals.

because of global interconnectedness but also because of the long time horizons and uncertainties associated with impacts on the Earth system. Accordingly, it becomes tempting for individuals to say that "the global quandaries of the Anthropocene are just so vast that it does not matter what I personally do: I do not personally cause them, nor can I personally fix them" (Di Paola 2015: 193).

These concerns have prompted some thinkers to advocate virtue ethics as a basis for moral decision-making in the Anthropocene (Schmidt et al. 2016: 196; see also Jamieson 2014). Virtue ethics focuses less on fulfilling general duties or maximizing overall well-being than on cultivating qualities such as honesty or compassion. Di Paola (2015: 203–4) concludes that "an ethic for the Anthropocene must be based on individualized, self-starting, self-regulating, metropolitan, networked, resolute ecosystem stewardship whose backbone is active, virtuous engagement." He advocates two virtues exemplified by gardening: mindfulness and cheerfulness. But tending one's own garden can be a way of turning one's back on problems that extend beyond the gardener's own patch, thus avoiding the collective efforts required to address those problems. If everyone else were cheerfully tending their own gardens, the world might be better off; but when some are desiccating or poisoning the gardens of others, the need for collective responses cannot be ignored.

The problem with relying on personal virtue ethics is that it ignores the social and economic structures (produced under Holocene conditions) that force people to behave badly in order to function in society. We both live in Canberra, Australia, home to a highly educated and environmentally progressive population that drives vast distances every day—because the sprawling Holocene layout of the city induces them to take to their cars. Thus even if people's attitudes change, this may be insufficient to overcome structural impediments to achieving justice. In the presence of such structures, virtuous individual behavior may even be counterproductive if it induces self-satisfaction and complacency.

If the virtues of gardening are to be relevant for the Anthropocene, they must also extend to collective stewardship (Marris 2011). Williston (2015) shows how a virtue-based account of Anthropocene ethics can be achieved while remaining attuned to broader societal concerns. For Williston, justice is one of three core virtues (along with truthfulness and hope) required to live ethically in the Anthropocene. His analysis is most compelling when it contrasts the virtue of justice—"the disposition to accord each member of the moral community his fair share of socially distributed benefits and burdens"—with the vice of greed, that is, "taking more than our fair share of a scarce resource" (Williston 2015: 80, 82). Williston emphasizes that cultivating justice in individuals and institutions can help to overcome collective action problems such as climate change which defy resolution because agents are unwilling to restrain their self-interest (or greed) until other actors do the same (p.83).

Some virtues, then, can provide a valuable way of thinking politically about justice and ethics in the Anthropocene.[3] Later in this chapter we will argue that ecological reflexivity becomes a particularly important virtue for political institutions in the Anthropocene. But virtue ethics alone cannot provide much guidance unless it moves beyond the individual and maintains a commitment to justice.

ARE EXISTING THEORIES OF JUSTICE SUFFICIENT?

Other critics accept the concept of the Anthropocene but contend that there is little need to rethink what justice means (Gardiner 2011a: 38; Heyward 2015).

Philosophers have indeed long thought about the just use of natural resources. The seventeenth-century philosopher John Locke sought to specify the conditions under which people may justly appropriate resources from nature. Locke's famous "proviso" states that individuals may acquire property rights over common resources such as land and water as long as there is "enough, and as good left in common for others" (Locke 1988 [1690]: paragraph 27). However, Locke thought that natural resources were so bountiful that the world's population could never use them up (Wolf 1995: 797–8). Some recent adaptations of Locke's proviso recognize that, with a rapidly growing global population consuming ever more resources, the "ecological space" available for each person is rapidly shrinking (Hayward 2006). Locke's proviso could still be adapted so that what counts as leaving "enough" resources for others is whatever is required to meet basic human needs, rather than allowing everyone to consume as much as the world's wealthy currently do. But the rapid depletion of the world's natural resources poses a much deeper problem for theories of justice.

Theories of justice rest on a set of background assumptions about the state of the world that makes the pursuit of justice both necessary and possible; these are often referred to (beginning with Hume 1739: book 3, part 2, section 2; and elaborated in Rawls 1999b: 109–12) as the "circumstances of justice." One of these assumptions is the existence of moderate—but not extreme—scarcity of resources. In a world of great abundance justice would be superfluous, whereas in a world of extreme scarcity justice would be unattainable. There is a long history of extreme scarcity at a local level accompanying famine, so the idea that it may be impossible to secure justice in dire conditions is not entirely new. But the risk of catastrophic state shifts in the Earth system now raises the

---

[3] See also Muller and Huppenbauer 2016, who advocate (in addition to justice) the virtue of sufficiency or temperance as having close affinities with sustainability. The Epicurean idea of living within nature's limits could also be thought of a societal as well as individual virtue.

possibility that even if moderate scarcity prevails globally for now, it may become extreme in future. Whether the circumstances of justice would hold at all under extreme scarcity remains debated (Wienhues 2017); at the very least the requirements of justice would need to be very different. Thus Mulgan (2011) envisages a "broken world" in the aftermath of ecological catastrophe. In a world where not everyone's needs could be met, he argues that "equal *chances* to survive might replace *guaranteed* survival as the minimum requirement of justice" (Mulgan 2011: 15; emphasis in original).

The limitations of existing theories of justice do not stop there. As we outline in later sections, the Anthropocene also underscores the need to overcome other blind spots in prominent conceptions of justice, including inadequate recognition of duties of justice towards people living in other countries, future generations, and non-humans. These represent what Nussbaum (2006) calls "frontiers of justice."[4] Some necessary rethinking has begun along these dimensions, particularly on duties of global justice (Beitz 1999; Caney 2005), but it is rare to find an integrated treatment of all three dimensions.[5] Philosophers of global justice often concentrate on duties of justice to the world's poor living today (e.g. Pogge 2008; Barry and Øverland 2016), with less emphasis on future generations. Intergenerational concerns are generally more prominent in thinking on climate justice (Page 2006; Gardiner 2011c; Shue 2014). We will draw extensively on this thinking, but there are three reasons why advances on climate justice do not exhaust the need to rethink justice for the Anthropocene. First, theories of climate justice have not engaged fully with obligations towards non-humans (Nolt 2011; Hayward 2012; Palmer 2011). Second, aspects of the Earth system beyond climate change have received very little attention, notably questions of justice in conserving biodiversity (Martin, McGuire, and Sullivan 2013). Third, despite the efforts of some climate ethicists to contribute to political debates, ideas of climate justice have hardly been reflected in the policies and practices of governments and international organizations (Heyward and Roser 2016). This

---

[4] Nussbaum's list of frontiers—disability, nationality and species membership—complements our own, with some important differences. Nussbaum's book focuses on theories of justice (such as that of Rawls) based on the idea of a hypothetical social contract under which citizens agree on the duties of justice they owe to each other. While these theories frequently struggle to address questions of justice for people with disabilities, this dimension can be accommodated more readily by other theories (e.g. those built on the idea of rights or capabilities), so we do not address it here. Nussbaum does not deal with justice for future generations because she contends (2006: 23) that Rawls's theory adequately deals with this aspect, but we argue that further rethinking of intergenerational justice remains necessary.

[5] Rawls's theory of justice includes a principle of "just savings" for future generations (Rawls 1999b: 255), but elsewhere (Rawls 2005: 21) he acknowledges that his theory has trouble handling the three dimensions of justice we have identified. His subsequent attempt to specify very limited duties of justice among nations (Rawls 1999a) is widely recognized as flawed (Nussbaum 2006: 23). Some theorists have tried to extend Rawls's principles to address some of these limitations, but rarely in the integrated fashion we advocate.

underscores the need for political analysis to identify how principles of justice can be translated into practice.

ARE HOLOCENE CONCEPTIONS OF JUSTICE PART OF THE PROBLEM?

The inability of Holocene ideas about justice to comprehend fully the conditions of the Anthropocene is not the end of the matter. Even worse, existing ideas of justice could be complicit in accelerating the ecological risks that humanity faces in the Anthropocene. Here we encounter again the problem of pathological path dependency: what if conventional ideas of justice, like other social institutions, are fundamentally compromised by their avoidance of feedbacks from the Earth system?

Clive Hamilton argues that existing ethics—among whose main concerns is justice—can no longer provide any guidance for the Anthropocene. First, he and co-authors contend, the timescales of the Anthropocene are fundamentally different to those of conventional ethics: "talk of ethics renders banal a transition that belongs to deep time, one that is literally Earth-shattering. In deep time, there are no ethics" (Hamilton, Gemenne, and Bonneuil 2015: 8). (It is ironic that Hamilton is a professor of public ethics.) Rhetoric aside, really Hamilton is simply arguing for longer time horizons, which is still a matter of ethics. Second, Hamilton argues that both religious and secular moral codes, by fixating on how humans should relate to one another, fail to provide sufficient guidance for how they should relate to the Earth itself (Hamilton 2017: 155). But thinking on ecological justice can still provide a starting point for contemplating human–non-human relations. Many forms of ethics (including non-Western ones) do not maintain a strict divide between humanity and nature (Schmidt, Brown, and Orr 2016: 189). Conversely, there are risks in wiping the slate clean: "simply rejecting conventional ethics could legitimate and amplify historical inequalities if coupled with claims that previous ethical conventions are no longer applicable despite the obligations created by them" (Schmidt, Brown, and Orr 2016: 189). In other words, dismissing ethics in its entirety could open the floodgates to all kinds of injustices.

A more important problem is that advances in justice may rest upon the same economic growth that has undermined the ecological conditions for human flourishing. What are we to make of the fact that the rise of social movements in the second half of the twentieth century—which yielded remarkable advances in addressing injustices associated with gender, sexuality, race, and national origin—coincided with the Great Acceleration in material consumption and production? Or that by far the greatest-ever reduction in numbers of people in poverty has been achieved by China's rapid economic growth over several decades? Or that governments have relied on continuing economic growth to maintain welfare states that help to alleviate social inequalities (Gough and Meadowcroft 2011: 495)? In this vein, Chakrabarty (2009) argues that "the mansion of modern freedoms stands on an ever-expanding base of fossil-fuel use."[6]

The pursuit of justice does not have to be yoked to economic growth and so to ecological degradation. There may be times when distributive justice and environmental protection conflict—but there are also times when they do not. The relationship between economic growth, income inequality (as a rough proxy for social injustice) and environmental degradation is complicated (see e.g. Stern 2004; Baland, Bardhan, and Bowles 2007; Chancel and Piketty 2015). Norway has one of the lowest levels of income inequality in the world, but its economy remains highly dependent on the export of oil and gas. Meanwhile, its neighbor Sweden has similarly low levels of inequality, yet its ecological impact is far lower: Swedes emit less than half the level of greenhouse gas emissions per person of Norwegians (World Bank 2017). And there is at least a possibility that countries can eschew economic growth altogether while still pursuing justice (we will have more to say on this in chapter 5). But there is little evidence to suggest that the pursuit of social justice will inevitably lead to ecological ruin.

In addition, if ever there was a tight relationship between economic growth and greater social justice, it may have come to an end. While in many countries average prosperity is increasing, it is now mostly accompanied by rising inequality, to the extent that very few of the benefits trickle down to the poor (Milanovic 2016). The idea that justice needs growth is yet another Holocene idea whose time has passed—but one that refuses to go away. To be clear: the core problem with Holocene justice is not that there *is* a necessary connection between economic growth and the promotion of justice, but that may people *believe* there is.

Holocene conceptions of justice do not, then, *necessarily* cause ecological degradation, even though those that are premised on unending material growth do so. It may even be that injustice drives degradation (Martinez-Alier 2002). Colonial exploitation of natural resources through the oppression of Indigenous peoples and the expropriation of their land is perhaps the starkest historical example here. But there is also evidence from contemporary societies that ecosystems in which Indigenous peoples' and local communities' rights to land tenure are not recognized tend to suffer higher degradation (Stevens et al. 2014).

A final reason not to discard Holocene justice in its entirety is that advances in extending the reach of justice—in relation to slavery and colonialism, for example—have often come about through convincing people to recognize

---

[6] Mitchell (2011) makes the somewhat more nuanced argument that the exploitation of coal and oil reserves helped both to open up and to constrain possibilities for democracy.

broader duties based on principles that they already hold (Crawford 2002: 102). Even if justice does need to be overhauled, failure to explore how much could be done through resolving inconsistencies in existing beliefs (e.g. the reasons why people consider humans but not animals as subjects of justice) would deprive political advocacy of an important motivational tool.

From environmental justice to planetary justice

How should we start rethinking justice for Anthropocene conditions? We take as our point of departure the idea of environmental justice, now deployed by social movements around the world (Schlosberg 2007; Walker 2012). Earlier theories of environmental justice focused mainly on distribution, with special reference to how environmental harms such as toxic pollution fall disproportionately on poor and marginalized people. More recently the net has been cast more widely to include procedural justice and justice as recognition (Schlosberg 2007; Martin, McGuire, and Sullivan 2013). Procedural justice concerns the fairness of decision-making processes (e.g. rights of participation and access to information, and responsibilities of power-holders to be accountable), while recognition involves validating the moral standing of other humans (and perhaps non-humans).

The idea of environmental justice could be seen as a corrective to an environmentalism that privileged nature conservation to the neglect of social justice and economic inequalities (Dobson 1998: 19). The often uneasy relationship between the environmental justice community and other environmentalists sometimes results in an overly rigid boundary between environmental justice that addresses relations of social justice among people, and "ecological" justice to the non-human world (Schlosberg 2007: 3; Walker 2012: 10).

At present we lack an overarching term and common framework to encompass both environmental and ecological justice, despite the fact that the two are closely intertwined. Schlosberg (2004: 43–4) observes that "the origins of environmental injustices are as much in the treatment of the non-human realm as in relations among human beings." Thus many of the environmental harms to people—from polluted air and water to droughts induced by climate change—are also products of contempt for the non-human world. More fundamentally, it is difficult to say what is owed to humans (or for that matter to non-humans) until we have a broader picture of the entire moral community, human and non-human, that has claims on finite resources.

Schlosberg (2004: 43–4) suggests that theories of environmental justice, including his own, are beginning to embrace justice for non-humans. But the distinction between ecological and environmental justice establishes a useful conceptual division of labor, while acknowledging the possibility of linkages between the two. So a different overarching term is needed. The idea of "social-ecological justice" is apt, not least because of its alignment with the social-ecological systems discussed in chapter 1.[7] The notion of "planetary justice" is for our purposes preferable because it denotes justice that relates to the Earth system as a whole (rather than to local or regional systems).[8] Thus climate justice and biodiversity justice—along with hitherto unexplored ideas such as nitrogen and phosphorus justice—could all be seen as facets of planetary justice.

The reach of planetary justice

We now address three ways in which the scope of planetary justice needs to reach beyond Holocene thinking: by escaping state-centric accounts of justice; in extending justice to future generations; and through encompassing justice for non-humans (see Figure 4.1). These extensions can be seen as continuing

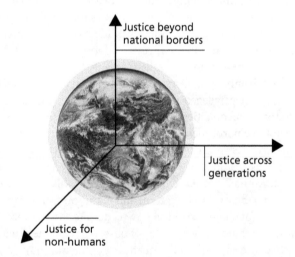

Figure 4.1. Dimensions of planetary justice

Earth photo source: NOAA/NASA (https://www.nasa.gov/sites/default/files/thumbnails/image/abi_full_disk_low_res_jan_15_2017.jpg)

[7] This term has been mentioned sporadically in the environmental justice literature, but to our knowledge Gunnarsson-Östling and Svenfelt (2018) are the first to include the term in the title of a work.

[8] To our knowledge the first use of this term in a sense that approximates our own can be found in Singer (2009). More recently, the Earth System Governance Project (2018) has launched a taskforce to explore this idea.

what Schlosberg (2013) calls the "expanding sphere" of environmental justice discourse.[9] None of these extensions is entirely new to the theory or practice of justice, but they are often neglected in favor of measures to address readily observable injustices to human compatriots living now.

JUSTICE BEYOND NATIONAL BORDERS

Like it or not, it is hard to see how the world could feasibly move beyond a system of states in the short term. But that does not mean national borders must dominate our thinking about justice.

The state exerts a strong gravitational pull on some well-known theories of justice, which hold that duties of justice apply exclusively or overwhelmingly among fellow members of a nation state (see for example Rawls 1999a; Blake 2001; Nagel 2005).[10] But an approach bounded by a social contract among fellow citizens proves incapable of comprehending the increasing global interconnectedness of human societies and individuals which results from their pervasive influence on the Earth system. Central to the challenge of grappling with the Anthropocene is the fact that the actions of individuals and entire societies now have far-reaching consequences both for the Earth system itself and so for other inhabitants of the Earth far removed in space and time (Schmidt, Brown, and Orr 2016: 192). When, for example, an Australian parent drives their children to school in a petrol-fueled car, they are contributing to the store of greenhouse gases in the atmosphere that is already harming people in low-lying river deltas in Bangladesh, Vietnam and beyond. But state-centric theories struggle to come to terms with injustices that cross national borders.

Recent thinking about global justice has recognized the need to think about duties of justice held by citizens of one country towards those in other countries (see for example Caney 2005; Pogge 2008; Valentini 2011). Theories of environmental justice have likewise expanded in scope. Early thinking and activism in this area focused primarily on the uneven distribution of local environmental harms, such as the siting of toxic waste dumps in disadvantaged communities. Over time environmental justice has expanded to confront injustices arising from the global distribution of environmental risks, such as the vulnerability of poorer countries to the impacts of climate change (Schlosberg and Collins 2014). However, the institutions of the welfare state (which we discussed in chapter 2) overwhelmingly emphasize securing justice

---

[9] See also Walzer's (1983) seminal account of spheres of justice (although it is unlikely that the shape of the planet informed his choice of metaphor).

[10] These theorists recognize that certain kinds of relationships across national borders (e.g. coercion or cooperation) may trigger other kinds of moral duties, but these generally do not amount to duties of justice.

for one's own citizens. Despite significant flows of global aid over recent decades, international mechanisms for protecting the vulnerable are far less developed than their domestic equivalents. Domestic welfare mechanisms remain vitally important, but the absence of a robust international system for social protection provides another example of how Holocene path dependencies may obstruct meaningful responses to the Anthropocene.

JUSTICE ACROSS GENERATIONS

A second priority for rethinking justice in the Anthropocene concerns the responsibilities that people living today owe to future generations for protecting the Earth system, and the responsibilities that the present generation holds for remedying the environmental damage caused by those who lived before. Problems of intergenerational justice are particularly acute because human influence on the Earth system is the result of cumulative environmental degradation across multiple generations, with far-reaching consequences for the future. For example, given that greenhouse gases can persist in the atmosphere for centuries, those who burn fossil fuels today are harming the life prospects of future people who will have to contend with harsher conditions and higher sea levels. Carbon dioxide released from coal that was burnt in nineteenth-century England continues to affect the global climate, even though the overwhelming bulk of humanity's cumulative greenhouse gas emissions has entered the atmosphere since the Great Acceleration began in the mid-twentieth century (Höhne et al 2011). When species become extinct today, they are permanently lost to future generations.

The task of rethinking intergenerational justice involves more than encouraging political institutions to outgrow their myopia; it also involves thinking specifically about what kind of Earth system conditions the present owes to the future. Should future generations inherit Earth system conditions that are roughly the same as those that the present generation inhabits, or is it permissible to bestow a warmer world provided that we also pass on technologies and infrastructure that will enable people to adapt? Questions such as these relate closely to how we should think of sustainability in the Anthropocene, and we return to these in the next chapter.

Such problems notwithstanding, we can be confident of at least two things. First, humans living today have a strong responsibility to ensure that future generations can live in a world where the circumstances of justice still prevail, particularly the ecological preconditions necessary for them to pursue justice (see also McKinnon 2009: 194). This means we must avoid causing extreme scarcity in the future because, as we observed earlier, the essential circumstance of justice is moderate scarcity. Second, consistent with the idea that ecological reflexivity requires anticipating the possibility of catastrophic state shifts in the Earth system (and the extreme scarcity they would cause), intergenerational justice requires current generations to minimize the possibility of those state shifts occurring in future.

JUSTICE FOR NON-HUMANS

A third priority is to rethink the duties of justice humans owe to non-humans (other living organisms as well as ecosystems that comprise both living and non-living things). These duties could flow from the intrinsic moral worth of these other entities—but also, ultimately, could derive from the value of non-human life for human well-being too. The Anthropocene casts relations of justice between humans and non-humans in a paradoxical light. On the one hand, as Hamilton (2017) emphasizes, the arrival of the new epoch underscores the distinctive nature of the human species, given its unique influence over other species and the dynamics of the Earth system. In this way, the Anthropocene could be seen as justifying a new anthropocentrism that place humans even more firmly at the center of the moral universe; Hamilton (2017) argues in favor of such an enterprise, in which the world really is all about us. Conversely, greater entanglements between human and non-human nature point to the need to recognize our moral as well as physical commonalities. In the Anthropocene, nature is not quite so non-human. Can this paradox be resolved?

The ever greater vulnerability of other species to human interference adds new urgency to longstanding calls by environmental ethicists to extend obligations of justice to non-humans.[11] Even so, we need a positive argument beyond vulnerability for generating obligations of justice; after all, concrete is vulnerable to humans wielding jackhammers, but that in itself does not mean concrete has any particular moral interests or value that must be protected.

One way to think about recognizing non-humans as subjects of justice involves extending the idea of capabilities (as proposed by Schlosberg 2007 and others).[12] Capabilities safeguard the potential for entities to flourish; capabilities-based theories of justice specify that protecting the ability to flourish becomes the central point of justice. Flourishing in turn can apply to human and non-human life, as well as entire communities and ecosystems such as forests or wetlands. The capabilities approach could serve as a basis for understanding planetary justice, grounding obligations to safeguard the capabilities of people living across national borders, and of future generations of

---

[11] For a related vulnerability-based argument for protecting the environment, see Goodin (1985: 179–86).

[12] See also Nussbaum (2006: 326) for a more limited extension of capabilities to individual animals (but not to species as a whole nor to ecosystems).

non-humans and humans alike.[13] The specific capabilities of individuals and communities may need to be redefined to take account of a changing Earth system. Especially important here is what Holland (2008) calls the "meta-capability" of "sustainable ecological capacity" that is necessary for all other human capabilities (such as political liberties, social opportunities, health, and education) and non-human capabilities to be secured.

Even in the absence of political consensus on the kinds of substantive capabilities or rights that non-humans possess, procedural justice requires that the interests of animals and other relevant entities be formally represented in decision-making. This need not involve the direct presence of "cats in congress or penguins in parliament" (Schlosberg 2007: 191), but could be achieved through humans acting as guardians of non-human interests in political settings. Could such rights be safeguarded in practice? To some extent we already see prominent types of ecosystems being represented in decision-making at the international level. Wetlands, for example, have a voice of sorts in international biodiversity negotiations through the participation of representatives of the Ramsar Convention on Wetlands of International Importance as well as the non-government organization Wetlands International. But the representation of other ecosystems remains patchy and could be formalized to ensure that all major biomes or ecosystem types—including, for example, frequently overlooked ecosystems such as grasslands and Arctic tundra—have a seat at the negotiating table.

Efforts to represent nature have seen more notable breakthroughs at the domestic level. The government of New Zealand has declared the Whanganui River and Mount Taranaki as living entities bearing the same legal rights as humans, with human custodians to be appointed to represent them and protect their interests. The government of India has done the same with the Ganges (Roy 2017; Safi 2017). These cases follow an earlier decision by Ecuador to grant rights to nature in its 2008 constitution (Kotzé and Villavicencio Calzadilla 2017). But even where ecosystems such as rivers are granted legal personality, there remain daunting barriers to protecting their interests, including the presence of competing and often highly vocal interests of farmers and other commercial water users. We will have more to say about representing non-human nature in our discussion of democracy in chapter 7.

What about the moral status of the Earth as a whole? Does humanity have any obligations of justice towards the Earth system itself? Di Paola (2015: 195–6) sums up the difficulties facing such a claim:

Climate change, biodiversity loss and whatever we may call the toughest ecological quandaries of our time are such only for us humans (and many other species), but of no matter whatsoever to *the planet*. Cosmically speaking, they are of no matter

---

[13] For an application of the capabilities approach to future generations, see Page 2007.

whatsoever at all. On this view, we cannot *owe it* to Earth, as such, that we avert these quandaries through our stewardship—unless it can be shown that it would somehow be a loss *for* Earth that, say, its morphology or atmosphere changed, and humans or other species were to fare much worse, or even go extinct altogether.

Nevertheless, the planet as a whole may matter. One reason the Death Star in *Star Wars* is so evil is that it destroys whole planets—not just a few troublesome rebels. It may be possible to think of justice towards the planet itself through anthropomorphizing the planet as "Mother Earth" who, in countries such as Bolivia, is viewed as having rights of her own.[14] Whether or not Mother Earth is seen as a living being literally or only metaphorically, the idea underscores the dependence of human and non-human life on the planet's fecundity. Just as ecosystems may acquire moral value by *sustaining* as well as *containing* living things, the Earth system may do so as well. Even if the planet itself is indifferent to its own future existence, we can still maintain that disrupting the Earth system's functioning is wrong because of the resultant harm to the capabilities of species and ecosystems that inhabit it.[15]

Responsibility for planetary justice

Any account of justice in the Anthropocene needs to identify who is responsible for minimizing and remedying Earth system damage.[16] The far-reaching scope of planetary justice we have outlined renders this task enormously complex. Not only does the number of subjects who are owed duties of justice multiply to include people in other countries, species and generations; the range of people who may collectively hold duties towards those subjects becomes vast as well. Damage to the Earth system and the resulting injustices are often the cumulative effect of many millions of individual actions in (for

---

[14] The 2030 Agenda on Sustainable Development also reaffirms "that planet Earth and its ecosystems are our common home and that 'Mother Earth' is a common expression in a number of countries and regions" (UN 2015b, paragraph 59; see also UNFCCC 2016, Preamble).

[15] Whether the wrongness of harming the Earth system is necessarily *unjust* remains a matter for debate, particularly if we think that an entity must have interests of its own to qualify as a subject of justice. However, one could respond that disrupting the Earth system involves at the very least a *derivative* injustice, in the form of the setbacks to the interests of those (including humans and potentially non-humans) who clearly are subjects of justice.

[16] By "responsibility" we mean prospective responsibility or duty to act—such as a responsibility to remedy an injustice or to prevent one from occurring—as distinct from deserving praise or blame (retrospective responsibility) for a past action (Erskine 2003: 8; Miller 2007: 97–8). If someone is to blame for a past injustice, this could be an important reason why they should be held responsible for remedying it (in which case we can talk about their "liability" for fixing the problem), but this need not be the case (e.g. if someone has done nothing to cause the problem but has the greatest capacity to fix it). The principle of "common but differentiated responsibilities" discussed in this section blurs these two senses of responsibility.

example) contributing to greenhouse gas emissions, or consuming environmentally destructive products. An account of planetary justice therefore needs to be capable of apportioning responsibility across the complex chains of production and consumption that are driving the Great Acceleration, in particular by determining the respective responsibilities of producers, exporters, and consumers. Crucially, the challenge is not just to find theoretically plausible reasons for allocating responsibilities; it is as much a matter of finding politically feasible ways of motivating agents to fulfill their responsibilities. Rather than treat questions of motivation and feasibility as secondary to the theoretical task, we see the political dimensions of justice as integral to thinking about what the pursuit of justice should mean in the Anthropocene.[17]

IS RESPONSIBILITY TO ACT INDIVIDUAL OR COLLECTIVE?

Debates about who is responsible for addressing the injustices resulting from Earth system damage typically feature two contrasting perspectives: one that pinpoints individual wrongdoers and another that aims for a more collective account.[18] The global climate regime's evolution has been marked—and often hindered—by conflicting views about liability for causing climate change, and hence about the responsibility that countries should bear for combating climate change. In chapter 3 we saw how understandings of "common but differentiated responsibilities and respective capabilities" (CBDR&RC) had evolved in global climate change negotiations. Despite consensus on this broad principle, developed and developing countries have clashed over what it means in practice. Numerous developing countries—Bolivia most vocal among them—have argued that developed countries are liable for a "climate debt" for their past emissions (Pickering and Barry 2012). This debt, they argue, arises because the countries that industrialized earliest (notably the US, UK, and other European nations) have used up more than their fair share of the atmosphere's limited ability to safely absorb greenhouse gases, leaving little space for countries that are industrializing later to pursue their development aspirations. Developed countries should repay their climate debt by drastically reducing their own emissions and by providing funding to help developing countries acquire cleaner technologies and adapt to the impacts of climate change.

While developed countries have been willing to acknowledge their historical contributions to climate change (as recognized in Article 3.1 of the UNFCCC),

---

[17] On the role of feasibility in justice generally, see Gilabert and Lawford-Smith (2012), and in climate justice, see Heyward and Roser (2016).

[18] Whereas previous sections drew a distinction between individual and collective virtues, the distinction we draw in this section between individual and collective approaches is somewhat different. Here it refers to the difference between the responsibilities of (i) individual members of a group and (ii) the group as a whole. Thus an "individual" could be a single state (even though it is a collective agent composed of individual people), as it is one member of a group or community of states.

they have been highly reluctant to countenance the possibility that they may be held liable for their historical emissions. Thus the chief climate negotiator for the US objected:

I actually completely reject the notion of a debt or reparations or anything of the like.... Let's just be mindful of the fact for most of the 200 years since the Industrial Revolution, people were blissfully ignorant of the fact that emissions cause the greenhouse effect. It's a relatively recent phenomenon. It's the wrong way to look at this. We absolutely recognize our historical role in putting emissions in the atmosphere that are there now. But the sense of guilt or culpability or reparations, I categorically reject that.   (Samuelsohn 2009)

To date wealthy countries have been able to dodge claims they are liable for the damage caused by their pollution of the atmosphere. While the Paris Agreement includes a provision to address loss and damage incurred by developing countries as a result of climate change (UNFCCC 2016, Article 8), the accompanying COP decision also contains a caveat that the relevant provision "does not involve or provide a basis for any liability or compensation" (UNFCCC 2016, Paragraph 51).

While there is a broad spectrum of views on CBDR&RC among parties to the UN climate regime, the positions of Bolivia and the US on climate debt represent two prominent understandings of responsibility for addressing risks to the Earth system. These understandings can be described as individualist and collectivist respectively. The first, encapsulated by the idea of climate debt, emphasizes (i) pinpointing individual agents (in this case industrialized countries) as liable for the injustice they have created; (ii) backward-looking (or historical) attribution of liability and so responsibility for action; and (iii) an adversarial strategy for pursuing justice that focuses on confirming liability and fulfilling rights or entitlements for those who have suffered. In contrast, the position of those opposed to climate debt stresses (i) a more generalized account of collective responsibility that shies away from finger-pointing; (ii) forward-looking moral considerations, including the agent's present capacity to remedy the situation; and (iii) a cooperative strategy involving negotiation to pursue collective action.

These contrasting views find parallels in Iris Marion Young's (2006; 2013) distinction between the "liability model" and "social connection model" of responsibility to overcome injustice. Young argues that many prevailing understandings—which she groups under the liability model—are excessively backward-looking, and their reliance on pointing the finger of blame at individuals makes them ill-suited to dealing with structural injustice. Structural injustice exists

when social processes put large groups of persons under systematic threat of domination or deprivation of the means to develop and exercise their capacities, at the same time that these processes enable others to dominate or to have a wide range of opportunities for developing and exercising capacities available to them.   (Young 2013: 52)

Instead, Young proposes a social connection model based on the idea that "individuals bear responsibility for structural injustice because they contribute by their actions to the processes that produce unjust outcomes" (Young 2013: 105). Rather than assigning blame or fault to individuals, responsibility under the social connection model is "essentially shared" among those contributing to unjust processes, and "can therefore be discharged only through collective action" (Young 2013: 105).

While Young's ideas about structural injustice focus on the exploitative underside of economic globalization, they are also relevant to the problems of the Anthropocene. Yet Young's interest in motivating collective action comes at a substantial cost (Barry and Ferracioli 2013; Neuhäuser 2014). Notably, she prioritizes forward-looking responsibilities to the virtual exclusion of backward-looking liabilities; history enters the picture mainly as a means of understanding how present institutional structures continue to produce injustice (Young 2013: 185). This approach risks blurring important distinctions among those involved in unjust processes. While Young emphasizes that those with greater privilege may need to do more than the disadvantaged to remedy injustice (Young 2013: 181, 186), she is too quick to put aside the idea that those that have contributed more to creating a structural injustice should likewise do more than those that have contributed less.

A further problem is Young's implication that backward-looking liability must mean guilt or blame (Young 2013: 97–8). The trouble with this view is vividly illustrated by the chief climate negotiator for Bolivia, Pablo Solón Romero, who retorted to the US comments on climate debt (cited above) as follows:

Admitting responsibility for the climate crisis without taking necessary actions to address it is like someone burning your house and then refusing to pay for it. Even if the fire was not started on purpose, the industrialised countries, through their inaction, have continued to add fuel to the fire.... We are not assigning guilt, merely responsibility. As they say in the US, if you break it, you buy it.   (Climate Citizen 2009)

Solón Romero's remarks underscore that responsibility to make amends for past actions need not flow from malicious intent but could be founded on recklessness or negligence. In the specific case of greenhouse gas emissions, the US government has been aware of the problem since at least 1965 yet still fails to do much about it. Our concern here is not to define a specific set of principles for ascribing responsibility but to emphasize that a political conception of responsibility for justice should and can accommodate both backward- and forward-looking considerations.

This emphasis might imply that when it comes to responsibility for responding to Earth system damage, a collectivist account should be favored over an individualist account, as long as the former can incorporate backward-looking considerations. In practice, courts have been reluctant to grant compensation or other remedies for climate-related harm (Bodansky, Brunnée, and Rajamani 2017: 286). Claims for compensation frequently founder on the difficulty of establishing that adverse impacts were caused by climate change—a task that is complicated by the presence of natural climate variability—as well as attributing harm to the actions of specific actors. Nevertheless, individualist strategies should not be dismissed. Legal action has achieved some successes in requiring governments to take action on climate change, notably with the *Urgenda* case, brought by 886 citizens organized by the Urgenda Foundation, which in 2015 successfully argued that the Dutch government had a duty of care to its citizens to increase its target for reducing greenhouse gas emissions (van Zeben 2015).

For the foreseeable future there will continue to be some environmental injustices where there are clear perpetrators; consider, for example, the burning of oil fields in Kuwait in the late stages of the Gulf War, or large-scale illegal logging of tropical rainforests. There may also be egregious cases where states or corporations have negligently or recklessly endangered the Earth system, as with ExxonMobil's efforts to sow confusion about climate science, or the Trump administration's cavalier disdain for environmental protection. Even in cases where negligence is less clear, the material origins of some Earth system risks may be concentrated in a relatively small group of actors: the United States and China alone accounted for around 42 per cent of greenhouse gas emissions in 2015 (Global Carbon Project 2017); and one study has traced around two-thirds of cumulative greenhouse gas emissions from fossil fuel and cement production since the mid-nineteenth century to just ninety "carbon major" corporations (Heede 2014). Nevertheless, Earth system disruption is ultimately driven by a broader range of actions—from air-conditioned offices in India and Australia to school buses in Norway and China—and for this reason the individualist pursuit of justice cannot be the whole solution.

BRIDGING THE INDIVIDUALIST–COLLECTIVIST DIVIDE

While attributions of individual liability for climate debt or other forms of past wrongdoing may help mobilize social movements for justice, and may sometimes advance the legal pursuit of justice, they face an important political limitation. Even where it may be possible to apportion responsibilities for Earth system damage, individualist and adversarial approaches may be ill-suited as a rhetorical foundation for international cooperation. Given that damage to the Earth system often involves "global commons" problems that are not extensively regulated by international law (no one has property rights over the atmosphere), global cooperative action is often the only feasible way forward. Dividing the world into climate debtors and creditors may work as "bonding rhetoric" for like-minded developing countries and activists, but not as the "bridging rhetoric" needed to span differences among actors with different values and worldviews (Dryzek 2010; Pickering and Barry 2012). Rhetoric that emphasizes guilt and blame may stifle cooperation if it prompts defensive reactions or blame-shifting (Täuber, van Zomeren, and Kutlaca 2015; Pickering 2016).

But just to complicate matters, it is sometimes possible that individualist calls to remedy the injustices posed by climate change and other Earth system risks can help to build momentum for cooperative solutions to these injustices. Thus Khan and Roberts (2013: 178–9) argue that the threat of liability was an important factor explaining the UNFCCC's decision in 2012 to take action on the issue of loss and damage resulting from climate change, as the spread of climate litigation

> may sound an alarm to governments and corporations that it may be better to settle the scores through negotiations, which could be cheaper than court-based settlements with more costly verdicts and never-ending uncertainty on their outcomes.
>
> (See also Doelle 2014: 38)

Similarly, the fossil fuel divestment movement has proved highly successful in painting coal and oil companies as the "enemy" (Mangat, Dalby, and Paterson 2018), but this framing has been accompanied by a strategy that emphasizes the power of any asset-holder to divest if they choose, rather than relying on a third-party adjudicator such as a court to impose liability on polluting companies (Ayling and Gunningham 2017: 141). In this way, the divestment movement simultaneously recognizes that responsibility for tackling climate change does not fall only on the large companies that extract or burn fossil fuels, but also on others along the supply chain, including investors and consumers. Activists argue that by helping to revoke the "social license to operate" of fossil fuel companies, divestment can pave the way for governments to roll out more ambitious climate policies (Ayling and Gunningham 2017: 136, 142).

Thus both individualist and collectivist approaches are important, and as we have seen may be connected in a sequence beginning with individual liability and ending in collective action. Finally, under conditions of persistent moral disagreement procedural justice becomes especially important (Holland 2017: 394). Even if it is impossible to reach consensus on substantive questions of justice—such as which principles should inform each country's fair share of the costs of protecting biodiversity or the atmosphere—it may be possible to craft procedures for resolving these questions that are accepted as just (Pickering 2015).[19] For example, any procedure to determine these contributions ought to

---

[19] The assumption that it is always easier to agree on matters of procedure than substance remains open to challenge (see for example Ceva 2012: 191).

include representatives of those most responsible for causing damage, those most capable of doing something about the damage, and those who have suffered most from the damage in question (Eckersley 2012).

Conclusion: planetary justice and ecological reflexivity

Justice, Rawls famously asserted in his highly influential work, is the "first virtue of social institutions" (Rawls 1999b: 3). In chapter 3 we suggested in contrast that ecological reflexivity is the primary requirement for institutions in the Anthropocene. This does not imply that justice is unimportant—far from it, as this chapter attests—but it underscores that the continuing vitality of core societal values such as justice depends now more than ever on their ability to co-evolve with a changing Earth system. Ecological reflexivity gives a dynamic twist to justice, which resonates with Sen's (1999) ethics of "development as freedom," in which the elements of justice should be amenable to continual rethinking in participatory public reason (which we would call deliberation).

The need for reflexivity highlights a crucial role for procedural justice: to safeguard the capacity of humans to engage in political contestation about what justice should mean in changing conditions.[20] This capacity may be thought of both as a procedural right akin to some other civil and political rights as well as a more general freedom of conscience. Protecting this capacity in turn becomes a requirement of justice. Engaging culturally diverse understandings in this contestation can help to reveal and correct blind spots in conventional approaches to justice. Notable here is the value of looking to non-Western understandings of morality. While many non-Western theories took shape well before the advent of the Anthropocene, they may nevertheless provide valuable insights, for example in thinking about how non-human nature could be treated as a subject of justice (Schlosberg and Carruthers 2010).

Enabling people to access the information needed to understand changes in the Earth system that may affect their lives—a crucial ingredient for practicing ecological reflexivity—likewise becomes a requirement of procedural justice (Vanderheiden 2015; see also Fricker 2007). There is clear potential for injustice where people are deprived of the ability to access knowledge due to a lack of educational opportunity, or where others intentionally disseminate false information or propaganda that aims to dispel ecological concerns.

Some aspects of justice need not change radically when seen through an Anthropocene lens. The notion that certain basic interests should be protected

---

[20] For a similar argument on the right to contest the meaning of democracy, see Dryzek 2016a.

as a matter of justice—particularly civil and political rights such as freedom from torture or arbitrary detention—is unlikely to be overturned under planetary justice. Rethinking justice for the Anthropocene is likely to broaden rather than narrow the scope of basic interests that are deemed necessary for human flourishing. Yet, as we have shown, the Anthropocene presents major challenges to prevailing notions of justice and how to achieve it.

In all this, the concept of planetary justice is crucial. The route to planetary justice starts by:

- Recognizing that the emergency of the Anthropocene need not and should not suppress questions of justice.
- Acknowledging that the cultivation of individual (and even collective) ethical virtues does not obviate the need to think about the organization of social justice.
- Accepting that different people (for example, from different countries) can be motivated by different understandings of justice.

The content of planetary justice then entails:

- Viewing humanity's relationship with the Earth system as central to planetary justice, rather than keeping justice in splendid isolation from the Earth system, as many Holocene accounts (such as that of Rawls) were wont to do.
- Thinking about how to detach the practical pursuit of justice from unending economic growth.
- Expanding justice beyond the confines of state boundaries.
- Extending justice to non-humans, future generations, and the Earth system in its entirety.
- Joining individualist and collectivist approaches to responsibility for minimizing and remedying damage to the Earth system, while recognizing that in the end, individualist approaches must yield to the need for collective action.
- Safeguarding a capacity for people to contest what justice should mean under a changing Earth system.

While justice in the Anthropocene is multifaceted, we cannot end with a simple celebration of pluralism, because different ideas about justice can point in different directions. That is why one of the most important requirements of justice is the need for good processes for deciding what to do when difference exists. Sen (2009) calls the process "public reason"; we believe that "deliberative democracy" better captures what is required. In the context of different views about what justice requires, deliberation should aim not for consensus on principles of justice, but rather for a "meta-consensus." Such a meta-consensus consists of mutual recognition of the legitimacy of disputed values by the parties to a dispute (Dryzek 2013a: 338). It would involve for example those (such as developing countries) who take an individualist approach to assigning liability for climate change coming to see the point of a collectivist approach to shared responsibility—even if they do not agree with it—and vice versa. While the deliberative construction of meta-consensus is hard work, it is difficult to envisage much in the way of progress without it.

Justice, while of crucial moral importance, is not the same as sustainability. The two appear closest to convergence when it comes to the intergenerational distribution of resources and risks, and a social-ecological view of justice helps to ensure that environmental interests are not sacrificed for human well-being. Yet we cannot simply assume that justice guarantees sustainability, or vice versa. Accordingly, sustainability also requires rethinking in the Anthropocene, and we do this in the next chapter.

5   Sustainability

Sustainability is a hugely popular way of thinking about environmental governance—and its linkages with other areas of governance. The idea of sustainable development has been around for several decades longer than that of the Anthropocene. Yet the popularity of the idea is matched by persistent shortfall in practice. Indeed, an apt way of summing up the consequences of the Anthropocene so far is "an age of unsustainability" (Dauvergne 2016: 390). Levels of resource use and environmental stress already far outstrip what the planet can sustain. This overshoot finds expression in the "ecological footprint" indicator, which compares humanity's use of natural resources with the Earth's capacity to regenerate them. By 2012, the world was using 1.6 Earth's worth of resources each year, and this figure is expected to increase to 1.75 Earths by 2020 (WWF 2016: 83). This state of affairs is unsustainable. Technological and institutional change have brought some notable improvements in how efficiently resources are produced and consumed, not least through higher agricultural productivity and energy-efficient appliances. But increasing wealth threatens to increase resource pressures on many fronts. The problem is no longer confined to excessive consumption by wealthy countries and global elites, as a rapidly growing middle class in the global South acquires the means to consume more, whether by buying cars or air conditioners, or by eating more meat, dairy, and fish.

We will argue that the Anthropocene means that sustainability must be rethought along more reflexive lines, and identify five key characteristics of such an account. Sustainability needs to be open, ecologically attuned, dynamic, far-sighted, and integrated with values such as justice. We then turn to a case study of one of the largest recent global efforts to advance sustainability and related values: the UN Sustainable Development Goals adopted in 2015. Do the goals and the process of shaping them show signs of reflexive sustainability? Our answer is that they do so to a limited degree, but many opportunities to go further were lost. Our focus throughout is mainly on the global scale, although we recognize that multiple levels are closely interrelated.

Sustainability and sustainable development: conceptual signposts

Sustainability and its close ally sustainable development are terms whose proper meaning is the subject of continued disagreement (Lafferty 1996).

Both terms have attracted a diverse array of interpretations. Indeed, we can speak of a broad discourse of sustainability, containing a number of interpretations of what sustainability means and what it requires of political institutions and actors.

Sustainability refers to the capacity of a process or state of affairs to be sustained or maintained over a long or indefinite period of time. But what exactly should be sustained? Over what time period? Attaching the term "development" to "sustainable" provides some anchoring, though the nature of development itself is contested too. Lélé's (1991: 609) definition of development as "a process of directed change" provides a useful starting point. The change in question is often considered by its proponents as synonymous with "progress."[1] Even so, there remains the question of what dimensions of development are to be sustained. Sustainability is often interpreted as *ecological* sustainability, but it may encompass social and economic dimensions as well. The "three pillars" of sustainable development are often described as environmental, social, and economic (Kates, Parris, and Leiserowitz 2005); however, as we will see, the metaphor provides a misleading account of the relationships across the three dimensions.

Sustainability is a wider term than sustainable development. Thus, sustainability could encompass other answers to the "what" question, including sustainable agriculture, sustainable finance, sustainable food, or sustainable fashion. However, in research and international policy debates, sustainability and sustainable development are often used interchangeably, and in this chapter we will generally do the same.

A final point to note about the concept of sustainability is its long time horizon and its emphasis on the relationship between the present and the future. Sustainability spans at the very least multiple generations of human life. Thus the Brundtland report, whose definition of sustainable development remains a touchstone for contemporary debates about the concept, defines the term as development that "meets the needs of the present without compromising the ability of future generations to meet their own needs" (World Commission on Environment and Development 1987: 8). While not explicitly encompassing the thousands or millions of years spanned by geological epochs, there is no reason in principle why sustainability could not extend equally far into the future.

---

[1] Even if development is understood in this broad sense, it could be objected that the notion of progress is too linear, and that it would be preferable to work with ideas such as harmony or balance (Kothari, Demaria, and Acosta 2014). While harmony and balance deserve far greater emphasis, we are reluctant to depart from the idea that progress (suitably understood) is something worth pursuing.

Is the idea of sustainability unsustainable?

Since its rise to prominence, the discourse of sustainability has come under attack from different quarters. Here we address three persistent concerns that take on added force in light of the Anthropocene: that sustainability is too static to serve as a societal goal; that the term has been co-opted by vested interests; and that sustainability is no longer possible given past or projected ecological degradation.

IS SUSTAINABILITY TOO STATIC?

Benson and Craig (2014: 777) argue that "the continued invocation of sustainability in international talks, development goals, and other policy discussions ignores the emerging realities of the Anthropocene." Their concerns reflect recognition of the complexity of the Earth system and the possibility of abrupt, non-linear changes. Sustainability, they argue, is too static to come to terms with these dynamics. They call for "the end of sustainability" and its replacement by resilience.[2]

Benson and Craig are justified in viewing social-ecological systems as dynamic. If sustainability could be viewed only in a static sense of conserving natural resources or ecological conditions exactly as they are today (or were at some other point in time, such as the pre-industrial era), Benson and Craig's critique would cut deeper.[3] However, sustainability is not inherently static. Standards of sustainable development are generally measured against values such as human needs (as in the Brundtland definition) or social-ecological well-being, and these may change over time; so may the kinds of natural and manufactured resources required to safeguard needs or well-being. But as long as we assume that future generations will come into being and that their well-being is closely tied to choices made today, sustainability will remain relevant even in a changing Earth system.

We elaborate on a dynamic conception of sustainability below. Here we note one further point about the relationship between sustainability and resilience. We saw in chapter 3 that resilience as conventionally understood may attract a similar criticism to that which Benson and Craig level at sustainability: the concept of resilience may be too conservative or normatively ambiguous to serve as an overarching goal for social-ecological systems. Rather than rivals, resilience and sustainability may be complementary and possibly even interdependent. So for example, sustainable development could

---

[2] For a more general discussion of resilience, see chapter 3.
[3] Similarly, we saw in chapter 1 the problems associated with tying planetary boundaries to the conditions that prevailed in the Holocene.

help address the objection that not all types of resilience are desirable: it may be desirable to cultivate only those types of resilience conducive to sustainable development, and to overhaul or discard institutions (such as capitalist markets that profit from ecological degradation) that are resilient but remain locked into pathological path dependencies.[4]

HAS SUSTAINABILITY BEEN CO-OPTED?

It is common to observe that that the discourse of sustainability has become reconciled to dominant discourses such as neoliberalism, and co-opted by actors whose interests are in fact inconsistent with sustainability. If so, championing sustainability could reinforce rather than disrupt problematic path dependencies established in Holocene institutions and ideas. Many governments and businesses have embraced the language of sustainability while doing precious little to restrain their ecologically harmful practices.

Corporations continue to proclaim sustainability to help sell their products, though brazen "greenwashing" has arguably become less prevalent as social media has enhanced the public's ability to detect hypocritical claims (Bowen 2014). Some businesses have become more sophisticated in articulating commitments to sustainability, and often seek to differentiate themselves from obstructive governments (such as the Trump administration in the US). But even when complemented by actions to recycle and reduce waste, corporate sustainability measures generally fail to address underlying drivers of ecological degradation, notably a materialist culture that embraces cheap, disposable products (Dauvergne 2016). Unless the problem of consumption is addressed, corporate sustainability commitments will at best make very marginal contributions, and at worst provide cover for ongoing ecological depletion.

The failure of the Rio+20 summit in 2012 to question conventional understandings of sustainable development—in particular the idea of a "green economy" in which sustained economic growth is happily coupled with moderate ecological restraints—can be attributed in large measure to the sway that business actors continue to hold over governments (Clémençon 2012).

But does this mean that the idea of sustainability should be discarded? Not necessarily. The risk of co-option also holds for other values such as justice and democracy, which have been marshaled to serve innumerable unjust and undemocratic projects over time. Concepts such as resilience are likewise far from immune from co-option. The risk of co-option is likely to be present whenever a social value is open to contestation; powerful actors can seek to bend the domain of contestation to suit themselves.

---

[4] Sustainable development is in fact often invoked as the "desired state" in the related literature on adaptive governance (Chaffin, Gosnell, and Cosens 2014: 7).

It makes no sense to abandon worthwhile values just because they have been abused, and to quarantine them from misuse would be impossible. Instead it is necessary to explore whether the public discourse surrounding sustainability can be redeemed for the pursuit of common rather than private interests. As Dauvergne (2016: 387) contends, "the narrative of sustainability is too valuable to surrender to business." Recent thinking has sought to deepen the discourse of sustainability through advancing ideas such as "sustainable materialism" (Schlosberg and Coles 2016) that are concerned with the material flows that feed into and out of consumption and "just sustainabilities" (Agyeman 2013). However, efforts to revitalize sustainability discourse should not crowd out exploration of alternatives to sustainability, such as the Latin American idea of *buen vivir* (living well), the Indian idea of ecological *swaraj* (self-sufficiency; Kothari, Demaria, and Acosta 2014), or the Chinese idea of "ecological civilization" (Jiang et al. 2017).

IS SUSTAINABILITY IMPOSSIBLE?

Efforts to co-opt the discourse of sustainable development often presume that environmental sustainability is compatible with indefinite economic growth. But endless material growth is impossible in a finite Earth system. If sustainable development necessarily requires continuing economic growth, it may remain an impossible ideal even if pursued in good faith.

However, the idea of development does not rely on such a presumption. As Daly (1990: 1) observes, "growth is quantitative increase in physical scale, while development is qualitative improvement or unfolding of potentialities. An economy can grow without developing, or develop without growing, or do both or neither." Thus it remains conceptually possible that well-being could be sustained in a steady-state (or zero-growth) economy (Jackson 2009). However, as Raworth (2017) points out, it is hard to imagine human development being possible in the poorest countries without economic growth in the short to medium term, even if the case for further economic growth in industrialized countries is far less clear. Reflexive institutions should be capable of asking whether, where, and under what circumstances economic growth is desirable, and if necessary of rethinking any core commitment to growth. At any rate, sustainability should not be equated with growth.

A related concern is that sustainability is no longer possible because humanity has already so depleted the Earth system's regenerative capacity that we cannot bequeath a safe planet to future generations. But even if the world that future generations will inherit is vastly different from the one that prevailed before the Great Acceleration, it is by no means clear that we have passed the point at which the future can no longer support the flourishing of human and other forms of life.

Sustainability meets reflexivity

What then should a reflexive understanding of sustainability look like in the Anthropocene? Any efforts to institutionalize reflexive sustainability should begin by recognizing the need to overcome the pathological path dependencies we identified in chapter 2. The inattention of Holocene institutions to social-ecological feedbacks means that those path dependencies entrench unsustainable practices.

Chapter 3 identified several qualities that reflexive *institutions* should exhibit when rethinking core social values, including capacity to recognize and respond to the results of interactions between institutions and social-ecological systems, and capacity to anticipate shifts in the Earth system. Here we deploy these qualities to highlight five attributes that a reflexive conception of sustainability must have: it must be open, ecologically grounded, dynamic, far-sighted, and integrated with values such as justice (see Figure 5.1).[5]

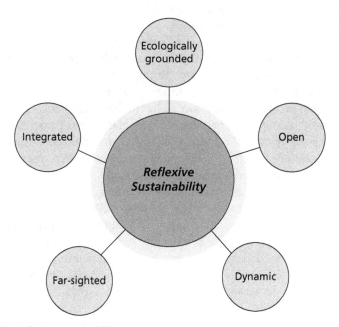

Figure 5.1. Reflexive sustainability

---

[5] For another typology, see Waas et al. (2011: 1645), who set out four principles: normativity, equity, integration, and dynamism. See also Leach, Scoones, and Stirling's (2010) idea of "dynamic sustainabilities," which we discuss later in this chapter.

OPEN SUSTAINABILITY

Reflecting on how sustainability should be rethought under Anthropocene conditions, Arias-Maldonado (2013) argues for a move from a "closed" to an "open" understanding. This argument extends a strand of thinking that has been present for at least two decades. Torgerson (1994) argued for a "de-centered" approach to sustainability that would involve multifaceted and multilevel experimentation in practicing sustainability—and exploring its practical meaning.

On a closed understanding of sustainability, its meaning is determined through an expert-driven process, whereas an open understanding exposes the meaning of sustainability to public debate. Thus sustainability can be seen as "a process of reflexive re-organisation of the socio-natural relation without pre-arranged shape," such that "only a democratic society guarantees the necessary conditions for its achievement" (Arias-Maldonado 2013: 429, 441). Openness cannot of course mean being open to pursuing every orientation towards sustainability—such as those that seek to co-opt sustainability or subordinate it to neoliberal discourse. Openness must be accompanied by deliberation that is capable of exposing and eliminating bad arguments and the manipulation of discourses.

An open or democratic approach to sustainability is justifiable in so far as sustainability is a societal goal rather than a purely scientific concept whose meaning can be definitively fixed through experiment or observation (Robinson 2004: 382). Accordingly, understandings of sustainability are likely to differ. For example, people are likely to have different views on the desirability of "strong sustainability" (which places firm constraints on the ability to substitute natural resources for higher material standards of living) vis-à-vis "weak sustainability" (which countenances greater scope for trade-offs between natural and manufactured resources).[6]

Open sustainability complements the view of sustainability as a continuing process rather than an ideal state (e.g. Robinson 2004) as well as those who equate reflexive governance with openness (Smith and Stirling 2007). Yet seeing sustainability as radically open-ended is risky. If sustainability remains perpetually open to debate that never reaches resolution (however provisional), it will be impossible to make collective decisions that could actually serve the cause of sustainability. We saw in chapter 3 the high environmental

---

[6] On the distinction between strong and weak sustainability, see Neumayer 2003. Note that the argument for democratic rethinking of sustainability need not assume that public participation is inherent in the definition of sustainability itself, as some claim (see the discussion in Lélé 1991: 615–16). There is arguably no conceptual contradiction involved in imagining non-democratic forms of sustainable development, even if there is empirical evidence to support a link between democracy and sustainability in practice (see chapter 7).

price that the world has paid for prolonged talks on climate change that failed to crystallize into action.

Sustainability cannot, then, be completely open. Openness remains vital for imagining new options and criticizing existing practices, but a degree of closure is required in order to govern and thereby to safeguard the values at stake. Thus there is more to reflexive sustainability than openness alone. In particular, it must be ecologically grounded.

ECOLOGICALLY GROUNDED SUSTAINABILITY

Reflexivity in the Anthropocene must be distinctively ecological: that is, it must recognize the interactions between institutions and the Earth system at large, and acknowledge the risks of instability and state shifts in the system as a result. What is true for reflexivity in this regard is just as true for sustainability.

Even an open conception of sustainability cannot be free of substantive ecological content, not least because "some socio-ecological thresholds are not to be crossed, in order to avoid major imbalances that may render any possible version of sustainability unattainable in the future" (Arias-Maldonado 2013: 439). In this light, standards for sustainability should be "contestable and open to review" while still reflecting available scientific knowledge (Arias-Maldonado 2013: 439–40).

The ecological dimension means that any view of sustainability that clashes with the ecological conditions for human and non-human flourishing must be ruled out. Ecological grounding represents an essential bulwark against efforts to co-opt sustainability discourse.

Ecological grounding also challenges the notion that the ecological dimension of sustainability is only one of three pillars (alongside economic and social sustainability). A better metaphor is one of concentric circles, in which the economy is embedded in society which in turn is embedded within social-ecological systems and the broader Earth system (Costanza et al. 2013). This understanding is reflected in the approach of Griggs et al. (2013: 306), who infuse Brundtland's phrasing with an Earth system perspective, and define "sustainable development in the Anthropocene" as "development that meets the needs of the present while safeguarding Earth's life-support system, on which the welfare of current and future generations depends."

The idea of ecological grounding also suggests that public deliberation must attend not only to evolving scientific knowledge about environmental change, but also to the experiences of communities affected by environmental change and to signals from the non-human world (concerns to which we return in chapter 6). Relatedly, this grounding suggests that deliberation should open up space for ecocentric (rather than purely anthropocentric) ideas of sustainability.[7] Questions of what is sustainable—and what kinds of resources can be substituted for one another—may look very different once the perspectives of non-humans are taken into account, not least because the abilities of animals, plants and ecosystems to adapt to higher temperatures or habitat loss may be far more limited than the adaptive capacities of humans.

DYNAMIC SUSTAINABILITY

There is a danger that positing an ecological grounding for sustainability could entail a static view of ecological constraints upon sustainability. As we noted earlier in this chapter, a static view is poorly equipped to cope with abrupt and non-linear changes in the Earth system. Understandings of sustainability need to be responsive not just to changing values (as allowed for by the attribute of openness) but also to changing *interactions* between humanity and the Earth system, and to resulting changes in the Earth system itself.

A static view of sustainability would involve fighting against deleterious changes in the Earth system with the help of fixed targets or guideposts. Fixed targets can be informed by analysis of past conditions in which ecosystems were not so damaged by human activity, even if they do not strictly require a return to those conditions (Hourdequin 2013). Thus the original proposal for planetary boundaries (which we encountered in chapter 1) defines the "safe operating space" for humanity informed by the conditions that prevailed in the Holocene (Rockström et al. 2009). If we have already moved out of the Holocene, a backward-looking baseline cannot be definitive when it comes to decisions about managing risks to the Earth system. So, for example, global average temperatures have already risen roughly 1°C compared to pre-industrial times, and the Paris Agreement aims to keep temperature rise "well below" 2°C and to pursue efforts to limit it to 1.5°C above pre-industrial levels. On a static conception of sustainability, a 1.5°C goal would be self-evidently better than 2°C, as it is closer to the Holocene baseline. But if we continue this line of thinking, a 1°C goal or even a 0°C goal would be even better. Yet even Rockström et al. (2009) propose a target that exceeds pre-industrial levels.[8] The problem here is that relying primarily on a retrospective benchmark may ignore other important considerations, not least the technical, political, and economic feasibility of returning to Holocene conditions, and

[7] Recall that in chapter 4 we argued for a conception of justice that is not limited to humans but also recognizes non-human life. On the distinction between ecocentrism and anthropocentrism in environmental politics, see Eckersley 2004.

[8] Their proposed boundary for climate change is an atmospheric carbon dioxide concentration of 350 parts per million, which is not precisely equivalent to a temperature goal but is more consistent with a 1.5°C goal than a 2°C goal.

the trade-offs that may need to be made not only to sustain other determinants of human development (e.g. investments in education and health) but also to invest in other dimensions of environmental sustainability (e.g. protecting biodiversity from agricultural expansion). Instead, we can imagine a forward-looking, dynamic approach that understands safety and sustainability in terms of the conditions that humans and non-humans require to flourish. The Holocene may still serve as a rough heuristic for conditions that we know were amenable to human flourishing, but safety and sustainability also need to be understood with reference to changing societal values as well as the technologies available for pursuing sustainability and adapting to environmental change.

There is however a risk that a dynamic account of sustainability could lure humanity into a different trap: detaching sustainability from any appreciation of the world that we have inherited, and the relatively modest role that humans have played within its longer history. Some commentators (e.g. Wapner 2014) argue that the Anthropocene confirms the end of nature.[9] But completely eliding the distinction between human and non-human nature may open up argumentative room for strategies that are pursued in the name of sustainability but ultimately endanger the Earth system—such as geoengineering. An argument of this kind could run as follows (compare Barrett 2014: 251–3): if humans are already manipulating the global climate by burning unprecedented amounts of fossil fuels, is manipulating the climate by other means (such as reducing incoming solar radiation by injecting sulfate aerosols into the atmosphere) really all that different? Geoengineering proposals, as we argued in chapter 3, pose grave risks for sustainability and global governance. Other controversial interventions in natural processes—such as genetically modifying crops to withstand higher temperatures—may still have a place in deliberation about sustainability. But a dynamic conception of sustainability must also remain ecologically grounded in the sense that humans and non-humans are integral parts of complex systems, in which human hubris must be avoided.[10]

FAR-SIGHTED SUSTAINABILITY

In order to give due weight to the idea that sustainability is strongly oriented towards the future, and consistently with the way we defined ecological

---

[9] For a widely cited invocation of the end of nature that preceded the Anthropocene debate but has subsequently informed it, see McKibben 1989).

[10] Dynamism is paramount in Leach, Scoones, and Stirling's (2010) notion of "dynamic sustainabilities." Their account shares some affinities with ours, including the need to open up deliberation about sustainability while retaining a commitment to normative values such as human well-being, equity, and environmental integrity (Leach, Scoones, and Stirling 2010: 5). However, in our view dynamism is best seen as one among several important attributes of a broader notion of reflexive sustainability.

reflexivity in chapter 3, conceptions of sustainability must also be *far-sighted*. This means that the current generation should take responsibility for the potential social-ecological consequences that its actions will have for the planet's future. Far-sighted sustainability complements our analysis of intergenerational justice in chapter 4.

Foresight presents multiple challenges. Projections of the future are inherently uncertain. In the Anthropocene this uncertainty is exacerbated by the possibility of thresholds and tipping points in the Earth system (Bai et al. 2016). Now, we cannot know definitively what kinds of values future generations will hold, what conceptions of sustainability they will prefer, and what kinds of trade-offs they will be willing to make between different kinds of resources. It may even be the case that while certain types of natural resources or ecological processes seem of little importance to us now, they will prove critical for human flourishing in future. Remember that what we now call wetlands were once dismissed as swamps that harbored little more than mosquitoes and noxious vapors, and were considered as places to be drained rather than protected. We now recognize their vital role in regulating water flows, storing carbon, and providing a home for many species of plants and animals. But even though it is hard to predict all future wants, needs, and values, it is relatively straightforward to recognize the need to keep open the ability of future generations to make their own choices on these dimensions— rather than foreclose them.

Foresight complements the other attributes of sustainability highlighted above, in that a longer-term view can help to foster an ecologically grounded approach that pays more attention to ecological cycles than to electoral ones. In addition, open participatory processes may prove capable of yielding a better approximation of the diversity of future interests than closed approaches that rely on the views of a handful of experts. Even so, far-sighted sustainability may provide a counterbalance to a radically open-ended view of sustainability, for it suggests the need to hold current institutional conceptions within limits so as to keep options open for future generations, notably by ensuring that the essential components of the Earth system remain in good working order.

INTEGRATED SUSTAINABILITY

Finally, reflexive sustainability must be integrated in two senses. Internal integration involves linkages across sustainability problems, such as the possibility that measures to repair the ozone layer could either mitigate or accelerate climate change. Internal integration also includes thinking about sustainability across multiple scales. Environmental law and policy have grappled more commonly with localized problems but increasingly need to take account of their global interconnections (Stephens 2017). External integration (which we focus on here) involves coupling reflexive rethinking about sustainability with reflexive rethinking of other core societal values. For example, understandings of what open sustainability requires should take into account how ideas of democracy need to change under Anthropocene conditions (a topic we discuss further in chapter 7). Similarly, far-sighted sustainability needs to be understood in light of a recast notion of intergenerational justice (as highlighted in chapter 4).

One important concern is whether it is possible to achieve an integrated view of sustainability and justice. Some accounts of sustainable development see "social sustainability" as a synonym for equity and justice, thus subsuming justice under the banner of sustainable development. In contrast, Dobson (2007: 93) argues that, except for their convergence on matters of what is owed to future generations, the two objectives may not be compatible, as "sustainability is about preservation and/or conservation; justice is about distribution." Social justice and environmental sustainability may find themselves at loggerheads when environmental protection will benefit future generations but impose costs on the present generation, especially today's poor. Regardless of whether justice is seen as extrinsic or intrinsic to sustainable development, the challenge remains: either to integrate sustainable development with justice (on the extrinsic view), or to integrate the environmental and social justice components of sustainable development with one another (on the intrinsic view).

Debate over the tension between environmental sustainability and social justice has flared up over a proposal by prominent biologists and ecologists that half of the Earth's area should be preserved for future generations (Noss et al. 2012; Wilson 2016). Büscher et al. (2017) argue that implementing the "Half Earth" proposal could have disastrous consequences for the world's poor if areas of land on which they depend for food and livelihoods were converted into inaccessible protected areas. Kopnina (2016: 177) responds that objections to the proposal "falter because they neglect the need to treat nonhuman beings justly," and that justice requires a fair sharing of the world's resources between humans and non-humans. Kopnina (2016: 177–8) also contends that Half Earth does recognize the need to ensure that conservation efforts do not unjustly treat human communities. More broadly, the debate suggests that the merits of preserving half the Earth cannot be divorced from thinking about the implications for both humans and non-human nature, underscoring the need for a social-ecological understanding of justice, as outlined in chapter 4.

One notable attempt to integrate justice and sustainability with the Earth system in mind is that of a "safe and just operating space" for humanity, first set out in Raworth (2012) and elaborated in Raworth (2017). The safe and just operating space is represented by a "doughnut" shape: its outer rim represents an ecological ceiling based on the planetary boundaries framework (the "safe operating space" that we encountered in chapter 1), while its inner rim represents a social foundation informed by human rights and minimum standards for social and economic well-being. On this understanding, the Earth system functions both as an enabler of and a constraint upon measures to advance social justice. This approach sees a sustainable Earth system as a prerequisite for efforts to foster just societies, while cautioning that measures to advance justice through material prosperity cannot afford to ignore their ecological impacts.[11]

The idea of a safe and just operating space valuably reminds us that, while avoiding dangerous instability in the Earth system is important, the pursuit of justice remains vital too.[12] However, the view that sustainability defines the ecological ceiling while justice defines the social foundation is an oversimplification that falls short of fully integrating safety and justice. For even when it comes to defining minimum conditions for safety or sustainability, concerns of justice already come into play. As we argued in chapter 1, any attempt to define planetary boundaries inevitably involves value judgments about degrees of acceptable risk. As the impacts of planetary risks will be unevenly distributed across the globe, choices about acceptable risk are themselves bound up with questions of distributive justice. Moreover, procedural justice requires that those affected by how the safe operating space is drawn should be involved in deliberating about those choices. Deeper integration of justice and sustainability is therefore necessary and possible.

"Transforming our world": deliberating on the Sustainable Development Goals

To explore in greater detail how the politics of sustainability works in practice, we now turn to an especially prominent international effort that explicitly tries to advance sustainability: the UN Sustainable Development Goals (SDGs) adopted in 2015. The title of the UN resolution setting out the SDGs—"Transforming our World"—is doubly significant from an Anthropocene perspective. Not only does it voice an aspiration to change the world for the better but it also (and perhaps less deliberately) gestures to the fact that humanity is already transforming the world in myriad ways, not all of them desirable. By assessing how the process to craft the SDGs fares against the

---

[11] For another account that seeks to integrate justice and sustainability, see Agyeman, Bullard, and Evans's (2003) idea of "just sustainabilities." Agyeman's (2013: 51) subsequent restatement of the idea links it to the idea of planetary boundaries and Raworth's "doughnut."

[12] Recall our argument in chapter 4 on why justice remains important even at a time of planetary crisis.

criteria of reflexive sustainability we have outlined, we can better sense whether current institutions of global governance can rethink sustainability and overcome the barriers that lie in its path.[13]

OPEN?

The SDGs succeeded the UN Millennium Development Goals (MDGs), which were launched in 2001 and expired in 2015. As the name indicates, the MDGs were about development, not *sustainable* development. They set out eight global goals for achieving human development, including reducing income poverty, expanding access to education and health, and advancing gender equality. While the MDGs gained widespread attention in media and public debate and helped to reverse the post-Cold War decline in global aid (Fukuda-Parr and Hulme 2011), they attracted criticism for having been created "through a top-down donor-driven process noteworthy for the absence of broad consultation" (Fox and Stoett 2016: 560). Agreement to launch a new process to formulate the SDGs was one of the few noteworthy outcomes of the Rio+20 Summit held in 2012 (Clémençon 2012).

The Rio+20 outcome specified that the SDGs should be developed through "an inclusive and transparent intergovernmental process . . . that is open to all stakeholders" (UN 2012: paragraph 248). Accordingly, the UN launched an extensive range of consultative processes to garner the views of people around the world on what the SDGs should look like. These processes included consultations held by a High-Level Panel of Eminent Persons on the Post-2015 Development Agenda; eleven global thematic consultations, including one on environmental sustainability; over ninety national and regional consultations; consultations with the research community through the Sustainable Development Solutions Network and with the business community through the Global Compact; and the MY World survey, which asked people about the issues that matter most to them (for details see Fox and Stoett 2016 and Sénit, Biermann, and Kalfagianni 2017). The MY World survey was able to garner an impressive 9.7 million responses as of October 2017 (UN 2017). The UN's Major Groups of stakeholders (originally established at the 1992 Rio summit and covering ten groups, including women, Indigenous peoples and farmers) also provided input at various stages. In addition, the intergovernmental Open Working Group's year-long, eight-session stocktaking stage included engagement with civil society, scientific evidence, and expert testimony. According to Chasek and Wagner (2016: 406), by the commencement of the drafting stage the stocktaking process helped to build "a high level of cohesion, a common

[13] For more on the SDGs process, see Kamau, Chasek, and O'Connor (2018).

sense of purpose, a shared understanding of the issues, and receptiveness to new ideas."[14]

All in all, these processes amounted to what the UN Secretary-General described as "the most inclusive and transparent negotiation process in UN history" (UN 2015a). Even so, the process did not take up proposals to hold citizens' assemblies to inform the goals, which may have helped move the emphasis from "extractive" to "deliberative" forms of participation (Wisor 2012). Others argue that the Open Working Group declined to adopt civil society recommendations for more structured engagement in its work (Spijkers and Honniball 2015: 286, 292). Ultimately some of the most innovative forms of citizen engagement emerged through independent initiatives. The Participate Initiative, a coalition of participatory research organizations, conducted a series of "ground level panels" (an inversion of the UN's High Level Panel) to enable the voices of marginalized communities to be heard (Howard and Wheeler 2015). As the goals edged closer to adoption, the process narrowed down to a more conventional mode of intergovernmental negotiation (Chasek et al. 2016). While civil society organizations were still able to provide input at this stage, some of the most contentious issues— including how the goals would address climate change—were resolved in contact groups composed of government officials whose proceedings were closed to observers (Chasek et al. 2016: 12).

Whether the views exchanged during the more open stages of the drafting process were reflected in the final set of goals is a question that remains to be investigated further. However, there is some evidence that summaries of consultations did not fully represent the range of participants' views. Gellers (2016) finds that, in the online thematic consultations on environmental sustainability, contributions from North Americans and other English speakers were significantly more prevalent in summary reports than in the consultations themselves, suggesting that voices from other regions may have been under-represented in the information that filtered through to decision-makers. The Participate Initiative found that the High-Level Panel "listened closely to some of the issues raised by people living in poverty and marginalization," but that the report ultimately did not go far enough in recognizing the ability of those people "to act to address their own situation, and then [build] a global development framework that supports them rather than reinforcing existing powerful interests" (Participate 2013; see also Fox and Stoett 2016: 562). In chapter 6 we will suggest that the influence of the most vulnerable ought to be crucial in shaping collective responses to the Anthropocene.

What of the openness of the vision of sustainability presented in the 2030 Agenda itself? Although the SDGs are the product of closure or consensus

---

[14] This stocktaking process finds a parallel in the "information phase" often used in small-scale citizen deliberation (Goodin and Niemeyer 2003).

around a common global set of goals, a number of features of the Agenda remain open to plural understandings of sustainability. While the Agenda does not go as far as recognizing different conceptions of sustainable development, it does acknowledge the existence of "different approaches, visions, models and tools available to each country" for achieving sustainable development, and refers to the idea of Mother Earth as another such vision (UN 2015b: paragraph 59). In addition, the Agenda leaves it up to national governments to set their own national targets, rather than assuming (as the MDGs did) that global goals could serve directly as national goals. Nevertheless, the goals themselves do not contain an explicit commitment to democracy. "Democracy" is mentioned only once in the Agenda, where "democracy, good governance and the rule of law" are seen as being "essential for sustainable development" (paragraph 9). Instead, the Agenda prefers the language of "inclusion" (forty-five references) and "participation" (fifteen references).[15] The closest that the SDGs get to a goal for democracy is target 16.7—"Ensure responsive, inclusive, participatory and representative decision-making at all levels"—which seems carefully crafted to gesture towards democracy without mentioning it by name.[16] Even if the commitment to democracy were more explicit, there is no guarantee that it would extend to democratic contemplation of the meaning of sustainability itself.

The openness we do observe in the SDGs means that plural understandings can flourish. But plurality is not the same as engagement, which would involve a deeper interrogation of the meaning of sustainability in ways that would have consequences for the Agenda as a whole.

ECOLOGICALLY GROUNDED?

The MDGs were criticized for their limited attention to environmental sustainability: the environment was relegated to a single goal (MDG 7) that lacked precise targets and was not well integrated with the other goals, which placed stronger emphasis on economic and social development (Brandi 2015: 32). The reframing of the post-2015 goals as "sustainable development" goals was an early indication that a degree of rethinking had taken place.[17] One other notable feature of the later goals ought to be conducive to more holistic thinking about the Earth system. Whereas the MDGs focused on developing countries, the SDGs are now universal in scope: "These are universal goals and

---

[15] These totals include references to variations on each word, such as "inclusive" and "participatory."

[16] Langford (2016: 173) suggests that China lobbied to have references to democracy removed from the draft text.

[17] Note however that the convergence of the processes to formulate sustainable development goals and to create successors to the MDGs only occurred subsequent to Rio+20 in 2012 (Chasek et al. 2016: 8).

targets which involve the entire world, developed and developing countries alike" (UN 2015b: paragraph 5). This shift is vitally important given that some of the most intense pressures on the Earth system stem from high levels of consumption in industrialized countries, as well as rapidly rising consumption in middle-income countries (WWF 2016: 80).

Environmental concerns are far more evident in the SDGs than in their predecessor goals. Three of the seventeen goals—on climate change, oceans, and land-based ecosystems (SDGs 13–15)—are directly related to ecological concerns, while goals on other issues—such as on energy, sustainable cities and communities, and sustainable consumption and production (SDGs 7, 11 and 12)—have clear implications for sustainability. The broader 2030 Agenda also indicates a degree of concern for the Earth as a whole, with the preamble stating a collective resolve to "to heal and secure our planet." The declaration also cautions that "the survival of many societies, and of the biological support systems of the planet, is at risk" (paragraph 14). This statement echoes a discourse of limits and boundaries that is much less ambiguous than sustainability discourse when it comes to the ecological constraints on human activity.

Nevertheless, there are important ways in which the SDGs lack an ecological grounding that is sufficient to contend with the Anthropocene. First, the 2030 Agenda does little to challenge the "three pillars" approach to sustainability. The Agenda states that "we are committed to achieving sustainable development in its three dimensions—economic, social and environmental—in a balanced and integrated manner" (UN 2015b: paragraph 2), reinforcing the idea that environmental concerns are to be balanced against—and when necessary traded off with—economic and social concerns. The synthesis of thematic consultations on environmental sustainability had concluded that "the current growth-led economic model has to transform in order to redress environmental and social challenges. This entails reconsidering how we measure progress and value natural assets" (UNDP and UNEP 2013: iii). The 2030 Agenda makes a concession to the latter point through a commitment to develop "broader measures of progress to complement gross domestic product" (UN 2015b: paragraph 48). However, overall the goals reinforce an approach to development that relies not only on sustainable but *sustained* economic growth (SDG 8), and fails to question whether sustained growth remains desirable in the world's wealthiest countries, even if it may be necessary for the foreseeable future in the poorest.[18] Having said this, the broader package of goals could be seen as a more comprehensive way of conceiving and measuring human progress than by economic growth alone (Young et al. 2017: 55).

---

[18] Target 8.4 provides a degree of balance through a pledge to "endeavour to decouple economic growth from environmental degradation."

Second, the goals lack a coherent approach to addressing major risks to the Earth system. In the lead-up to their adoption, some commentators argued that the SDGs should refer explicitly to Earth system concepts. Hajer et al (2015: 1654–5) called for the adoption of the "safe and just operating space" discussed earlier in this chapter, while Brandi (2015: 33) argued that the SDGs should contain a goal to "safeguard Earth's life-support system" (see also Griggs et al. 2013: 305).[19] Neither of these approaches was taken up in the final document, nor does the 2030 Agenda refer to the Anthropocene or planetary boundaries. Moreover, to the extent that individual goals do address the Earth system, they vary greatly in their levels of specificity (Hoff and Lobos Alva 2017). Notably, SDG 13 ("Take urgent action to combat climate change and its impacts") does not set out a precise target for avoiding dangerous climate change, such as the 2°C or 1.5°C temperature targets that had been cited in previous UNFCCC decisions.[20] Some targets do draw attention to issues that have struggled to gain traction under existing international regimes, notably the target to "minimize and address the impacts of ocean acidification" (target 14.3). But many of the targets related to Earth system processes call vaguely for "significant" or "substantial" reductions in ecological degradation, rather than setting out ambitious, quantified goals that could help to motivate action and monitor progress. Across the SDGs more generally, Hajer et al (2015: 1653) observe that "environmental concerns are less often named in goals, less well-defined and more often addressed in targets under goals focused on the social and economic dimensions of sustainable development."

DYNAMIC?

The transition from the MDGs to the SDGs already suggests a degree of dynamism: international development goals do not remain fixed for the indefinite future but need to be revisited in light of changing circumstances, including shifts in ecological conditions. Moreover, participants in the SDGs consultations sought to learn from the experience of the MDGs and design the SDGs so as to address the shortcomings of their predecessor goals (UNDP and UNEP 2013: 16–17). While the 2030 Agenda allows for flexibility in national implementation and sets out processes for national, regional, and global reviews of the implementation of the goals (UN 2015b: paragraphs 72–91), it does not explicitly allow for the possibility of revising the goals and targets

[19] See also Norström et al. (2014) for a social-ecological systems perspective on how the SDGs should be framed.
[20] The lack of specificity in the climate change goal was partially due to the fact that the Paris Agreement (which does specify a temperature target) was still under negotiation at the time the SDGs were adopted.

themselves as new evidence emerges or trends in global development change. Nevertheless, because the SDGs are time-bound, there is a degree of built-in momentum to review the targets as their expiry date of 2030 draws closer, and if necessary to set new targets. But this possibility falls short of any permanent deliberative capacity to revisit core commitments in light of changes in the Earth system—least of all at the global level.

FAR-SIGHTED?

The 2030 end date for the SDGs extends well beyond the time horizons of short-term electoral cycles, though far short of addressing future generations in the plural. To that extent, the SDGs entail a degree of longer-term thinking than in conventional policy-making, although governments may find it easy to commit to targets so distant that they will not be held accountable for failing to achieve them.

Nevertheless, some aspects of the SDG process suggest short-term thinking. The MY World survey, for example, asked people to choose the top six issues that matter to them from a list of sixteen.[21] As Fox and Stoett (2016: 566) observe, "the survey was a snapshot of people's preferences at a fixed point in time. This was problematic in at least one unalterable respect: the evolution of people's preferences and the legitimate rights of future generations were not taken into account." Moreover, the way the question was asked induced respondents to focus on their personal interests—not any collective interests. The survey asked "which of these is most important for you and your family?"—not what is most important for the world, or indeed anyone else. It was not surprising, then, that "action taken on climate change" was ranked the lowest of all sixteen options, with the top three responses ("a good education," "better healthcare," and "better job opportunities") all attracting at least twice as many responses (UN 2017). In addition, the survey lacked contextual information about the risks to the Earth system (or for that matter about the links between different kinds of priorities) that might have encouraged respondents to take a more thoughtful perspective on development priorities. The example highlights the limitations of drawing on survey data to inform longer-term goals.[22] In contrast, the national consultations on the SDGs produced quite different outcomes on priorities, including "a real and growing awareness of the fragility of the environment and the threats to livelihoods from growth patterns which do not take into account environmental

---

[21] While the survey allowed respondents to add a further issue that was not included in the list, most responses remained within the fixed set of options.

[22] Nevertheless, surveys could be designed with the aim of eliciting people's views on the future, not just on the present (for an example, see Davies and Pickering 2017).

sustainability" (UN Development Group 2013: 46; see also Fox and Stoett 2016: 565).

In our view, there is no reason why the 2030 Agenda's vision—of "a world in which consumption and production patterns and use of all natural resources—from air to land, from rivers, lakes and aquifers to oceans and seas—are sustainable" (UN 2015b: paragraph 9)—could not serve as a far-sighted goal, taking the world well beyond 2030. A process that gave greater weight to the interests of future generations could have resulted in a set of goals that placed even stronger emphasis on longer-term concerns such as environmental sustainability.

INTEGRATED?

The call for an integrated approach to environmental sustainability resonated strongly in the SDG consultations (UNDP and UNEP 2013: iii). As mentioned above, the shift towards integrating environmental, social, and economic concerns is an especially prominent feature of the 2030 Agenda. Indeed the words "integrated" or "integration" are mentioned twenty-seven times in the Agenda, usually with reference to the unified approach of the Agenda as a whole (UN 2015b). A network analysis of the SDGs finds that integration across goals is stronger than in the MDGs, and that sustainable consumption and production (SDG 12) is the goal most extensively linked with other SDGs and targets (Le Blanc 2015: 180). However, the same analysis finds that important opportunities for stronger integration were overlooked, including links between climate change on the one hand and energy, industrialization, land use, water, and oceans on the other (Le Blanc 2015: 185).

While ideas of justice are made explicit in the Agenda, they are generally understood in narrow terms, mostly in conjunction with the notion of access to justice (i.e. an ability to seek legal means of redress, as in SDG 16 and target 16.3). By and large, concerns of distributive justice are couched in the somewhat less stringent language of "equity" (e.g. equitable access to education or drinking water). Still less is justice understood in ecological terms, as called for in chapter 4. Integration in the SDGs only goes so far.

SUMMARY

The process of formulating the SDGs was certainly more open than that associated with the MDGs. The SDGs achieved a stronger ecological grounding and better integration of sustainable development with other societal values, and showed a dynamic ability to learn from previous experience. Nevertheless, the SDGs still fall short in recognizing broader risks facing the Earth system, and in emphasizing the foresight needed to reverse patterns of unsustainable development that are undermining the conditions for the planet's future. Having said this, it is easy to find something to criticize in a multilateral process that sought to reach consensus across vastly different cultures and national circumstances. The challenge of cultural, national, and value pluralism will endure in future efforts to craft post-2030 goals, and it will be vital that those efforts learn from the SDGs. Equally, reflexive sustainability will require rethinking across other levels of governance, not least through deliberation on how the SDGs should be understood in local contexts and implemented at national and sub-national levels (Howard and Wheeler 2015: 566).

Conclusion

The inescapability of the Anthropocene means that sustainability, already elusive, becomes still harder to pursue than before, but not impossible. The pathological path dependencies we have identified in dominant institutions continue to pose serious obstacles to more sustainable societies. A reflexive conception of sustainability is needed, not only to overcome these path dependencies, but also to cultivate a capacity to rethink what sustainability should mean in light of shifts in the Earth system as well as changing technologies and values. That reflexive conception needs to be open (within limits), ecologically grounded, dynamic, far-sighted, and integrated with other values. That is a lot to ask for, although as we have seen we can find intimations of what is required in real-world processes, such as that which yielded the Sustainable Development Goals. But who exactly will engage in this kind of rethinking, and how? We explore this question in the next chapter.

6 Who will form the Anthropocene?

The contours of the Anthropocene will, for better or worse, be shaped by humans (though in conjunction with non-human systems). In this chapter we try to pinpoint who exactly might shape it for the better. In chapter 3 we developed the idea of ecological reflexivity as the primary requirement for governance in the Anthropocene. Reflexivity refers to the capacity of structures and systems to question their own core commitments and values such as justice and sustainability, then make changes if necessary. But somebody or something must do the questioning and responding, which brings us to the idea of agency. The "somebodies or somethings" are agents.

In the context of the Anthropocene, when agency is discussed it has been mainly in terms of what humans have done to the Earth system. For example, Oreskes (2007: 93) argues that "humans have become geological agents, changing the most basic physical processes of the earth" (see also Chakrabarty 2009: 206–7). While the Earth system has always been shaped by geological *forces*— from asteroids and glaciers to volcanoes and oceans—it is only in the Anthropocene that geological *agents* have begun to shape it too. However, agency entails more than this sort of influence or causation. Agency involves the capacity to think and then act. It is associated most straightforwardly with individual humans, and is arguably part of what it means to be human. It is also possible to think of collective or group agents, when people are organized into a body such as a corporation, social movement, international organization, political party, or state (List and Pettit 2011).

Our stress on pathological path dependency as the key deficiency of Holocene institutions draws on a tradition of analysis that emphasizes not agency, but structure. The agent–structure debate has a long history in social science. That debate continues an even longer history of dispute about the role of freedom and determinism in the human world. An extreme structuralist position would have no room for human agency at all, but would see history in terms of the remorseless operation of impersonal forces. A structural account of the rise of environmental policy would stress not the efforts of environmentalists but the increasing incidence and depth of risks and hazards accompanying economic development which eventually threaten to undermine the political and economic order, thus requiring response. MacNeil and Paterson (2012) deploy this kind of analysis to show how the neoliberal political economy of the United States forced environmental regulation to adopt policy instruments short of a comprehensive regime of greenhouse gas control. Social-ecological systems analysis in the field of ecology often sees social change through a structuralist lens, as human social systems respond to the causal force of ecological constraints. We saw in chapter 3 how resilience theory grounded in ecology has struggled to come to terms with human agency and power relations. Structuralists can often be found in the discipline of sociology. According to Dusenberry (1960: 233), whereas "economics is all about how people make choices[,] sociology is all about how people don't have any choices to make." This stereotype perhaps no longer holds, though structuralists can be found in plenty of other disciplines, not just sociology.

It is important to recognize both structure and agency. Structures constrain agency, but do not fully determine what agents can do. Some accounts of the Anthropocene privilege agency at the expense of structure by viewing humans as super-agents (e.g. Hamilton 2017; see also the advocates of a "good Anthropocene" discussed in chapter 1). Others lose sight of the role of individual decisions in shaping planetary impacts by emphasizing remorseless economic forces such as those producing the Great Acceleration since the mid-1940s. Accounts of the Anthropocene may also neglect agency to the extent that they emphasize people's vulnerability to global environmental change without due recognition of their ability to think and act in ways that can help to reduce their vulnerability.

One way of thinking about reflexivity is that it involves advancing a desirable kind of agency which requires listening, reflection, foresight, and anticipation against the structural determinism of path dependency, such that agents can become more capable of rethinking and transforming structures to good effect. However, as we argued in chapter 3, institutional structures may themselves either enable or obstruct the exercise of reflexivity, so reflexivity can also be an attribute of institutional structures. Whatever happens, structures will still exist, and will still constrain agency to some extent.

Agency can be seen not just as a way of explaining how people interact with the world, but also as a morally important quality of human life. Human agency—in particular the freedom to think and reflect on one's goals in life and to pursue them in practice—is something to be cultivated and safeguarded; its opposite, being a victim of circumstance or a pawn in someone else's machinations, is something to be overcome (Sen 1999; Crocker 2008).[1] At the same time, not all kinds of agency are morally desirable, since humans and institutions can exercise agency for nefarious or self-destructive ends.

In this chapter, we take a close look at the agents who could give better shape to the Anthropocene by critically questioning and changing institutions

---

[1] Agency may also be morally significant as a prerequisite for assigning moral responsibility for harmful or beneficial actions, but this is not our concern here (see generally Erskine 2001).

and practices. The actors on whom we focus are "discourse entrepreneurs" (leaders or activists capable of advancing the standing of discourses), scientists and other experts, cities and other sub-national governments, and those most vulnerable to the negative impacts of ecological change. We will pay less attention to powerful actors such as states, international organizations, and corporations which are vitally important and must change their ways—but we do so only because we think the motive force for change must come from elsewhere. Non-human nature has some but not all of the attributes of agents, and we will address how it could still play an active role in how the Anthropocene gets shaped.

Formative agency

The previous two chapters drive home the point that what we mean by justice and sustainability must be determined in ongoing political processes. The most important actors in these processes can be termed *formative agents* (a concept first introduced in Dryzek 2015), so called because they give form to what justice, sustainability, and related concepts should mean in practice. While they can draw on more general ideas, formative agents shape the principles that ought to be adopted in particular contexts (such as the governance of biodiversity or climate change). Thus they affect questions such as whether sustainability should involve economic systems, ecological systems, or social-ecological systems; whether or not principles of justice should extend to non-humans; the degree to which we should care about future generations of people, if doing so may hurt specific categories of people in the present; and whether the units of obligation and concern when it comes to global environmental issues should be states, or individuals irrespective of which states they happen to live in.

Formative agents can be involved in determining what broad principles should apply to any case at hand. For example, to what extent should the principle of respect for private property rights be applied in pollution control policy, and how should that principle be balanced against other concerns such as the integrity of affected ecological systems?

These examples show that formative agents can be active on questions as small as what it might mean to restore a damaged local ecosystem (if the baseline condition of the ecosystem is controversial), or as large as what principles should be the basis for global governance. Given the pressing need to change dominant institutions and practices for the better, we will emphasize the exercise of formative agency on the big questions.

We need to examine what happens when actors exercise (or fail to exercise) formative agency, why that exercise (or lack of exercise) can sometimes be problematic, especially in Anthropocene conditions, and how the problems might be corrected. Formative agents can sometimes act wisely, but sometimes their actions can be disastrous—for example, if they decide to create or perpetuate institutions and practices that refuse to respond to feedback on the condition of social-ecological systems. We need to examine the conditions that make it more likely that formative agents will act to good effect.

There is more to agency than formative agency. Notably, once actors decide to adopt a principle (such as the precautionary principle when it comes to pollutants, which means government acting to forestall potential harm before it is proven), they are agents—but not formative agents. O'Neill (2001) refers to "primary agents" upon whom the obligation to promote justice rests; she has in mind corporations and NGOs, as well as states. But formative agency is logically prior to primary agency, because it determines what values such as justice should mean to begin with. Primary agents implement principles, rather than form them. Particular actors can, though, sometimes act as formative agents (for example, in helping to craft a treaty), at other times as primary agents (for example, when they subsequently take actions to implement the treaty they helped to craft).

Formative agency in action

To illustrate how formative agency operates, consider the case of biodiversity and the related concept of ecosystem services. Now, biological diversity per se is very old, and for almost all of its history there were no humans around to worry about what it should mean. Perhaps the simplest way of thinking about biodiversity is to consider the total number of species on Earth, though that proves hard to count. There is plenty of scope for thinking in terms of anything from the fate of a species in a particular location to the distribution of species across locations, the variety of ecosystems, and aggregate global rates of species extinctions (Mace et al. 2014). But in practice, biodiversity has come to mean much more than numbers. Many concerns that once came under the heading of conservation or wilderness preservation have been brought under the biodiversity heading in the past two or three decades.

The biodiversity concept was first used in the 1980s as a contraction of "biological diversity," initially by academic scientists (for a history, see Takacs 1996 and Jeffries 2006: ch. 1). Biologists Thomas Lovejoy and Edward O. Wilson were prominent in publicizing the idea. Before long the idea gained political traction, as the International Union for the Conservation of Nature (IUCN) advocated the establishment of a global convention. This call met with a response at the 1992 Earth Summit (United Nations Conference on Environment and Development) in Rio de Janeiro, which established the

Convention on Biological Diversity (CBD). By then it was apparent that diversity could refer to genes, species, or ecosystems; simply counting species in an ecosystem without reference to the functions they performed was too simplistic.

If biodiversity matters, that means it is valuable. But in what terms? The scientists and philosophers who initially thought about this value would see it in terms of ensuring the healthy workings of ecosystems—or possibly as something intrinsically valuable, irrespective of whether or not it served material human purposes. But eventually economists entered, with attempts to put monetary value on biodiversity through reference to the "ecosystem services" that biodiversity provides to humans—in recycling wastes, in rendering ecosystems productive in the resources they can yield, in providing human habitat and facilitating human health, in moderating climate, and so forth. The importance of the economic interpretation of biodiversity was confirmed in 2012 in the title of the newly established global scientific assessment body, the Intergovernmental Science-Policy Platform on Biodiversity and Ecosystem Services (IPBES). In the global aggregate, the monetary sums that could now be attached to the value of biodiversity were astronomical. One study puts the value of ecosystem services at US$125 trillion per year in 2011, or almost double the value of the global economy as conventionally measured by gross national income (Costanza et al. 2014).

At least for the economically minded, nature's hefty price tag should constitute a knock-down argument in favor of conservation. But at more local levels, thinking in monetary terms meant that biodiversity could be traded off against the money to be made from housing developments, or mining, or the construction of large dams, or logging, or land clearance for agriculture. In the United States, the Nature Conservancy came to treat non-human nature as a repository of "natural capital" that can be cultivated to provide quantifiable ecosystem services. This interventionist approach appalls conservation biologists led by Michael Soulé, who believes this kind of thinking facilitates attacks on biodiversity and may even enable ecological collapse (Miller, Soulé, and Terborgh 2014). The debate between Soulé and the Nature Conservancy illustrates formative agency in action, as the two sides struggle on behalf of their competing meanings of conservation. Similarly, within IPBES the Bolivian delegation—led by the anthropologist Diego Pacheco—vocally opposed the adoption of a conceptual framework built around ecosystem services, arguing instead that the idea of Mother Earth better captured Indigenous understandings of nature's value (Borie and Hulme 2015).

We noted in chapters 1 and 5 that concepts such as conservation, preservation, and restoration need to be reconsidered if the Anthropocene brings permanent ecological instability and change, undermining the idea of baseline ecological conditions. The dispute between the Nature Conservancy and conservation biologists does not reach the right territory because on one side the attempted treatment of nature in economic terms deploys a mode of thought developed in Holocene institutions—the discipline of economics— and on the other side conservation means that nature should be protected for its own sake and kept wild. Restoration ecology has perhaps progressed further: rather than refer to baseline conditions that should be the target of restoration, the idea is to stop degradation, and promote beneficial processes in the context of shifting conditions (Higgs 2012).

In 2009 Rockström et al. identified "biodiversity loss" as one of the nine planetary boundaries we discussed in chapter 1. The indicator associated with this boundary was the rate of species extinctions relative to the rate that would occur in the absence of human intervention. In light of the previous three decades of rethinking, this was perhaps a retrograde step as it involved counting individual species. Critics could point out that biodiversity loss is something whose damage is generally experienced locally, not globally, and that extinction rates do not capture other important signals of biodiversity loss, such as changes in the abundance and geographical distribution of surviving species and in the ways that ecosystems function (Mace et al. 2014). The 2015 version of planetary boundaries (Steffen, Richardson, et al. 2015) renamed this boundary "biosphere integrity"—though retaining the extinction rate indicator on an interim basis, pending the availability of data on species variability, while adding a "Biodiversity Intactness Index" that can be applied regionally, for example to biomes. The scientists involved in both the 2009 and 2015 versions showed a capacity to learn and exercise formative agency in relation to the meaning of biodiversity, even if the precise indicator they retained in 2015 did not quite reflect this learning.

We see that when it comes to the practical bite of biodiversity there are clear changes over time, as well as continued disputes over meanings and values— and these changes and disputes are the result of the activities of formative agents. These agents can be viewed as constituting a community of inquiry; not one that proceeds in dispassionate scientific terms, but one that mixes science and politics. The practical meaning of biodiversity is the outcome of the interactions of these agents. This meaning is always provisional and can change with time, as its elements are contested. Putting the meaning into policy practice is an essential part of the process—though, as the case of planetary boundaries suggests, often hard to achieve.

Global biodiversity governance has seen struggles for formative agency not only over the meaning of biodiversity itself but also over what values such as justice should mean in this context. In the CBD, claims for justice are voiced most forcefully by Indigenous peoples and local communities, who frequently maintain a close relationship with highly biodiverse ecosystems, but whose rights to access and protect the resources within them remain limited (see for example Marion Suiseeya 2014). Many calls for justice in the CBD remain tied to the claims of particular communities, rather than portraying justice in biodiversity as a matter that affects everyone worldwide. In this regard, the contrast with global climate governance—where a diverse set of movements for global climate justice has emerged—is striking (Pickering 2017): an analogous movement for global biodiversity justice is yet to emerge. The ability of participants in the CBD to rethink the global dimensions of biodiversity justice is limited by the text of the Convention itself, which affirms countries' sovereign rights over the biological resources within their territories, thus confirming the priority of state-level concerns over local and Indigenous concerns. Here we encounter again (as we did in chapter 4) a form of pathological path dependency that restricts the penetration of global justice.

How to exercise formative agency: reason, rhetoric, and deliberation

The preceding discussion looks at how formative agency achieves practical effect in the real world by creating and changing meanings—though the impact of those meanings has been variable, mixing some local success with plenty of local failures in identifying and conserving biodiversity. Recognition of the Anthropocene requires formative agency that can question and disrupt problematic path dependencies in institutions, practices, and their supporting ideas. In this section we will look at how formative agency might be exercised; in the next section we move to who might exercise it. Our stress will be on the use of language in creating and questioning meanings, which must be central to any account of formative agency. Language can involve reason, rhetoric, and deliberation. Formative agency can also be exercised through non-linguistic means, in protests, leading by example, violence, coercion, and visual representation. But these alternative means are always accompanied by language that transmits their meaning.

Ideas underpin institutions, and can be complicit in their path dependency when actors in institutions benefit from the persistence of ideas (Hay 2006: 65). It is no surprise that fossil fuel corporations finance think tanks such as the Heritage Foundation and American Enterprise Institute that question climate science and help perpetuate a set of ideas that underpin institutions and practices supportive of fossil fuel production and use. Institutions work because of a convergence of ideas, expectations, and understandings, not just formal rules (Schmidt 2008). So for example market-oriented globalization is so powerful in large measure because it permeates the understandings of actors in institutions such as banks, corporations, government finance departments, and international economic organizations such as the WTO and IMF (Hay and Rosamond 2002). Policy deviations from its orthodoxy (such as redistributive social policies, or significant taxes on corporate profits) are punished not just by impersonal market forces but also because people in key positions in financial and economic institutions believe those deviations will have negative economic consequences, and so (for example) disinvest in the deviant state. In global financial affairs, this set of understandings has so far been largely impervious to disruption by reasoned scrutiny, rhetorical interventions, or anything else, but that is not necessarily the case in other areas, as we shall now see.

REASON

The most obvious way to exercise formative agency is through argument on behalf of action, principles, concepts, positions, and interpretations. In the case of biodiversity (just discussed), those arguments might come from different directions, concerning what the term means to begin with, why biodiversity should be conceptualized as a global phenomenon, why instead it makes more sense to think in terms of regional or local levels, why everybody should care about it, why it should be valued first and foremost for the material benefits it provides to humans, why there is much more to its value than such narrow materialism. In some ideal logical world, collective outcomes such as the commitments embodied in global treaties or the policies of governments could be the result of such argument, reflecting the strength of the points made by different sides.

How important are arguments in disrupting problematic path dependencies in institutions and governments? The argument that Anthropocene conditions dramatize and change the way we ought to think about governance and politics has been made by others as well as ourselves. The book you are reading is our attempt to argue on behalf of a way to think about the Anthropocene, which we hope will have some influence (though we are also aware of the limited reach of academic books). It is fair to say that arguments about the Anthropocene have yet to have much of an impact on the real world of politics and policy. Yet perhaps we should not be too despondent: it took over a century from the recognition of human-caused climate change as a theoretical possibility to the point at which the world showed any sign of doing much about it. The history of climate change suggests that rarely is there a single knock-down argument made by one actor that persuades others enough to produce an identifiable policy outcome. Instead, arguments (and their rebuttals and refinements) accumulate over time; with luck this cumulative impact can make some difference. Once a sufficiently large number of people are persuaded, social change can happen remarkably quickly. A similar pattern of accretion and cascade can be found in some of the largest social movements in recent centuries, including struggles to end slavery and colonialism (Crawford 2002).

An optimistic view of the power of reason in international environmental governance is advanced by Peter Haas, who has explored the influence of "epistemic communities" built around scientific findings, though their membership extends beyond scientists to supportive actors inside and outside government. Haas (1992) believes such a community was central to successful efforts to protect the ozone layer, including the adoption of the 1987 Montreal Protocol. Orsini and Compagnon (2013) look at the impact of reasoned argument and deliberation (as opposed to bargaining) in the context of the international biodiversity negotiations—though their analysis is limited to negotiators meeting behind closed doors, especially in small "friends of the chair" or contact groups.

RHETORIC

Yet the Montreal Protocol also illustrates the limits to argument based on science—and the need for something extra to persuade the world to act. According to Litfin (1994) widespread support among scientists for the theory that human activities were depleting the ozone layer was already evident some years before the Protocol's adoption. What changed in the mid-1980s was a combination of accumulating scientific evidence along with the arrival of a new rhetoric adopted and advanced by scientists and environmentalists that highlighted the idea of an "ozone hole" in the southern hemisphere, which in turn dramatically advanced the standing of what she calls a "precautionary" discourse that then underpinned the Protocol by making global agreement possible.[2]

The ability of rhetoric to disrupt path dependency can be further illustrated by the history of how sustainable development came to be the dominant discourse in global environmental affairs following the 1987 delivery to the United Nations of the report *Our Common Future* (World Commission on Environment and Development 1987), generally known as the Brundtland report. The invocation of the idea of sustainable development by Brundtland was an attempt to show that environmental concern (and social justice) did not have to challenge conventional material growth. Incompatibility between environmental protection and economic growth had been a mainstay of thinking about environmental affairs, and was crystallized in the 1970s in *The Limits to Growth*, which we discussed in chapter 2. Brundtland did not prove or really even argue that reconciliation was possible, but rather asserted it with great force. Thus the rise of the discourse of sustainable development

---

[2] The ozone hole rhetoric was underpinned by research published in 1985 that showed a dramatic seasonal drop in ozone levels over the Antarctic. Benedick (1991: 18–20) argues that the ozone hole discovery had a greater influence on public opinion than directly on the Montreal talks.

on the world stage was secured. The net environmental effects of its rise to global prominence remain debatable, as the years since Brundtland have seen sustainable development become ever more reconciled to conventional ideas about economic growth (Parr 2009) and the neoliberal political economy that is home to these ideas. In this light, though Brundtland did change the terms of global environmental discourse, her report did not disrupt the path dependencies associated with the dominant global economic order, its governance institutions, and its supportive discourse. What happened instead was that sustainable development discourse was pulled into progressively closer association with the dominant order.

The moral we take from this discussion is that effective formative agency is not just a matter of argument: it can also involve rhetorical moves. Now, for some people the idea of rhetoric calls to mind either an attempt to divert attention—denigrated as "mere rhetoric"—or an appeal to emotions that cloud reason. There is no denying that demagogues have deployed rhetoric for nefarious purposes. But rhetoric per se is neither good nor bad. Rhetoric does enable an audience to be moved when reason alone fails. The solution is to hold rhetoric to critical standards: notably, does it induce reflection and open up possibilities for effective dialogue (Chambers 2009)? Does it help build bridges across difference, or does it demonize those who are not part of the group? (Dryzek and Lo 2015 show how a rhetorical appeal to a popular tax that finances health care in Australia brought climate change skeptics into a productive dialogue on carbon pricing.) Does it facilitate or impede an effective deliberative system? (We will have more to say about deliberative systems in the next chapter.) Most importantly, does it make reflexivity more or less likely? The Montreal Protocol eventually yielded a good example of what de Búrca, Keohane, and Sabel (2013: 780) call "experimental global governance," featuring "deliberative, joint rule making." If they are right, then the rhetorical intervention highlighting the ozone hole facilitated effective institutional reconstruction that embodied a measure of reflexivity in ozone governance.

DELIBERATION

Recognition of the importance of discourses in underpinning institutions suggests that human agency can disrupt structural historical forces. Disruption may be hard work, but the recognition can help identify points of leverage for the advancement of reflexivity.

Reason and rhetoric are capable of changing the relative weight of different discourses and ideas, as the examples of sustainable development and ozone both suggest.

Crucial here is not just the exercise of persuasion, but its reception. Those to whom argument and rhetoric are directed are not just passive receptors: ideally they are also interlocutors, capable of listening, reflecting, and responding. This ideal points to a deliberative process in which established institutions can be questioned rather than taken for granted.

Some very large claims have been made for the efficacy of deliberation in social-ecological contexts (Smith 2003; Baber and Bartlett 2005). The claims include deliberation's ability to integrate the interests and perspectives of diverse actors (scientists, public officials, activists, and others) concerned with different aspects of complex issues, promote public goods and common interests, enlarge the perspectives of participants by bringing to mind those not physically present (such as future generations and non-human nature: Goodin 1996b), and organize feedback on the state of social-ecological systems into political processes.

There is some empirical support for the effectiveness of deliberation in promoting environmental values. So for example World Wide Views ran citizen deliberations on climate policy in thirty-eight countries on the same day in 2009 using the same model; in just about every country participants favored stronger action than their governments were prepared to undertake (Rask, Worthington, and Lammi 2012). The exercise was repeated for biodiversity in 2012, with similar results (Rask and Worthington 2015). The results were presented to the respective COPs of the UNFCCC and CBD. However, this sort of effectiveness does not necessarily translate into the ability of deliberation to enable formative agency that is effective enough to overcome problematic path dependencies in dominant institutions and practices. World Wide Views had no such effects.

More promising lessons might be gleaned from our analysis of the UNFCCC in chapter 3. There we examined a process with some deliberative elements that led to the emergence of hybrid multilateralism as an alternative to the problematic extremes of top-down and bottom-up global climate governance (though this development involved more than formative agency).

If we cast a broader net, some evidence from other areas illustrates the transformative potential of deliberation. Ackerman's (1991) analysis of three transformative moments in the history of the United States provides some clues. These occasions were the Constitutional Founding, the Civil War amendments to the constitution, and the New Deal. What characterized all three moments was intense deliberation encompassing all the institutions of government—and much of civil society—simultaneously, in response to a great crisis of the state. This kind of intense engagement, featuring deep reflection about what constitutes the common good (though nothing like unanimity in how that good should be defined), was on Ackerman's account very different from politics as usual.

Ackerman's analysis suggests that a systemic crisis may be necessary for deliberation to take hold effectively. While in chapter 3 we pointed to the danger of relying on transformation amid crisis, deliberation does increase the likelihood of positive response to (for example) a crisis of legitimacy of the sort that occurred in the United States around 1970. As we pointed out in chapter 2 this provided an opening for the environmental movement to be brought into government by the Nixon administration, and helped create a new regime for environmental protection.

OTHER WAYS TO EXERCISE FORMATIVE AGENCY

There are other ways to exercise formative agency for which language per se is less central—though these other forms are generally accompanied by argument, rhetoric, and/or deliberation. These forms include:

- *Protests.* Protests can sometimes have the aim of reconfiguring the established order, and occasionally find some success in so doing. Large-scale protests have sometimes played a part in the downfall of authoritarian regimes. Anti-globalization/global justice protests are credited by former World Bank Chief Economist Joseph Stiglitz (2002) with eventually leading the Bank to take on social and environmental concerns that it had previously downplayed. UNFCCC events are often accompanied by large-scale protests, and while much of the time they do not appear to bring much that is new to the negotiating agenda or facilitate progress in tackling climate change, perhaps those protests have stimulated more effective recognition of climate justice.

- *Leading by Example.* Rather than advocate something different, some movements mainly try to live something different—and hope that the example may make a difference. Consider for example the Transition Town (or Transition Initiative) movement (Felicetti 2016), designed as a response to global and national failure to act on climate change and resource scarcity; or "sustainable materialist" movements that emphasize ethical and sustainable consumption (Schlosberg and Coles 2016). To date the broader impact of these movements has been marginal.

- *Violence.* Historically, some of the most effective formative actions that disrupt path dependency have been violent. Violence can involve imposing one's will on reluctant others (think of imperial conquests, or revolutions). While it is hard to imagine violence being put in the service of ecological reflexivity (and of course we do not endorse violence as a way of exercising formative agency), the aftermath of violence—in particular, total war—has in the past led to comprehensive reconstructions of the international order, though never in a way that had much to do with social-ecological concerns.

WHO WILL FORM THE ANTHROPOCENE? **115**

While some forms of radical environmental protest have been dubbed "ecoterrorism" (Vanderheiden 2008), environmental social movements have overwhelmingly sought to bring about change through non-violent means. Even supposed "ecoterrorism" has never led to any human casualties, only property damage; which is why it is more accurately described as "ecotage" (ecological sabotage).

- *Coercion* can involve the threat rather than use of force. There is a sporadic history of thinkers who advocate coercive rule by an ecologically enlightened elite. While again there are no obvious positive examples from the past, some observers think authoritarian China is well placed to construct what its leaders (including President Xi Jinping) have occasionally referred to as an "ecological civilization," which if it ever came to pass really would involve significant disruption of economic path dependency. However, to set China on that path would also require plenty in the way of reason, rhetoric, and deliberation—"ecological civilization" is itself a rhetorical move.

- *Visual Representation* can seek to disrupt complacency by depicting injustice or imagining different ways of life.[3] Although it is rare for these forms of communication to alter path dependency in isolation, they have nevertheless been important in mobilizing dissent and social movements. Of particular importance for emerging understandings of the Earth system is the iconic "blue marble" photo of the Earth taken from space by US astronauts in 1972. The image became a symbol for the environmental movement and is often credited with helping to shift popular imagination of the planet as a unified and fragile entity (Petsko 2011).[4] A more recent example (employed to dramatic effect in *An Inconvenient Truth*, Al Gore's cautionary film on climate change, and frequently attacked by climate skeptics) is the "hockey stick" showing rapid temperature rise in recent decades compared to far longer periods of cooler temperatures.[5]

This, then, is the repertoire of formative agency. We now get to the core business of this chapter: who exactly might exercise formative agency for the Anthropocene in positive fashion? What are the obstacles to effective agency, and how might they be overcome?

---

[3] A similar argument could be made for creative media that mix linguistic and non-linguistic communication, such as music, theatre, and film.

[4] In 2017, an article by one of us (JD) entitled "Democracy Needs More Trees and Less Trump" was made into an artwork called "Forest Trump" by artist Darragh Gallagher, and exhibited in Basel, Switzerland. Gallagher created 600 origami trees, each from a sheet of paper with the article printed on it, and placed them in a landscape made of sand. Visitors could take home a tree and read it.

[5] One of the best-known and controversial examples of the "hockey stick" is found in Mann, Bradley, and Hughes (1998). The IPCC's Fifth Assessment Report presents an updated version (Masson-Delmotte et al 2013: 409).

Who exactly will form the Anthropocene?

A catalogue of formative agents could look like a standard list of powerful political actors: governments, international organizations, lobby groups, corporations, foundations, labor unions, voters, political parties. Rather than go through every conceivable category of agent, we will be a bit more selective. What we have in mind, then, can be called in Lea Ypi's (2012) terms "avant-garde political agents" (though her main concern is limited to people who inspire their fellow citizens to pressure their governments to promote global justice).

One way to be very selective indeed is to identify just one kind of agent, and pin our hopes on that. Shearman and Smith (2007) call for authoritarian expert governance instead of failed democracy in response to climate change (echoing Ophuls 1977: 163 on "ecological mandarins"). According to a widely quoted sentiment—questionably attributed to anthropologist Margaret Mead—one should "Never doubt that a small group of thoughtful, committed citizens can change the world; indeed, it is the only thing that ever has."

Seeking deliverance through one kind of agent, be it experts or citizens, is simplistic. We will be a bit more sophisticated than that, but still selective in emphasizing the most promising sorts of agents when it comes to moving the world beyond pathological Holocene path dependencies. Correspondingly, we downplay the actors stuck most severely in these path dependencies. Stuck actors—notably states, corporations, and international organizations—can be moved, and it is vital that they be moved. But they are unlikely to do the moving themselves.

Agents associated with or commissioned by states or international organizations can still do some moving. To illustrate, the UNFCCC revealed a degree of reflexivity (as described in chapter 3) in adopting orchestration as a mode of governance in the 2015 Paris Agreement. But it was not the UNFCCC as a whole that motivated the change; rather it was a smaller "quartet" composed of the Peruvian presidency of the 2014 Conference of the Parties (COP), the French presidency of the 2015 COP, the Secretariat of the UNFCCC, and the office of the United Nations Secretary-General (Widerberg 2017). We prefer to think of movers such as this quartet as norm or discourse entrepreneurs, rather than lump them into the organizations that they work for or with.

NORM AND DISCOURSE ENTREPRENEURS

Some actors specialize in promoting social change, and as such might enthusiastically put up their hands if we ask who will form the Anthropocene. International relations scholars speak of "norm entrepreneurs" (Finnemore and Sikkink 1998), who organize knowledge and advocate on behalf of norms. Successful entrepreneurs manage to get their favored norms internalized in the practices of states, international organizations, and others as "norm cascades" take effect. Norm cascades illustrate the power of feedback effects in social systems, where states or other actors adopt a norm because others have already done so. For example, Sikkink (2011) charts the emergence and institutionalization of the norm that heads of government and other high officials can be prosecuted for human rights violations. We believe that speaking only of norms is unnecessarily narrow, so we will add a category of "discourse entrepreneurs" who advance different ways of understanding the world—discourses. Any discourse is comprised not just of norms, but also assumptions about which entities are recognized as existing, or should exist; who or what has the capacity to act to make a difference; key metaphors and other rhetorical devices; and taken-for-granted relationships such as hierarchies, competition, cooperation, equalities (see Dryzek 2013b for a catalogue of environmental discourses). Norm entrepreneurs often take the existing institutional landscape as given; they just want to change what actors can, should, and must do within that landscape. Discourse entrepreneurship can be more thoroughgoing to the degree that it targets the underpinnings of existing institutions.

To illustrate what we have in mind, consider the history of states. States have over time changed themselves in quite fundamental ways: for example, to become capitalist states, or welfare states. The transformation to becoming welfare states was in large measure a response to the rise of the organized working class, to provide some security to the disadvantaged who now proved capable of disrupting political and economic order. Yet that simple task could have been accomplished just by some targeted social policy expenditures. The more thoroughgoing institutional transformation that the "welfare state" terminology connotes was spurred by discourse entrepreneurs (perhaps most famously, William Beveridge, in a landmark 1942 report to the UK government) who advocated, among other things, universal participation in welfare state programs. The rise of welfare states involved something more than expanded poor relief: it amounted to a fundamental shift in what it meant to be a member of a (national) society, and involved the establishment of an institutional structure (such as comprehensive public health services) to reflect that.[6] In this light, contemporary environmental policy generally resembles poor relief much more than it resembles the welfare state: as yet there are no green states that have established environmental concern as a core priority on a par with national security, economic growth, or social welfare. The welfare state parallel would suggest that the development of the green state depends

---

[6] Welfare states did of course eventually come under attack from another set of discourse entrepreneurs: neoliberal privatizers and marketeers.

on three requirements: crisis threatening the stability of the system (such a crisis already exists); broad recognition of that crisis (such recognition does not exist); and discourse entrepreneurs advocating alternative underpinnings for institutions (who do exist, but so far with limited impact).

Who might effective discourse entrepreneurs now be? Discourse entrepreneurs may be high-profile political leaders. Gro Harlem Brundtland and her 1987 Commission were largely responsible for establishing sustainable development as the dominant discourse in global environmental affairs (though as we have seen, it has not fared well in its struggle with competing economic discourses, and those who want to dilute it). They can also be religious leaders. Pope Francis played an important role here with his encyclical entitled "*Laudato Si'*: On Care for Our Common Home," which mobilized a religious discourse for environmental responsibility. *Laudato Si'* moved the Church to a position more consistent with St. Francis of Assisi's stress on reverence for all of God's creation, and away from an instrumental attitude toward non-human nature.[7] However, an opinion survey among US Catholics found that while the encyclical heightened concern about climate change among some individuals, it had the opposite effect on conservative Catholics and non-Catholics (Li et al. 2016). Not only did these groups dismiss the Pope's arguments, but they also sought to protect their own beliefs by casting doubt on the Pope's credibility to speak about climate change. In the US, religion is now largely subordinate to political ideology. The fact that these responses were polarized along party political lines highlights that discourse entrepreneurs typically operate in a field in which they must contend with powerful existing discourses, not least market liberalism. Discourse entrepreneurs could also be experts such as the chemist Paul Crutzen and the ecologist Eugene Stoermer, who are widely credited with having coined the term "Anthropocene." Tellingly, the proposal for a new geological epoch came from non-geologists (albeit a Nobel Prize-winning non-geologist in Crutzen's case), and the challenges that the term has faced in gaining the approval of the International Commission on Stratigraphy attest to the enduring power of established discourses within epistemic communities. Discourse entrepreneurs can also be public intellectuals. Nisbet (2014) compares the ideas of three sets of public intellectuals active on climate issues: "ecological activists" (such as 350.org founder Bill McKibben and Naomi Klein), "smart growth reformers" (such as Al Gore and Nicholas Stern, who led the UK Government's highly influential Stern Review on climate change), and "ecomodernists" (who include the proponents of a "good Anthropocene" we encountered in chapter 1).

---

[7] The Umbrian phrase in the encyclical's title translates as "Praise be to you," and derives from a canticle of St. Francis of Assisi which continues, "Praise be to you, my Lord, through our Sister, Mother Earth, who sustains and governs us" (Pope Francis 2015: 3).

Social movement organizations and political activists specialize in social change. They are highly visible in global environmental governance (somewhat less visible in other crucial areas such as economic and financial governance, despite some high-profile campaigns on fair trade, aid, debt relief, and tax evasion). Much has been written about the roles they can and do play. What about their roles when it comes to effective formative agency in questioning—and if necessary disrupting—pathological path dependencies associated with the norms and discourses that underpin established institutions and practices? Very few organizations and activists have this kind of role in mind: often their work is very instrumental, focused on achieving a substantive goal (be it halting rainforest destruction, securing a more just distribution of environmental benefits and risks, or implementing more sustainable technologies). However laudable such goals may be, their effective pursuit is not sufficient to constitute an effective response to the Anthropocene.

Yet there are times when social movements can act as discourse entrepreneurs in a way that can enable more fundamental change. The very concept of "the environment" had no political weight until the 1960s; the idea of a comprehensive environmental policy was then made possible by the discourse advanced by the emerging environmental movement. Environmentalism destabilized the dominant discourse of industrial society (Torgerson 1999: 51)—though, as we have already observed, it fell short of changing states in a way that would resemble earlier seismic transformations such as the Westphalian creation of the system of states in 1648, or of the development of welfare states in the twentieth century.

Still, the hope remains that social movements can achieve instrumental goals while also changing the tenor of public discourse. So, for example, the fossil fuel divestment movement has been remarkably successful in making the case that assets in coal and oil constitute a bad business proposition. At the same time, it has called upon investors to see themselves not simply as relentless maximizers of shareholder wealth, but also as moral agents who need to take into account the social and environmental impacts of their decisions (Ayling and Gunningham 2017).

Discourse entrepreneurs are crucial when it comes to shaping the Anthropocene. But they cannot do it alone.

SCIENTISTS AND OTHER EXPERTS

Individual scientists have long been active in trying to influence environmental governance. Influential biologists have included Aldo Leopold, propounding a "land ethic" in 1949; Rachel Carson, warning of the dangers of pesticides in her 1962 *Silent Spring*; and Garrett Hardin, who in 1968 publicized "the tragedy of the commons." However, until more recently scientists were not part of any collective and comprehensive efforts to reorient environmental policy and governance. With a few individual exceptions (e.g. Paul Ehrlich) they were conspicuous by their absence from the *Limits to Growth* political action of the 1970s that we discussed in chapter 2.

Gradually that changed. Beginning in the 1980s, "epistemic communities" grounded in science and advocating action began to emerge; earlier in this chapter we discussed the case of the 1987 Montreal Protocol for the protection of the ozone layer. Since then, scientific assessments have proliferated. The most visible is the Intergovernmental Panel on Climate Change (IPCC), established in 1988. The IPCC periodically summarizes the relevant climate science in its assessment reports—but also projects the likely consequences of acting, and failing to act, on what the science tells us about the trajectory of climate change and its consequences. The award of the Nobel Peace Prize to the IPCC in 2007 (along with Al Gore) crystallizes the fact that the IPCC does not just summarize science, but also tries to make a difference in global governance. Other prominent scientific assessments now include the Intergovernmental Platform on Biodiversity and Ecosystem Services, and the one-off Millennium Ecosystem Assessment.

Scientists sometimes think that solving problems requires merely doing research and then arguing for the logic of what should be done in response. If theory and logic corroborated by empirical test suggest that X causes Y, and if Y is desirable, then we should do X. For example, Y might be a two degree limit to average global temperature rise above the pre-industrial baseline, X might be the cumulative level of greenhouse gas emissions that will cause two degrees of warming (estimated by the IPCC's fifth assessment report as around the equivalent of a trillion tons of carbon dioxide, though some uncertainty surrounds this figure); therefore if we want to limit warming to two degrees we need to limit the cumulative level of emissions to the equivalent of a trillion tons—and then cease emitting. However, sometimes judgment rather than proof is necessary. Consider for example the arguments associated with planetary boundaries, which among other things are based on judgments about how and where each boundary should be located (there is no scientific finding which says the boundary for human freshwater use is 4,000 cubic kilometers per year; it is a judgment informed by many findings). These judgments are informed but not determined by science; the overall prescription for the world to stay within the "safe operating space" defined by the nine boundaries rests on a series of such calls.

Scientists have, then, become more assertive in articulating the meaning and advocating the importance of concepts such as planetary boundaries. The role they play is vital and indispensable. Without science we could have no conception of climate change, or ozone layer depletion, or the Anthropocene, or the Earth system. The role of the Resilience Alliance is especially noteworthy because its members have explicitly tried to develop a science of complex social-ecological systems, and recognize the problematic character of existing governance arrangements within those systems (though we discussed the limitations of their analysis at some length in chapter 3).

What could possibly go wrong? The cases of greenhouse gas emissions and planetary boundaries show that when science and associated arguments confront politics and enter governance, they do not necessarily spur effective action. Planetary boundaries proved to have implications that were unpalatable to too many states negotiating the declaration of the 2012 United Nations Conference on Sustainable Development (Rio+20) and so were left out of the final declaration. The assertiveness of scientists has encountered deep opposition from those who do not like the implications of the findings; this eventually developed into a full-scale assault on science and scientists. In the US (and to a degree in the UK, Canada, and Australia), climate scientists have been vilified by organized climate change deniers. Most US Republican politicians now subscribe to this denial, and some are in the forefront of attacks. These developments flourish in and feed a post-modern world of "post-truth politics" and "alternative facts," where everything is ideological, including science; so climate scientists are treated as "warmists."

Consequently scientists are no longer surprised when the advice that seems so obvious to them fails to gain traction in the political world. This doesn't stop scientists trying (note the push since 2009 by scientists to get the idea of planetary boundaries broadly accepted). When scientific advice collides with path dependencies in dominant institutions and practices and their supporting ideas, it is generally the science that loses out. But we should not give up on the effective agency of scientists; we just have to think a bit harder about how it might be exercised, given that simply publicizing findings and giving advice has limited effect.

Scientists themselves have begun to think a bit harder in these terms. In order to deflect criticisms that it has become overly politicized, the IPCC has sought to tread a careful line by describing its findings as "policy relevant" but not "policy prescriptive" (reflecting a commonplace distinction between experts as being "on tap" rather than "on top"). Edenhofer and Kowarsch (2015) seek to capture this distinction in more vivid terms by describing experts as "mapmakers" and policy-makers as "navigators" who chart their preferred directions across the maps of policy options drawn by experts. It is possible for experts to map the landscape of values as well as that of facts. One chapter of the IPCC's Fifth Assessment Report was co-authored by ethicists who surveyed scholarly knowledge about how ideas of justice apply to climate change (Kolstad et al. 2014).

The distinction between experts/mapmakers and policy-makers/navigators is illuminating but more complex than it first appears, because what is selected to be put on the map depends on many judgments about what is important and how it ought to be conceptualized; think again of planetary boundaries. Central to the field of Science and Technology Studies (STS) is the idea that scientific knowledge and social order (with a values aspect) can be "co-produced" in the activities of scientists. As Jasanoff (2004: 2) puts it, "the ways in which we know and represent the world (both nature and society) are inseparable from the ways in which we choose to live in it." The map-makers versus navigators formulation of the division of labor between experts and policy-makers will, then, fall short unless it can account for the full potential of experts as formative agents. The essence of formative agency is the creation of meaning. Meaning refers here not only to the creation of new scientific terms (such as "gene" or "Higgs boson") that facilitate scientific explanation, but also to concepts and bodies of knowledge that have implications for action. Asking scientists to keep their scientific work completely separate from value judgments about how to act upon scientific knowledge is too restrictive, because scientific practices are interwoven with normative values. Those values inform which problems are deemed worthy of scientific investigation and may underpin whole fields of research (Kitcher 2011: 36–8). For example, it is no surprise that ecologists care about the integrity of ecosystems. Scientists and other experts may legitimately engage in this kind of meaning creation. In other words, they may legitimately enter debates about which maps should be drawn and why.

The ways in which problems and possible solutions are conceptualized can in turn have clear implications for political institutions. Planetary boundaries were conceptualized not in the service of scientific curiosity but to inform collective action. In other words, the proponents of planetary boundaries were not simply making a map but also arguing that there were some paths on the map—those leading to a more dangerous Earth system—that should not be traveled. In a well-functioning democracy the role of experts can and must reach beyond that of mapmakers to include what Pielke (2007) calls "issue advocates"; that is, experts who call for certain kinds of action (e.g. conserving a particular ecosystem or staying within planetary boundaries) that are informed not only by their scientific knowledge but also by the values that they hold as citizens. To avoid the risk that scientists become (or are perceived to be) the mouthpieces for partisan ideology, the actions that scientists prescribe and the underlying value judgments should face robust public scrutiny and deliberation. We will address in the next chapter how the formative agency of scientists can get some help from other sorts of agents in dialogue with science.

THE MOST VULNERABLE

It is frequently noted that those most vulnerable to the instabilities of the Anthropocene and least able to adapt to changing conditions also have very little in the way of political power to do much about it. Examples here are people in small island states and low-lying river deltas (such as much of Bangladesh), poor people living in the path of cyclones and hurricanes (even in relatively rich places like New Orleans and Houston), Indigenous peoples displaced by deforestation, sub-Saharan Africans who will experience worse droughts and heat stress with climate change.

Why then do we emphasize their agency? Beyond intrinsic questions of justice, which require a more effective voice for the most disadvantaged (see chapter 4), the most vulnerable have moral authority precisely because they are the ones upon whom the burden of risks falls most heavily. They are in a position to dramatize what is happening—to themselves in the present, but what will happen to many others in the future. There is a sense in which they could be what Ypi (2012) calls avant-garde political agents—though they may not necessarily describe their role in the same terms. So, for example, the Marshall Islands poet and climate activist Kathy Jetñil-Kijiner (2014) delivered a moving call to action to world leaders gathered at the UN climate summit in New York, reading a poem addressed to her new-born daughter pledging that the world would not abandon small island countries such as theirs that are threatened by rising seas.

Those hit most by disasters can constitute what Curato (2019), discussing typhoon-hit cities in the Philippines, calls "communities of misery." As well as developing effective democratic locations for rebuilding and advocacy on their own behalf, such communities remind us that those who have suffered from disasters do not just hold out a begging bowl, but can be very active players in the recovery of their communities. They are also in an especially good position to transmit what Plumwood (2002: 86) calls "the bad news from below" that dominant institutions can be so bad at hearing.

The fact that the most vulnerable have immediate concerns related to subsistence and survival means that they may not always be well placed to make their voice heard. Immediate concerns may also mean that the most vulnerable cannot readily engage abstractions such as the Anthropocene and its implications—no matter how vital its consequences may be when it comes to their own suffering, and that of others in future. What then happens is that advocates step in on their behalf. So for example Oxfam is an organization active both in delivering relief and in advocacy. This advocacy extends beyond poverty alleviation to environmental concern. Oxfam publicizes salt-water intrusion into aquifers as a result of sea level rise in Tuvalu, deaths caused by flooding in Bangladesh, the effect of drought on nomadic pastoralists in East Africa; and is active on the global governance of climate change. Hence the question "Who Elected Oxfam?," as *The Economist* asked in a 2000 article. Now, representatives need not be elected in order to be effective and legitimate representatives of the vulnerable—consider, for example, carers who represent the interests of severely disabled people, or organizations campaigning for animal rights. Thus Rubenstein (2014) argues that the more important issue is not whether NGOs such as Oxfam were elected, but whether or not NGOs misuse the power they hold as representatives or advocates. Nevertheless, advocates can be criticized for being out of touch with those whose suffering they claim to represent. Along these lines, Thompson (2014) criticizes the "new abolitionists" who, like white anti-slavery activists in the nineteenth century, seek to rescue vulnerable non-whites, this time from the ravages of climate change, in the role of "white savior" that "presumes that the impoverished and non-white communities on the frontlines of climate change cannot speak for themselves."[8] These problems and criticisms mean we need to think about connections between advocates and the most vulnerable— which we will do in the next chapter, in the context of larger deliberative systems. There we will also address ways in which the most vulnerable can make their voice heard more directly, without advocates as intermediaries.

CITIES AND SUB-NATIONAL GOVERNMENTS

Barber (2013) argues that we would be much better off "if mayors ruled the world." When it comes to climate change, Barber believes that city governments—responsible for over half the world's population, and the majority of the world's greenhouse gas emissions—can do a much better job than nation states, mainly because they do not have to care about asserting sovereignty and protecting borders. Cities have developed networks such as the ICLEI Local Governments for Sustainability and C40 Cities Climate Leadership Group to share information and technology, coordinate actions, and ratchet up commitments on (say) emissions reduction (Bulkeley 2011). Barber imagines cities together taking on much greater roles in global governance—in our terms, potentially disrupting the problematic path dependencies that characterize a system of global governance dominated by states and international organizations. Mainly he envisages cities together setting up an alternative system of global governance that is pragmatic, dynamic, and far from the nationalistic and populist currents that hobble nation states. These currents now seem to flourish most amid rural life. In this light, cities can be "agents of sustainability and resilience" (Barber 2017: 11).

When in 2017 President Donald Trump announced that the United States would pull out of the 2015 Paris Agreement on climate change, he declared: "I was elected to represent the citizens of Pittsburgh, not Paris." Trump's choice of the US city, known for its lost steel industry, proved to be a poor one. The mayor of Pittsburgh, whose inhabitants had voted overwhelmingly in

---

[8] Thompson's implicit criticism of anti-slavery activists is a bit odd; would slaves really have been better off without their efforts?

favour of Trump's rival Hillary Clinton in the 2016 presidential election, swiftly retorted: "Pittsburgh stands with the world and will follow [the] Paris agreement" (Gambino 2017). Mayors of over 180 US cities representing over fifty million people were likewise quick to announce they remained committed to the goals of the Agreement. Many large US corporations, as well as governors of states such as California and New York, joined them in supporting the Agreement (We Are Still In 2017).

The reason we stress cities and other sub-national governments such as US states here rather than corporations is that these sub-national governments are challenging the structure of the global governance order in a way that corporations are not. These governments are essentially saying that global governance is not something to be negotiated only by sovereign states, that when it fails to perform on a vital issue like climate change the line-up of key players needs to be reconfigured.[9] The corporations, in contrast, are not claiming a new formative role in governance beyond the (large) role they already play.

There are limits to this rosy picture of cities and other sub-national governments. Bulkeley (2011: 470) points out that there is a gap between the declared ambitions of cities and their achievements in greenhouse gas emission reduction (though this is a matter of what we described earlier as primary agency, not formative agency). And cities are selective in their focus: they may be active when it comes to climate change, but nowhere to be seen when it comes to biodiversity, or the nitrogen cycle. Cities vary in their degree of autonomy and are often highly constrained by national-level policies (Bulkeley 2011: 471). Cities in developing countries are often under-resourced and not easily capable of putting commitments into local practice, let alone taking part in global leadership networks. Moreover, Bulkeley et al. (2013) find that few climate initiatives based in cities have an explicit concern with justice. This is not conclusive evidence of their inability to rethink ideas of justice, but suggests that there may be structural constraints on the targets of their formative agency. We believe it is wrong to expect cities to do everything— "to rule the world" in Barber's terms. Again, we need to examine how they might productively combine with other key actors.

NON-HUMAN NATURE

The Anthropocene means that human influences are decisive in affecting the parameters of the Earth system; but the instability so induced means humans must pay much more attention to how the system can surprise them, often in very unpleasant ways. Non-human nature becomes an active player in the way

---

[9] Hence, when the mayor of Los Angeles reaffirmed his support for the Paris Agreement, it prompted a headline that was only half in jest: "Los Angeles Says It'll Stay In the Paris Climate Agreement It Isn't In" (Rogers 2017).

the future unfolds; indeed, now that humans are reshaping the non-human world in so many ways, nature itself is not quite so non-human.

But can we speak of non-human nature as an agent? To do so would seem to fly in the face of hundreds (if not thousands) of years of Holocene thinking, be it in philosophy or what looks like common sense, about what separates humans from animals and the rest of nature: humans think, non-human nature does not. Agency requires the capacity to think before communicating and acting; traditionally, that capacity has only been associated with (some) humans. However, it is increasingly clear that many other animals—ranging from gorillas and elephants to octopuses and crows—are capable of complex thought, as demonstrated by their ability to solve problems, remember past experiences, and deceive others (Griffin 2001; Godfrey-Smith 2016).

We can also find meaningful communication in nature—within species, and sometimes between different species. Peter Wohlleben's (2016) *The Hidden Life of Trees* examines the subtle ways in which trees communicate with one another, to their mutual benefit. When giraffes start chewing on the leaves of acacia trees, acacia these trees emit ethylene, which induces other trees to pump toxins into their leaves to discourage the giraffes. Below ground, roots connect with networks of fungi that carry chemical signals—which can reach trees of different species. Other analysts have found something like democracy in the decision-making of groups of animals such as bees and deer (List 2004; Gagnon 2013).

All the same, communication and cooperation are not the same as the more complex forms of thinking typically associated with agency, including an ability to weigh up different courses of action. Even if we drop the requirement that cogitation is necessary before action, we can still find in nature what Bruno Latour calls "actants" as opposed to agents (see Bennett 2010; Latour 2014); quasi-agents that act in meaningful and consequential ways. Actants might be individual living things, or ecosystems. But agency then remains restricted to a more limited range of living things, principally humans and some other complex animals.[10] To expand agency too far into the material world would, as Hamilton (2017) cautions, diminish our understanding of an epoch defined by the consequences of human agency. When it comes to *formative* agency, it is likely that only humans have the capacity to engage directly in the abstract reasoning and sophisticated communication required to shape what core societal values and concepts should mean.

---

[10] An alternative way of embracing non-human agency (based on the idea of capabilities discussed in chapter 4) is that anything possessing capabilities to flourish could be considered an agent. But even if possession of capabilities could give a non-human entity such as an ecosystem moral status as a subject of justice, it does not follow that it is an agent, so long as it lacks the power to think. Relaxing the criterion of cognition would stretch the concept of agency too far.

Even so, non-human nature could still be involved in human efforts to exercise formative agency—albeit not on its own. The non-human world may be screaming in pain as we enter the Anthropocene, but we have devised institutions, practices, and discourses that render us very bad listeners. The remedy begins (but does not end) in better listening (Dryzek 1995; Dobson 2010), putting humans and nature together in a productive partnership capable of exercising what can be recognized as formative agency. One target of this agency ought to be to validate the very idea that non-human nature should have an explicit place in human institutions. We can see intimations of this in some of the examples mentioned in chapter 4, such as court decisions in New Zealand and India that recognize rivers and mountains as legal subjects with rights of their own; and the 2008 constitution of Ecuador, which recognizes the rights of nature (in the form of Pachamama, or Mother Earth) to exist and flourish. While such developments are to be welcomed, it is important to guard against the possibility that legal recognition may treat non-human entities as just another set of interests to be balanced against other more conventional ones within legal systems.

Conclusion

Shaping the Anthropocene is going to be hard work for many kinds of agents. We have shown how it can be done, and how formative agency can be exercised in the creation of meanings and principles to guide practices, even though it will always have to struggle against resistant structures and entrenched ways of viewing the world.

Discourse entrepreneurs, scientists and other experts, sub-national governments, the most vulnerable and their advocates, and non-human systems have parts to play. But all of them also have limitations; we should not put all our hopes for agents in one basket. In the next chapter we will show how limits and deficiencies can be overcome, and promise realized, in the social processes in which these agents are embedded. We will highlight democratic remedies that help overcome deficiencies. And we will show how the whole can be so much more than the sum of its parts when different categories of agents are joined in effective deliberative systems. The deliberative systems in question should be critical and transformative, not functional for some status quo; capable of producing significant change, not preserving stability. How agents act is important. In the next chapter we will show that still more important is their capacity to *inter*act to good effect.

7 Democratic Anthropocene

We concluded the previous chapter by reiterating the importance of formative agents who will give shape to what principles such as justice and sustainability will mean in practice in the Anthropocene. These agents can be engines of reflexivity. We also suggested that their interactions with one another are so much more important than their actions in isolation. We will now develop the idea of a "formative sphere" which encapsulates these interactions. The formative sphere is crucial in determining human—and more than human—responses to the Anthropocene.

The formative sphere can be thought of as the sum of activity encompassing the creation, questioning, and development of principles for collective action (see Figure 7.1). This activity can take place alongside other activities: for example when people pause to reflect on what they are seeking and why, in the middle of (say) negotiating an agreement. Equally, formative activity could also take place at some remove from other processes, as where activists or public intellectuals envision different ways of living. The formative sphere need not map onto any particular institutional configurations—indeed its ability to generate new principles may depend on a capacity to transcend or rethink institutional boundaries. The formative sphere also cuts across conventional distinctions between empowered or authoritative institutions on the one hand, and public space or civil society on the other, as formative agency could be found within either of those sites or in the interaction between them. Just as formative agency may involve a mix of linguistic and non-linguistic communication, with the linguistic aspect encompassing reason, rhetoric, and deliberation, the formative sphere has a correspondingly diverse repertoire.

We will show that the conditions of this formative sphere need to be democratic—but democratic in a particular way. Our intention here is not to offer a detailed model of democracy for the Anthropocene, but rather to show why democratic sensibilities and principles ought to pervade any processes of societal reconstruction in response to the Anthropocene. This in turn will enable us to reply to skeptics who do not think democracy is up to the task of effective Earth system governance.

The relationship between democracy and ecology has been debated at length over the decades (Dryzek 1987; Goodin 1992; Smith 2003; Eckersley 2004; Wong 2016). Political theorists who have contemplated the question mostly see a positive relationship between democracy and effective environmental

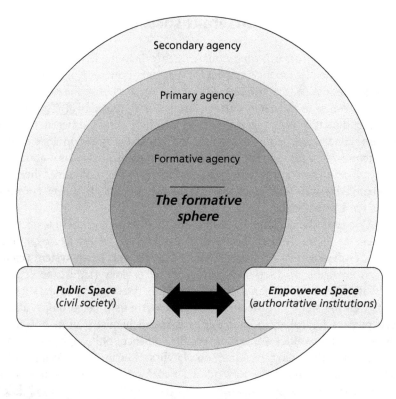

Figure 7.1. The formative sphere

problem-solving (though some disagree: Beeson 2010). In political practice, there is little evidence that authoritarian regimes do better than democratic ones in environmental policy performance, and substantial evidence that they do worse (Li and Reuveny 2006). We will not join that debate, but rather move in a different direction that follows from our stress on formative agency. The effective exercise of formative agency is essential but hard: it is hard for agents in isolation, and there are all kinds of ways for it to misfire or be overwhelmed by other forces. Democracy enables effective formative agency, though as we will see the democracy in question has to be deliberative as well as ecological.

Our discussion will highlight the formative agents we introduced in chapter 6: norm and discourse entrepreneurs, scientists and other experts, the most vulnerable, cities and sub-national governments, and non-humans (as quasi-agents). We inquire into the interactions they may profitably engage in, with one another as well as with additional agents such as citizens, which all require important democratic features if they are to work well.

Deliberation across different sorts of expertise

Scientists have been assertive in publicizing threats to the Earth system and in advocating principles (such as respect for planetary boundaries) for intelligent action in response to these threats. There are two sorts of problems that limit their effectiveness as formative agents. The first is the potential for incompatibility and difficulty of integration (even conflict) across different sorts of expertise. The second, more serious, is a seeming inability to convince enough other actors—citizens and publics as well as political leaders—about the severity of the threats and the need for change. The difficulties here are exacerbated by well-funded anti-scientific movements in a few countries such as the United States.

To begin with the question of multiple sorts of expertise: there is no single royal science of the Anthropocene that should take precedence over other sciences. Different sorts of specializations are relevant. Earth system science (itself an amalgam of disciplines), branches of ecology (landscape ecology, conservation ecology, human ecology, evolutionary ecology, population ecology, as well the study of different sorts of ecosystems), meteorology, atmospheric physics, hydrology, oceanography, and geochemistry all matter. Social sciences and humanities (including political science, philosophy, sociology, history, and anthropology) matter too (Lövbrand et al. 2015). While voices from many disciplines have now joined debates about the Anthropocene, those from natural science have been most prominent in interdisciplinary collaborations such as the Future Earth initiative (which coordinates a range of global environmental research programs). It is vital that fields that can shed light on the Anthropocene as a *political* phenomenon—albeit one in which expertise is not reduced to politics, as we argued in chapter 1—are recognized as having a valuable contribution here.

What happens when different sorts of expertise meet? There may simply be a fight of the sort we looked at in our discussion of biodiversity in the United States in the previous chapter, where conservation biologists who are committed to preservation take on economists for whom the idea of ecosystem services is central, such that the value of ecosystems is reduced to their instrumental benefits to humans. This clash involves one of ethics (biocentric versus anthropocentric conceptions) as well as different sorts of natural and social science. The encounter becomes productive to the degree that there is an opportunity for learning across the two sides of the dispute. This does not mean everyone (or anyone) has to compromise. But it could mean that (for example) "nature's contribution to people" is recognized, as it now is in IPBES proceedings, without necessarily being tied to monetary valuation of that contribution (Pascual et al. 2017).

What has this got to do with democracy? The interactions between different sorts of experts are crucial ingredients of larger political processes and, to the degree that they feature mutual respect and efforts to reach across differences in disciplinary background, they are consistent with deliberative democratic values.

To illustrate, consider Norgaard's (2008) analysis of the Millennium Ecosystem Assessment, which was a comprehensive synthesis of knowledge about the state of the world's ecosystems, involving 2,000 scientists and social scientists from many disciplines. The scientists had to find a common language in which to express their findings (many of which charted severe ecological degradation) and analyze ecosystems in all their complexity. This language was not an amalgam of specializations, still less one of the specializations that had to be learned by the others. Rather, it was a kind of scientific vernacular that also involved a degree of reflexivity, as it induced the participating scientists to address the limitations of their own discipline-based specializations such as forestry, different branches of ecology, biogeochemistry, and economics. Norgaard finds that the kinds of norms this involved were very much like those of deliberative democracy, as participants sought to express themselves in terms that made sense to those starting from different frameworks, enabling them to "form a collective analytical ability that was more than the sum of their individual contributions" (Norgaard 2008: 863). Here we find a solution to the challenge of different sorts of experts seeing the world in different ways. Equally important, in developing this vernacular, scientists inadvertently found a way to communicate more effectively with non-specialists beyond the assessment, because "personal or experiential knowledge played an important bridging role in the deliberative learning process" (Norgaard 2008: 863). Though Norgaard does not use our terminology, what he describes is a process by which scientists discovered how to exercise formative agency more effectively.

Experts, citizens, and publics

If scientists and other experts are to be able to exercise formative agency, they need to be able to reach political leaders and ordinary citizens, whose response is crucial in determining whether or not principles that seem obvious to experts get any traction in collective decision processes and policymaking. Norgaard's analysis shows how experts can at least develop a language to bridge the expert/lay divide. But there are still problems to be overcome. Simply communicating scientific findings to the public does not mean that their implications will be accepted—even if they are in intelligible language. People will not necessarily believe science just because it is true—or, rather, represents the best understanding available. In the previous chapter we noted that when scientific findings conflict with path dependencies in institutions and ideas, it is often the science that loses, meaning that the promise of expert contributions to broader societal questions—such as rethinking what sustainability means—goes unrealized.

How might matters be improved? A large part of any answer should involve experts and citizens joining more effectively in ways that would enhance the formative agency of both. This joining would have substantial democratic qualities. Reflecting on the experience of scientific assessments, Norgaard (2007: 381) suggests that "the lines between scientific ways of knowing and democratic ways of choosing continue to blur." Many of the judgments exercised by the scientists participating in the Millennium Ecosystem Assessment were not so dissimilar to those that lay citizens could contribute (for example) through deliberating the directions that research and technology should take, or how risks such as ecosystem collapse should be interpreted and evaluated. The Millennium Ecosystem Assessment did survey fifty-nine decision-makers on questions such as "What words would you use to describe the ideal state of the Earth's natural and human systems in 2050?" (Bennett, Peterson, and Levitt 2005). While the survey yielded some valuable insights, the Assessment did not engage a broader range of citizens for input on its scenarios, still less in a dialogical manner rather than a one-way consultation.

In deliberative settings, ordinary citizens can grapple effectively with expert knowledge without leaving behind their own ordinary knowledge and varied lay perspectives. The evidence here comes from designed citizen forums on issues such as genetically modified organisms in agriculture, human biotechnology, nanotechnology, and climate change. Hundreds of these citizens' forums, or "mini-publics" as they are often called, have been carried out around the world (Grönlund, Bächtiger, and Setälä 2014). Two popular designs (very similar to each other) are consensus conferences and citizens' juries, each made up of a small group of ordinary citizens recruited more or less at random (technically, through stratified random sampling). Citizens are given access to information and receive expert presentations. They can also receive presentations from advocates on different sides of an issue. The citizen-participants write a report recommending and justifying policy action. The report can reflect moral as well as technical judgments. Among hundreds of such cases in many different countries, it is very hard to find a single instance of citizens failing to comprehend scientific knowledge presented to them. Moreover, there is evidence to suggest that citizen deliberation can help overcome the biases and cognitive shortcuts that otherwise affect judgments about risk. In Kahneman's (2011) language, deliberation involves "slow" rather than "fast" thinking. Niemeyer (2014b: 184) shows how deliberation can bring citizens' considered judgments about what to do into line with their inner values and beliefs, as citizen deliberators can see through the misleading claims that often dominate partisan politics—and often lead people to have preferences about actions that are inconsistent with their own interests and values. So for example deliberation in an Australian forum enabled participants to reject misleading claims that Australia would be burdened unfairly by action on climate change compared to other countries (Niemeyer 2013: 442).

One finding from an analysis of citizen forums on genetically modified foods is that wherever these forums are conducted, they almost invariably reach a more precautionary approach to the issue than that adopted by policymaking elites, who are more committed to putting the technology to use in the interests of economic development (Dryzek et al. 2009). Here it is not risk aversion per se that indicates reflexivity, but rather risk recognition, which policymaking elites tend to repress in the interests of economic imperatives. This is a perfect illustration of deliberating citizens with access to scientists and expertise proving to be more reflexive than standard policymaking processes in their willingness to question society's basic normative commitments.

It is possible to think further about the role of deliberation in productively joining experts and citizens if we look at attempts to communicate climate change to the public, which we discussed in chapter 3. The traditional approach to communication assumed that the public simply needed to be educated in the findings of climate science. This one-way model has reached its limits, as members of the public who do care about the issue tend to process information through ideological filters. So at least in the United States, disbelief in climate science has become a marker of conservative political identity, while belief has become a requirement of liberal (left) identity. Surveying success and failure in communication on climate change and other issues, Moser and Dilling (2011) believe that the solution to failure in one-way campaigns lies in better engagement and deliberation involving scientists, advocates, and ordinary citizens. Citizens would play a more active role in helping to pose questions for science to study, prioritizing problems for inquiry, making sense of what scientific findings imply, reconciling lay concerns with the findings of science, and reasoning through the implications for policy. The hope is that this kind of engaged dialogue would enable participants to get beyond ideological filters and be involved in more reflexive scrutiny of established practices (Cornell et al. 2013).

The kind of process advocated by Moser and Dilling involves direct, face-to-face dialogue. An alternative way of thinking about expertise and participation would be to see each as different parts of a deliberative system (see chapter 1). A key insight from a deliberative systems perspective is that the qualities of the system as a whole need not depend on every component of the system exhibiting all deliberative virtues at all times (Mansbridge et al. 2012). Instead, some components of the system may place a greater emphasis on scientific rigor, some on reflection and judgment across competing arguments, others on including the most vulnerable, and so on, but they would still contribute in varying ways to the system's overall performance. In this light, there would be no strict need for experts and citizens to deliberate together all the time. Such a deliberative system might involve an expert assessment body—such as the Intergovernmental Panel on Climate Change (IPCC) or the Intergovernmental Science-Policy Platform on Biodiversity and Ecosystem Services (IPBES)—linking to familiar sorts of citizen forums. It may make sense for (say) scientists to spend some time just with other experts, and citizens with other lay citizens. What then becomes crucial is the nature of the connections between the two sorts of forums (and with inter-governmental negotiations, which should ideally be influenced). Communication from science to existing lay citizen forums is well established, because experts often testify to forums. The scientists who do so are usually there as individual experts, rather than representatives of an expert assessment panel. Communication in the opposite direction, from citizen forum to expert panel, is currently for the most part non-existent in global scientific assessments, and rare in other settings, though there is no reason why it could not be established.

One very clear institutional design implication is that bodies such as the IPCC and IPBES should foster ways of enhancing citizens' input into future assessments. This need not mean delegating to citizen forums the task of passing judgment on technical aspects of atmospheric chemistry or landscape ecology (or other sciences). Rather, these bodies could engage with citizens' perspectives in several ways: (i) assessing the current state of scholarly knowledge about public perceptions relevant to specific assessments (e.g. perceptions of risk, values that people assign to goods such as nature and a safe climate, and the sorts of problems that matter most to them); (ii) seeking reflective citizen assessment of risks; (iii) pinpointing similarities and differences between expert and lay knowledge; and (iv) providing insights into what kinds of language are likely to resonate with publics. IPBES has progressed considerably further than the IPCC in engaging stakeholders (Beck et al. 2014: 85). Nevertheless, both institutions could do more to take account of the knowledge held by citizens, including members of Indigenous peoples who may be particularly vulnerable to—and aware of—the impacts of climate change and biodiversity loss.

A second design implication is that citizens' perspectives should be represented in international policy processes that seek to manage Earth system risks. Proponents of the planetary boundaries concept sometimes offer a highly simplified account of how the concept could be translated into practice. Steffen, Rockström, and Costanza (2011: 64–5), for example, argue that

there will need to be an institution (or institutions) operating, with authority, above the level of individual countries to ensure that the planetary boundaries are respected. In effect, such an institution, acting on behalf of humanity as a whole, would be the ultimate arbiter of the myriad trade-offs that need to be managed as nations and groups of people jockey for economic and social advantage. It would, in essence, become the global referee on the planetary playing field.

In response to proposals such as these, critics warn that the Anthropocene could usher in "a dangerous new world of undisputed scientific authority and anti-democratic politics" (Leach 2013). If the task of "refereeing" the planetary playing field were left solely to experts, such an approach would struggle to achieve democratic legitimacy. Yet there may be ways in which citizens and experts could engage productively with one another on how to govern Earth system risks, without constraining the freedom of experts to propose responses to those risks. Assessments about how tightly planetary boundaries should be drawn (e.g. judging when climate change reaches a dangerous level) require more than scientific understanding about the dynamics of the Earth system and associated tipping points. Such assessments also involve an irreducible degree of normative judgment. Accordingly, Pickering and Persson (2018) argue that citizens' and policymakers' perceptions about risks to the Earth system are a crucial ingredient in efforts to define planetary boundaries and to shape institutions that could help humanity to stay within the boundaries. As a first step towards democratizing planetary boundaries, evidence about public risk perceptions could inform experts' own proposals for how to define boundaries. Perhaps even more importantly, public risk perceptions should play a vital role in shaping "planetary targets," that is, political targets (such as the 2°C target in the UN climate regime) that are informed by expert understandings of Earth system risks as well as by broader considerations of political, technological, and economic feasibility.

The kinds of processes linking experts and citizens we have discussed do not mean undercutting or diminishing the formative agency of experts. Rather, these processes can enable scientists and other experts to exercise formative agency more effectively in a democratic system.

One remaining question is how experts and citizens should interact on the meaning of the Anthropocene itself. Citizen scientists may well unearth objects that could help understand the Anthropocene as a geological epoch,[1] but our concern here is with interactions on the broader discourse of the Anthropocene. Debates about whether the Anthropocene should be viewed as good, bad, or inescapable need to reach beyond the walls of academic institutions. While there is already evidence of a robust public exchange on these questions, such an exchange should extend beyond the well-read audiences of the *New York Times* and the *Guardian* to reach a broader community. Nevertheless, a democratic Anthropocene need not require that every citizen recognizes the term "Anthropocene," much less knows exactly what it means.

---

[1] Zalasiewicz et al (2016: 13) note that "technofossils" ("a trace fossil produced by humans") such as plastic rubbish could serve as a useful stratigraphic indicator for the Anthropocene.

As with other terms that have emerged in expert discourse but have a bearing on people's everyday lives (ranging from disaster risk reduction to ocean acidification), citizens could still exercise formative agency through non-technical understandings of Earth system processes. For example, citizens could become more aware of the environmental consequences of their consumption habits and thereby rethink their relationships to other people and non-human nature. While there remains a role for experts in building public understanding of the Anthropocene concept and engaging in public debates on the term, they also have a responsibility to support citizens' efforts to exercise formative agency in ways that do not depend on possessing a high degree of technical knowledge.

The most vulnerable and their advocates

While those most vulnerable to ecological damage may have moral authority because of their exposure to risks and limited ability to counteract them, they often lack the capacity to give voice to their concerns—and so exercise formative agency. As we noted in chapter 6, what often happens is that others give voice on their behalf. The problem is that this substitution may detract from the moral authority of the advocacy. Doubts are raised about the validity of the representation claims of advocates—the "who elected Oxfam?" skepticism that we discussed in the previous chapter.

To redeem the moral authority of the most vulnerable, it is necessary to think about how their voice can be heard. Advocacy organizations can play a role here. Montanaro (2018) argues that the representative credentials of Oxfam and similar sorts of organizations can be legitimated to the extent that these individuals and organizations help create a constituency that could validate the representation in question by holding the representative to account. However, the advocate should not substitute for the constituency. It is up to the advocate to cultivate relationships with that constituency; and so enable the voices of the most vulnerable themselves to be heard.

For example, La Via Campesina is an international federation of peasants' movements. Its major concern is with livelihoods, fair trade, and food sovereignty, but it is also active on ecological issues—offering energy-efficient "peasant agroecology" as a key part of the global response to climate change. "We peasants can cool the planet!," as their slogan has it. La Via Campesina is an advocacy organization. But unlike Oxfam, whose existence was and is authorized by donors, La Via Campesina began (in the 1990s) as a social movement from the grassroots. Over the years it has tried to remain connected to the grassroots movements on which it is based, and to distinguish itself from NGOs that rely on wealthy donors. Historically, it developed in a bottom-up fashion, as various local, regional, and national organizations joined together. Its origins are in Latin America, but the idea behind its global organization is that peasants face globally organized threats—agribusiness and global finance—requiring a global response. The organization strives to retain the characteristics of a social movement, and to retain ties of accountability to the components of its federation. La Via Campesina therefore remains in a good position to receive and transmit the "bad news from below" in terms of the impact of the neoliberal global economic system on livelihoods and ecosystems—and as such can contribute to ecological reflexivity at multiple levels of governance. Its ability to make this contribution is reinforced by its internally democratic organization.

It is also possible to imagine more direct participation by the poor and marginalized in democratic assemblies. To date, positive examples come mostly from the local level. *Gram sabhas*, village assemblies mandated by the Indian government, can—at least in South India—operate in this fashion. Rao and Sanyal (2010: 147) describe *gram sabhas* as "arguably the largest deliberative institution in human history, at the heart of two million little village democracies that affect the lives of seven hundred million rural Indians." Their studies in the context of inequality and caste divisions show that *gram sabhas* can help correct for injustice by allowing low-caste individuals to perform as equals in public deliberation (p. 154)—with real consequences for the distribution of local expenditures. The individuals involved exercise formative agency as "deliberation shapes the meaning of poverty" (p. 164). There is little evidence that meaning-shaping in these forums extends into environmental governance—but there is no reason why it need not. There is plenty of evidence that local communities can devise cooperative institutions that regulate access to, and prevent abuse of, commons resources (Ostrom 1990). There is a challenge in moving this kind of direct participation by the poor and marginalized beyond the local level; but it could be tried. Wisor (2012) sketches a design for recruiting poor people directly into citizens' assemblies that deliberate on post-2015 development goals (i.e. the goals that eventually became the Sustainable Development Goals, as discussed in chapter 5). It is even possible to imagine targeted recruitment to global assemblies (Dryzek, Bächtiger, and Milewicz 2011). The recruitment could be done by something akin to the way participants for citizens' juries and citizens' assemblies are currently selected—but with a weighting toward marginalized status.

There have been a few transnational experiments in citizen deliberation—notably the 2009 Europolis Deliberative Opinion Poll, which involved citizens from many European countries deliberating on climate change and immigration. Other experiments, such as the World Wide Views initiatives on climate change and biodiversity discussed in chapter 6, involved citizens in numerous countries deliberating simultaneously, although each forum comprised citizens from the same country or region rather than bringing citizens from many nations into a single forum. These sorts of assemblies are especially good when it comes to listening to what advocates have to say, reflecting on the merits of different sides, and coming to well-thought-out conclusions. They are not so good when it comes to the justification of positions and making of arguments—which is why advocates are still necessary.

Advocates and discourse entrepreneurs in a deliberative democracy

One reason for the substantial attention paid to norm entrepreneurs in international politics is that they often seem to be a force for good in battling oppression—in spreading (for example) norms of human rights, inducing compliance from reluctant states. But is that always true? Not necessarily. No single discourse or set of norms is the repository of all wisdom or all morality. Nobody has all the answers. Even when discourses become widely accepted, that does not mean they are beyond reproach.

Norms and discourses advanced by entrepreneurs can be problematic. Consider for example resilience—which, as we argued in chapter 3, should be thought of as a discourse rather than a concept that can be defined with any precision. Resilience has plenty of enthusiastic advocates, but also critics, especially those who think resilience entails the capacity to soak up punishment on the part of those who would really be better off resisting the punishment. Other critics point to a failure to recognize the key differences between ecological systems (from which the resilience concept comes) and social systems (to which it is applied). To take another example (introduced in chapter 5), sustainable development discourse has been criticized for its too-easy accommodation with the dominant economic system, such that the discourse eventually provided cover for a conventional economic growth imperative. Discourses arising to challenge a problematic status quo can decay over time, as they get co-opted by dominant interests. Greenwashing of products by clever advertisers is a co-optation (and corruption) of environmental discourse.

All these problems can occur before we get to discourses that try to shut down reflexivity. Populism is an example of the latter kind of discourse, because one of its hallmarks is the view that all complex problems have simple and obvious solutions that can be implemented as soon as self-serving elites are overcome (think of the simplistic approach to politics espoused by Donald Trump and his supporters). Climate change denial is a discourse that was engineered into existence and prominence in a few countries by some wealthy vested interests such as ExxonMobil and the Koch Brothers, aided by a handful of scientists who had previously helped the tobacco industry to evade regulation (Brulle 2014).

In light of all these problems, how then can we think about the role of discourse entrepreneurs in shaping the Anthropocene in a way that advances rather than hinders ecological reflexivity? The effective engagement of different discourses is crucial here. The aspiration is not some fruitless pluralism, but a critical engagement in which deficiencies can be exposed and discourses rejected if they fail to stand up.

Fruitless pluralism exists when multiple discourses relevant to common issues fail to engage each other. So for example in global climate governance, there are enclaves formed by the discourses of mainstream sustainability and green radicalism that often fail to reach other enclaves (Stevenson and Dryzek 2014). Mainstream sustainability is oriented to market instruments for mitigating greenhouse gas emissions, green businesses and jobs, and ecologically benign economic growth. It is very much in evidence at side events sponsored and attended by businesses at the global climate change negotiations. Green radicalism emphasizes the need fundamentally to reshape prevailing institutions and practices in order to protect the environment, and often advocates decentralized or grassroots (rather than state- or market-led) strategies for sustainability (Dryzek 2013b: Part V). Green radicalism appears at different side events—and often in parallel civil society forums. There is very little traffic between the two sorts of forums, and very limited communication across them. Scientific discourses and forums, stressing ecological limits and boundaries, can form a third enclave. The result can be discursive echo chambers that are insensitive to their own limitations, with limited public impact, as advocates and activists communicate in terms that resonate with others within the enclave—but not to those outside. Hence, as we argued in chapter 4, there is a need not only for discourses that bond like-minded people together, but also for discourses that can bridge highly diverse worldviews and values.

Engagements can also work badly, which is why they need to be critical and inclusive. Consider again the decay of sustainable development. Over the decades, sustainable development *did* engage with neoliberalism, the dominant discourse in the global economy and its institutions (such as the World Trade Organization and International Monetary Fund) that emphasizes free markets, property rights, and free trade. This engagement helps to explain the decay, as neoliberalism induced acceptance of the compatibility of environmental concerns with very conventional economic growth. Sustainable development did not engage with an older discourse of ecological limits whose heyday was in the 1970s—either ignoring it or (as in the Brundtland Report) obscuring the question of limits in a fog of ambiguity. Sustainable development also managed to detach itself from more radical kinds of green discourses that might have enabled it to maintain a more critical attitude to the growth imperatives of the international economy and to resist the embrace of neoliberalism (Carruthers 2001).

The inclusive, open, critical, and consequential engagement of discourses involving capable representatives, advocates, and citizens ought to be the critical essence of deliberative democracy (Dryzek 2000). Engagement needs to be *inclusive* of all relevant discourses—though as already pointed out that does not necessarily mean that all discourses should survive. Engagement needs to be *open* to all those affected by an issue. Engagement needs to be *critical* to ensure that deception, misinformation, and manipulation of discourses are exposed; and so that reflectively acceptable positions and practices can flourish. And engagement needs to be *consequential*: it should make a difference when it comes to collective action, be it influencing the policies of governments, the outcomes of international negotiations, the practice of economic systems, or the ways that people behave toward each other (and toward non-humans). For the sake of reflexivity, the outcome of engagement should always be provisional and open to revision in light of new information, new challenges, better arguments, and further reflection. Consider for example the trajectory of a discourse of limits and boundaries over the decades since the 1970s. The original 1970s presentation involved a crude model of overshoot and collapse that drew on population dynamics in a hypothetical ecosystem where the population of one species grows out of control (for example because of a lack of predators) and then crashes as it depletes the food source on which it depends. This crudity was criticized by those who pointed to the presence of adjustment mechanisms (such as markets) in human systems. The more recent manifestation of planetary boundaries is subtler and does not rest on any idea of overshoot and collapse (though it does involve thresholds and tipping points), as it identifies much more precisely the key features of the Earth system that deserve respect. This does not imply the newer version is beyond criticism—as should be clear from what we ourselves have said about it.

Without engagement, problematic aspects of path dependencies in ideas and practices—embedded in dominant discourses—will go unexamined. Consider in this light Hajer's (1995) landmark analysis of environmental discourse. Hajer charts the emergence of ecological modernization in the Netherlands as a discourse that combines economic and environmental values under the idea that "pollution prevention pays." The emergence of ecological modernization—going beyond an older discourse that puts pollution control and economic growth in necessary opposition—is indicative of a measure of reflexivity, because it involves rethinking the basis for public policy. However, Hajer laments the degree to which ecological modernization adopts a reassuring technocratic attitude toward pollution control. He advocates instead the need for "reflexive" as opposed to "techno-corporatist" ecological modernization. Reflexive ecological modernization would distrust the privilege of experts, and ask critical questions about the composition of economic growth. But what would induce such critical examination and so reflexivity amongst ecological modernizers? One source would be scrutiny from the direction of more radical green discourses—including those that Hajer dismisses as "mediocre naturalist environmentalism" (p. 283). Such critical discourses may need nurturing in settings receptive to creativity and unorthodoxy, before entering the larger contestation of discourses. Here there is a role for enclaves of the sort we criticized earlier as obstructing engagement—but that role can only be provisional, a step on the road to more effective engagement.

Productive engagements in a deliberative democracy

The mere presence of multiple norms and discourses in an issue area does not mean that reflexivity will necessarily be generated. For example, global climate governance has long featured a very active multiplicity of discourses (Stevenson and Dryzek 2014: 41–54)—along with impasse and lack of progress in challenging dominant institutions and practices that have led the world to the edge of climate catastrophe (though the 2015 Paris Agreement showed some signs of hope—and, as we discussed in chapter 3, some signs of reflexivity).

Effective deliberative democracy requires more productive relationships across diverse values, judgments, preferences, and discourses. Here, we stress the pursuit of *meta-consensus* (Dryzek and Niemeyer 2006). Simple consensus means agreement on what is to be done, and why. Simple consensus is often precluded by competing norms and discourses, reflecting deep-seated differences in values and beliefs. Meta-consensus is less demanding in that it refers to agreement on the legitimacy of disputed values (such as livelihoods and nature preservation), the credibility of disputed beliefs (based for example on local experience of environmental damage versus epidemiological studies of health), the range of acceptable options (such as different kinds of policies for de-carbonization of the economy), and the acceptable range of contested discourses (for example, moderate and radical discourses on climate change as discussed earlier). Meta-consensus cannot be achieved unless people exercise a degree of scrutiny of their own positions as well as the positions held by others. This does not necessarily mean that individuals have to let go of the positions with which they began (though that is a possibility). But it does mean that these positions may have to be reformulated in a way that renders them understandable to others who do not share the position, who must themselves be equally willing to engage in self-scrutiny. Here, the pursuit of meta-consensus comes close to the essence of reflexivity. The achievement of meta-consensus may require hard work, especially when it comes to the need to construct bridges across conflicting positions.

Meta-consensus is not just a theoretical abstraction; it is observable in response to all kinds of real-world conflicts. In communicative approaches to dispute resolution, getting each side to recognize the legitimacy of the interests held by other sides is a key step on the way to a substantive agreement. The agreement itself is sometimes referred to as "consensus" (Susskind, McKearnan, and Thomas-Larmer 1999), but it is not consensus in the sense that the outcome is now the first preference of all participants. Rather, it is a workable agreement that the different sides can accept in comparison to the alternative of no agreement (Lo 2013: 92). Often this requires a measure of creativity to craft options that meet the interests of different sides—though those interests can and should themselves be open to reconstruction in deliberation.

We can see in global climate change negotiations the emergence of something like meta-consensus yielding workable agreement, in the path to agreement at the UN climate summit in Paris in 2015, in which the traditional division between developed and developing states was transformed into a more productive recognition that all countries had parts to play in reducing emissions. Attempts to quantify the part that each country should play (in terms of shares of the global mitigation effort) foundered on a collective inability to agree on a single metric or formula for sharing national emission reduction efforts (Pickering 2015). In the absence of simple consensus on a metric for effort-sharing, countries moved to an implicit meta-consensus that, while they retain discretion to choose the metric on which they base their national contributions to emissions reduction, they must publicly justify why their contributions are fair and ambitious (UNFCCC 2016: paragraph 27). Nevertheless, the overall process was only weakly reflexive, for deliberation did not reach as far as any questioning of dominant neo-liberal growth-centric models of development. Few countries have provided robust justifications for the fairness of their national contributions; this suggests that civil society will need to maintain an active role in clarifying what fairness means and requires, conducting independent assessments of the equity of national pledges and holding countries to account if their pledges are unfairly weak (Winkler et al. 2017).

A stronger example of meta-consensus comes from the global governance of biodiversity. One of the first tasks for IPBES after it was established in 2012 was the development of a framework to guide its future activities. The resulting framework reflects debate about whether the economic concept of ecosystem services (which we discussed at length in chapter 6) can capture the diverse ways in which individuals and cultures value nature, or whether it just treats nature as simply another commodity that can be bought and sold. The framework that was adopted was sensitive to this debate by pairing terms more commonly grounded in Western expertise, such as "ecosystem services" itself, with terms from other knowledge systems, such as "nature's gifts," under a common rubric—in this case, "nature's contributions to people." Borie and Hulme's (2015) description of how this framework was drafted suggests that the process, while not without shortcomings, engaged people representing a variety of knowledge systems and social groups in constructive dialogue. They conclude that "while no consensus could be found at the inception of the process, the [framework] allows different interpretations to coexist. It also makes possible the continuation of IPBES['s] work by providing a common framing for different groups of actors with multiple concerns" (Borie and Hulme 2015: 494).

Both the content of a meta-consensus and the process through which it is generated can be more or less defensible. We have discussed some positive examples. A negative example, involving sustained attempts to engineer a meta-consensus that undermines simple consensus, can be found in the efforts of those Oreskes and Conway (2011) call "merchants of doubt," who have managed to paralyze policy in the United States. These merchants are publicists and a small group of scientists who have tried to obtain public acceptance for the credibility (though not necessarily the truth) of claims challenging the view that smoking causes cancer and that climate change is occurring as a result of human activity. Policy inaction can then be justified on the grounds that there is legitimate disagreement over the underlying science. What these examples illustrate is that meta-consensus only contributes to reflexivity if it is generated through free and reasoned deliberative means, and if it is accompanied by reflection on one's own position, as opposed to self-serving manipulation of the terms of public discourse.

At the level of principle, there is no need to welcome into a meta-consensus a discourse such as organized climate change denial that is designed to undermine the conditions for effective public deliberation. There is a big difference between discursive engineering of the sort engaged in by the Koch Brothers alongside some fossil fuel corporations on the one hand, and deliberative democracy on the other. The more deliberative the process, the less likely it is to rest upon false claims that are designed to mislead the public (Niemeyer 2014a).

Communicating and learning beyond local experiments

We pointed out in the previous chapter that cities and other sub-national governments can be less constrained in their exercise of formative agency than states and international organizations. This exercise is consistent with enthusiasm for polycentric or experimental approaches to environmental governance—which do not need to involve only sub-national governments; they can also be initiated by businesses and non-governmental organizations, and transcend national boundaries. Reflexivity would arise inasmuch as these initiatives lead to scrutiny of dominant patterns of governance, and a resulting reconfiguration of these patterns if existing patterns are failing.

Here, reflexivity may begin with the ability of individuals and groups to organize into "niches" for innovation or experimentation that are partly insulated from external pressures to conform or immediately compete (Olsson, Galaz, and Boonstra 2014: 5; Westley et al. 2011: 767). Such experiments might involve anything from cooperative resource management to participatory approaches to local budgets to vehicle sharing schemes to local sourcing of food. These niches could also serve as sites of discursive experimentation or deliberative enclaves that foster the capacity of particular groups subsequently to engage in public debate. Of course much depends on what goes on in particular niches. It is entirely possible that a particular niche may be dominated by economic interests committed to development at all costs (Baber and Bartlett 2005: 129–30), and not interested in reflexive questioning of that imperative.

In a skeptical light, decentralization means mainly the fragmentation of governance, limited to partial and ineffective solutions. The implication is that there is no necessary reflexivity at the level of the system as a whole. So if we look for example at the numerous decentralized initiatives in climate governance celebrated by Hoffmann (2011), there is no systematic learning mechanism that transcends individual cases; still less any contemplation within the pattern of governance they constitute about how adequate those initiatives are in sum when it comes to addressing climate change. Hoffmann (2011: 159) himself recognizes that participants are not able to discern the system they are part of in the way he describes it, in which case it is hard to see how the system could be thought of in terms of promoting reflexivity.

The difficulty that decentralized approaches have in enabling more systemic reflexivity could be overcome by a deliberative learning mechanism that sorts lessons from particular cases and communicates them in persuasive and comprehensible terms to those in a position to advance initiatives in other locations. The best existing intimation of such a mechanism may perhaps be found in networks that link local governments concerned with issues such as climate change. The International Council for Local Environmental Initiatives (ICLEI) cities network is an information-sharing, advocacy, and capacity-building institution through which lessons from successful (and unsuccessful) local practices can be disseminated. The network has a voice at global climate change negotiations. Multilateral processes may also facilitate deliberation about the role and impact of decentralized processes, thereby increasing the prospects of diffusing successful initiatives. At the Paris climate summit, for example, parties to the UNFCCC agreed to establish a platform for exchanging experiences and best practices on mitigation and adaptation among Indigenous peoples and local communities (UNFCCC 2016: paragraph 135).

However, such information-sharing does not necessarily amount to a meaningful exercise of formative agency. Generally missing from such innovations is contemplation of how local actions contribute to consequential wholes and systemic effectiveness. These larger questions could involve how to promote learning that transcends individual cases, how to facilitate the broader recognition and take-up of successful niche ideas, how to coordinate partial actions into more consequential wholes, and how to incorporate expertise into fragmentary governance arrangements. Where then might we seek this kind of deliberation about the pattern of polycentric governance?

One possibility might be to establish productive linkages with multilateral governance processes. Here, it is noteworthy that sub-national actors have recently secured greater recognition in the UN climate framework. Thus, for the first time in a legally binding multilateral climate pact, the 2015 Paris Agreement recognizes "the importance of the engagements of all levels of government and various actors [...] in addressing climate change," albeit with a caveat that such engagement should occur "in accordance with respective national legislations of Parties" (UNFCCC 2016: Preamble). The Agreement and its accompanying decision by the Conference of the Parties explicitly acknowledge sub-national actors. This kind of recognition opens the door to thinking about how polycentric initiatives could be joined with multilateral processes such as the UNFCCC in a way that could mobilize the advantages of experimental governance for the purpose of scrutinizing the adequacy of the pattern of governance in its entirety, the principles on which it rests, and the values it should try to promote. A survey of sixty transnational climate governance initiatives found that their emergence "has taken place in the 'shadow' of the international [climate] regime and is firmly embedded within existing patterns of political economy" (Bulkeley et al. 2012: 603). Thus the challenge remains to forge linkages between sub-national and global action without reinforcing pathological path dependencies.

Listening in the Earth system

The Anthropocene heralds an Earth system whose functioning and parameters are heavily influenced by human activity. The "all-affected principle" in thinking about governance in general and democracy in particular requires that all those affected by a decision are entitled to a say in the decision.

Shouldn't the Earth system and its component entities therefore have a say in the crucial decisions that humans and their institutions make?

This idea contradicts persistent notions in Western thinking that draw a clear demarcation between humans and non-humans based on capacities to reason and act. But how deep is the difference really? Or how much does it simply reflect what Eckersley (2017: 994) calls "human chauvinism"?

This chauvinism is often justified on the grounds that only humans can communicate what they want in meaningful fashion. Yet, as we pointed out in chapter 6, if we take a look at the non-human world, we find that it is pervaded by meaningful communication. Moreover, researchers have found democratic decision-making processes in societies of animals such as bees, which communicate information by dancing in deciding (for example) where to establish a new hive (Seeley 2010). Animals use democratic processes to pool information that enables them to make good collective decisions (List 2004).[2]

Plants and animals are beginning to look better in communicative democratic terms at the same time as people are starting to look worse. The rise of post-truth identity politics means that identity determines what people believe, even if those beliefs are manifestly false—for example, many opinion surveys have shown that a large proportion of Republican voters in the United States were unshakable in their belief that President Obama was a Muslim born outside the United States. "Truthiness"—where a claim feels true because it accords with what one wishes rather than with facts—substitutes for truth, as American comedian Stephen Colbert put it. A similar process helps explain the extreme form of climate change denial, which is impervious to facts and argument.

In short, there seem to be fewer reasons to place humans in a hierarchy over non-humans when it comes to communicative democratic capabilities. Other species and ecosystems may not be like humans; but that does not mean they should be accorded lesser status than humans (Eckersley 2017: 994). For both humans and non-humans, meaningful communication ought to be able to overcome individual limitations in both information and cognition. And given the manifold ways in which humans and non-humans affect each other's lives, that communication should take place across species—not just within species.

As we pointed out in chapter 3, ecological reflexivity requires that humans listen more effectively to the screams of pain from the Earth system, from species extinctions, acidifying oceans, the death of waters that once were healthy, crashes in the number of insects in ecosystems, and so forth. The

---

[2] The capacity for democratic forms of decision-making does not necessarily entail a capacity for formative agency, unless an entity has the capacity to rethink the meaning of democracy itself. Hence the point here remains consistent with our argument in chapter 6 about the difficulties associated with viewing non-human animals as formative agents.

means of listening that are in question can involve science, the most vulnerable, and discourse entrepreneurs. A lot of what is going on in the Earth system—such as the condition of the nitrogen cycle, or the rate of climate change—can only be ascertained by science. Science can introduce into social systems a kind of listening, and thereby establish a communicative link from the ecological to the social. Those most vulnerable to disturbance in the Earth system are generally more effective listeners than those who are remote from these changes; and as a result are in an especially good position to transmit this information to dominant institutions. Here we note the role played by small island states in the UNFCCC—out of all proportion to their minuscule share of the world's population. Or consider the prominence of Indigenous peoples in global biodiversity governance (as discussed in chapter 6).

Discourse entrepreneurs could also play a role in promoting listening. One way of thinking about democracy is as a pattern of discursive representation (Dryzek and Niemeyer 2008). Whereas conventional representation involves acting on behalf of other people (e.g. a politician representing their constituents), discursive representation involves acting on behalf of specific discourses (e.g. an activist representing climate justice or a biologist representing biodiversity), even if the discourse is not associated with a well-defined set of people. Discursive representation is especially important in non-electoral contexts—such as global governance, where discourses such as sustainable development, human rights, transparency, and human security get represented, often by civil society organizations. In this context, there is scope for representing a discourse that emphasizes the conditions of non-human entities—though of course any such representation is done by human activists, who must themselves listen to, reflect upon, and interpret signals from the Earth system.

Yet listening alone is not enough. To illustrate, consider the finding of Ripberger et al. (2017) that ordinary people are quite good at perceiving "health and distress" in non-human systems. In a survey done in Oklahoma, they find that individuals' perceptions of climate anomalies largely match the data—though only when anomalies (in temperature and rainfall) are "large and persistent" (p. 2). At the same time, Oklahoma is a world leader in climate change denial. While Ripberger et al. present no data on the question, we might ask whether the perception of climate anomalies is followed by much reflection on the causes—let alone on whether there is any need for humans to act in response. Reflection is necessary, not just listening. And effective reflection is central to the idea of deliberation.

The need for deliberative processes that listen effectively to and reflect upon signals from the Earth system is not that much different from the need for deliberative processes to listen to and reflect upon signals from human systems—which are often puzzling and require interpretation. What did the referendum majority for British withdrawal from the European Union in 2016 really mean? Was the majority vote in favor of Brexit a gesture of protest against the political class, an expression of nationalist identity, an attempt to remove immigrants, or a sober calculation of economic costs and benefits? In a radically different context, trying to figure out the intentions of an adversary in an international crisis from behavioral signals can also benefit from deliberation. The exemplary case here is the well-documented deliberation of the Executive Committee convened by President John F. Kennedy to advise him during the Cuban Missile Crisis in 1962. The Committee's deliberations involved interpreting only one actor (the Soviet government), and took place in a committee. Signals from the Earth system have many more sources—which suggests that deliberation needs to be more inclusive and so more democratic, with many more channels for listening.

How then might more thoroughgoing listening and reflective capacities be inculcated so as to pervade human components of social-ecological systems? Here we can begin by noting that most individuals do not lack environmental sensibilities—it is just that these sensibilities are crowded out by other sorts of concerns. People living in poverty may understandably be preoccupied with meeting basic needs (although even then they may be acutely aware of their dependence on natural resources and their vulnerability to environmental harm). But in many societies environmental concerns are displaced by the deluge of advertising in market systems, by misinformation in the public sphere (reaching its worst in post-truth politics), by demagogues playing on fears about other categories of humans, and by the generally low quality of information circulating in the media and public sphere. Even high-quality information has its content largely determined by the imperatives of Holocene institutions—such as reports produced by the International Monetary Fund and the World Bank that reflect an uncritical stance toward economic growth. However, spaces of reflection that enable enlarged thinking do exist—and are demonstrably effective in bringing environmental sensibilities to the fore. Niemeyer (2014b) points out that designed citizen deliberations (such as citizens' juries) often yield such effects—for example leading citizens to recognize individual and collective responsibilities for acting on climate change. As Niemeyer (2002) also shows, simply taking deliberating citizens out into a rainforest whose fate they were deliberating had a positive impact in these terms.

Currently these sorts of initiatives remain on the margins of collective action. But it is possible to imagine giving them a more central role—for example, constituting the upper house in a legislature as a chamber of randomly selected citizens (Barnett and Carty 1998). More broadly, if deliberative conditions do indeed enhance ecological sensibilities, the challenge is to make systems of governance more deliberative. This can apply to the way parliaments work, to the content of electoral campaigns, to multilateral negotiations, to the role of civil society organizations in representing different ranges of concerns; in short, to the construction of a more effective delibera-tive democracy.

This construction has to involve much more than institutions. It must also involve a challenge to dominant discourses that effectively suppress distress signals from the non-human world. Such a challenge would help constitute a democracy whose engagements could open up spaces for listening and reflect-ing, and so entry points for non-human "actants" into deliberative systems. There are intimations of such possibilities in global biodiversity governance, as economistic discourse gives ground to alternative ways of thinking about biological diversity and human relationships to ecological systems; but much needs to be done to make such engagement consequential.

Redeeming democracy in the Anthropocene

Our defense of democracy here sheds new light on long-running debates about whether or not democracy needs to cede to authoritarianism in the face of ecological crisis. This debate first arose in the 1970s, with the first shots fired by eco-authoritarians dismayed by the seeming incapacity of liberal demo-cratic states to move fast enough and decisively enough. Those sorts of arguments faded from view in light of the failure of existing authoritarian states to perform well in environmental terms, and evidence about the higher capabilities of different kinds of democracies (especially consensual ones in which the divide between government and opposition is not especially marked). In recent years, eco-authoritarians have looked to China's decisive-ness in taking the lead on renewable energy and contrasted this leadership with the paralysis on climate change that we can see in the United States (Beeson 2010). Most of the debate on authoritarianism versus democracy has taken place at the level of problem-solving effectiveness, which assumes we know what the problems are and what needs to be done. But the formative sphere we have described—home to the exercise of formative agency—stands in logical priority to the sphere of problem-solving, because it enables identifi-cation of what problem-solving should be trying to achieve. And a flourishing formative sphere simply must be democratic, not in the thin and compromised terms of existing liberal democratic states, but in terms of deeper and more inclusive deliberation.

Thus the Anthropocene does not require a top-down, technocratic approach to governance that is at odds with democracy. Technocratic systems might be good at decisive implementation of investment decisions—again we note China's implementation of renewable energy. But they lack reflexivity of the sort that is essential to navigating the Anthropocene.

Skeptics might point out that most people, while not hostile to environmental concerns, accord them low priority in comparison with (say) immediate material interests about employment, income, and security.[3] Assuming this is the case, democracy—if it simply reflects what most people want—will be insufficient, or so they argue. This lack of priority is true enough, but again the solution is not to dispense with democracy but to seek more meaningful democracy (without losing sight of the urgency of safeguarding the Earth system). As we have seen, latent citizen dispositions toward ecological concern can be strengthened in deliberative settings.

A democratic Anthropocene will require more than democratizing the formative sphere alone. Although this chapter has not explored in detail the case for democracy outside the formative sphere, many of the arguments we have presented reinforce the case not only for a democratic rethinking of core values, principles, and meanings, but also for democratizing the collective decision-making needed to institutionalize and advance principles in practice. There is a common communicative and democratic theme to what we have said about interactions among different kinds of experts, between experts and citizens, between the most vulnerable and their advocates, between advocates and discourse entrepreneurs, across local experiments, across the human and non-human components of the Earth system. As humanity confronts the Anthropocene, a democratic sphere is vital to give meaning to key concepts such as justice, sustainability, biodiversity, ecological concern, planetary boundaries. The precepts that guide this formative sphere should be those of a deliberative and ecological democracy that is capable of questioning its own foundations.

---

[3] See, for example, the MY World Survey data discussed in chapter 5.

8 Conclusion: a practical politics of the Anthropocene

We began in chapter 1 with a look back over a couple of billion years to how cyanobacteria transformed the Earth system they once dominated—to their own eventual detriment, though not complete demise. Can humans do better than cyanobacteria? The preceding chapters suggest that they can, though the degree to which they actually will remains an open question. Humans will only do better if there is something like a state shift in the way human institutions operate, and in the way the people who make up those institutions think about them—in order to forestall catastrophic state shifts in the Earth system itself.

The broad contours of what we think the core problems are, and what needs to be done in response, should be clear by now. The core problem is pathological path dependency in institutions, practices, and ideas that developed under Holocene conditions, in ways that did not recognize the possibility that the Earth system could be anything other than benign (indeed, mostly did not recognize the Earth system at all). The solution is easily summarized, but much less easily achieved: to establish ecological reflexivity as a core priority of social, political, and economic institutions. In chapter 6 we discussed the agents who might make this happen. We have tried to show (especially in chapter 7) how that capacity can be advanced in so many ways by democratic communication that is ecological and deliberative.

The idea of ecological reflexivity is challenging because it means that thinking in terms of choice across alternative models of governance and economic systems will not suffice. Thinking in terms of the comparative attributes of different models is common. It can win people Nobel prizes. Elinor Ostrom's *Governing the Commons* begins in its first chapter with a comparison of three normative institutional models, featuring respectively central control of the commons, dividing the commons into chunks of private property, and cooperation among commoners.[1] She advocates the virtues of the third in the interests of maintaining the quality of the commons.[2] In 2016–17 the Global Challenges Foundation (based, like the Nobel Foundation,

---

[1] At the time of writing, Ostrom remains the only woman to have been awarded the Nobel Prize in Economics (she received the prize in 2009).

[2] See also Dryzek (1987: part II), comparing markets, administered systems, and polyarchy in terms of a common set of criteria. Ostrom (1990: 184 and 214) and Dryzek (1987: 244–5) eventually proceed to recognize the limits of models.

in Sweden) summoned efforts from numerous teams around the world in a competition—the "New Shape Prize"—to come up with the best new alternative *model* for global governance.

Reflexive governance involves a permanent capacity to question the foundations of political institutions, suggesting those foundations should not be too secure. We have argued that rather than think in terms of any model to aim for, it is much better to begin with where we are now and figure out positive moves on many fronts. Shortly we will go into some details of what this may involve in practice, but before we do let us respond to a challenge: that what we have said about reflexivity means that we should not be talking about institutions at all. For surely if institutions are reflexive all the way down would they not be permanently engaged in questioning their own foundations (even questioning their own questioning!), to the exclusion of providing the kind of stable environment for action, and for problem-solving, that the very idea of an institution connotes? To see why this need not be the case, let us take a look at the idea of living frameworks.

Living frameworks

If institutions are to respond effectively to the ecological threats posed by the Anthropocene, they must strike a balance between agility and durability (Young 2017: 218). A reflexive institution needs to be flexible enough to respond to feedback from public deliberation and changing environmental conditions, while stable enough to provide a framework for collective, large-scale responses to risks to the Earth system. An *ecologically* reflexive institution needs in addition to be responsive to signals from the Earth system, as well as capable of foresight to forestall future state shifts in that system. This kind of ecological grounding can benefit from establishing principles for action based on the conditions of the Earth system and rates of change in it. However, any such principles should not be seen as immutable; instead they require periodic rethinking as circumstances change. That is why, against those who contend that planetary boundaries should be institutionalized as hard, non-negotiable constraints, we believe they should be open to periodic reformulation in response not just to better scientific knowledge but also in light of changing values, public perceptions of risk, and changing technologies (see chapter 7).

In other words, planetary boundaries—matched with "planetary targets" adopted in international agreements and national policies—would be living frameworks. If they were reconfigured in this way, their centrality to deliberation about our planetary future would confirm and help solidify their influence, even as they were open to continual adjustment (to overcome some of the reservations we expressed about the concept in chapter 1). This mode of thinking can be applied to institutional configuration more generally. To navigate competing demands for flexibility and stability, as well as to preserve ecological grounding and a capacity for foresight, we propose thinking of institutions as "living frameworks." The term may call to mind the idea that a constitution can be a "living document" (as opposed to one that is, as it were, set in stone). More importantly, the term connotes the idea of a framework *for living*, that is, for flourishing under unstable conditions. Living frameworks should not be confused with the persistent but unsustainable frameworks of the Holocene (comprising the institutions we discussed in chapter 2), which might seem very much alive but, given their capacity to devour living things, are perhaps better seen as undead or zombie frameworks. Living frameworks always have sustainability in mind, while building in mechanisms that enable the frameworks to change in response to changing circumstances.

Some elements of living frameworks already exist in practice, though not yet at the kind of scale and depth that are necessary to make them central to governance. The global ozone regime provides an example of a robust yet flexible framework (Young 2017: 227). The regime was built up through an iterative process of treaty amendments that progressively tightened regulations on ozone-depleting substances in response to changing knowledge about the ozone layer and innovations that brought down the costs of substitute technologies (de Búrca, Keohane, and Sabel 2014). The Paris Agreement on climate change, which we discussed in chapter 3, sets out a long-term goal for limiting dangerous climate change, while incorporating rolling cycles of setting and reviewing national targets every five years. This represents a departure from the previous approach under the Kyoto Protocol (which required a treaty amendment for subsequent phases of cooperation to commence: see Pickering et al. 2018). This is not to say that the Paris Agreement meets all the conditions required for a living framework to bring about a shift towards sustainability. As we argued in chapter 3, the Agreement remains hampered by the large gap between the global goal and the national contributions to emissions reduction that countries have been willing to pledge. Other ingredients remain crucial for the success of living frameworks that are built around iterative efforts to lift global cooperation, including domestic political commitments to advance and rethink sustainability—although the presence of an international living framework could also help to galvanize domestic momentum. As it stands, the Paris Agreement falls far short of establishing a framework *for living*, because it competes with so many other national and global institutions with different imperatives—not least an international political economy (and its governance institutions such as the World Trade Organization and the G20) still geared toward the maximization of economic growth. Even so, there are important elements of the Paris Agreement that help to reveal shortcomings in other frameworks. For example, the Aichi Targets under the Convention on Biological Diversity provide a time-limited strategy for action up to 2020, but lack a longer-term framework or robust mechanisms for countries to set and review national targets. The Aichi Targets also lack a mechanism to "ratchet" national commitments upwards by specifying that countries should not backslide when they update their targets.

Living frameworks could also entrench or "constitutionalize" basic principles for humanity's interactions with the Earth system. Many constitutions now include some variation on a right to a safe or healthy environment (Gellers 2017). International lawyers and others have called for the recognition of such a right in international law, while French President Emmanuel Macron proposed a "Global Pact for the Environment" that would encode basic principles of international environmental law. The draft text of the pact includes duties to pursue sustainable development, prevent environmental harm, and safeguard procedural environmental rights (pactenvironment.org 2017). Kim and Bosselmann (2015) argue further that international environmental law would be better equipped to respond to challenges posed by the Anthropocene if it adopted the idea of protecting the ecological integrity of the Earth's "life-support system" as its basic norm or purpose (see also Bridgewater, Kim, and Bosselmann 2014).

Embedding rights and obligations in international law could help to convey the seriousness with which risks to the Earth system should be treated. However, entrenchment of this type has its own risks, not least because it may narrow the options of future generations to determine what forms of sustainability they wish to pursue (Beckman 2008). The risks of greater legal protections for sustainability need to be weighed up against the risks of failing to put robust sustainability measures in place at all, and some forms of entrenchment could be seen as necessary for securing the ecological conditions in which future generations can deliberate.

Laws, rights, and constitutions are not themselves enough to bring a framework to life, because they represent only the formal rules that regulate interactions. Informal understandings matter just as much, or perhaps more. Such informal understandings—especially dominant discourses such as neoliberalism—also need questioning. It may even be possible to think of discourses such as sustainability as potentially living frameworks (though not neoliberalism, which is a zombie framework; see Quiggin 2012). Discourses are like institutions in that they provide a stable context for action. Sustainable development has performed this role in global environmental governance for several decades (to questionable effect, as we argued in chapter 5). But discourses also need to be exposed to critical scrutiny that can only come from engagement with other discourses; as we argued in chapter 7, meaningful engagement of this sort is one of the key aspects of deliberative democracy.

Some practical suggestions

While we have stressed that an effective response to the Anthropocene requires institutions to cultivate unprecedented capacities for ecological reflexivity, development of those capacities has to start from where we are now (as opposed to some blueprint or model). We can group feasible actions into those that dismantle barriers to reflexivity, those that avoid new forms of lock-in, and those that introduce elements of reflexivity. Social movements and individual action will be vital for spurring the transition to more reflexive societies, but unless dominant institutions change, system-wide reflexivity will remain out of reach. Accordingly, the following recommendations focus mainly on pathways towards transforming states and markets.

DISMANTLING BARRIERS TO REFLEXIVITY

One key barrier that needs dismantling is lock-in to unsustainable practices. Many existing treatments of what could be called (somewhat paradoxically) unsustainable lock-in analyze carbon lock-in specifically, but there are other sorts (such as nitrogen lock-in when it comes to fertilizers used for agriculture, or pesticide lock-in). Different forms of lock-in may reinforce one another, as when government subsidies for fossil fuels help to suppress power prices and prop up energy-intensive households and cities.

Lock-in results largely from the kind of infrastructure that is built (and so not easily abandoned) and the kind of technology that has been adopted. In addition, institutions and the behavior of individuals and societies may become locked in to unsustainable practices (Seto et al. 2016: 427). It is easy enough to identify policies that would encourage societies to shift to more sustainable lifestyles, including funding research and development for cleaner technologies, subsidizing renewable technologies in the early stages of diffusion, investing in low-polluting transport infrastructure, and developing robust standards and labeling schemes for energy and water efficiency. It is much harder to see why institutions in the grip of path dependencies would be prepared to adopt such policies comprehensively. Other practical institutional reforms are needed that would at least ameliorate pathological path dependency, such as introducing restrictive rules on political donations to restrain the power of vested interests; overcoming the tax evasion practiced by multinational companies in order to reduce the sway they hold over governments and to enhance public expenditure on global environmental priorities; reforming trade rules that constrain environmental protection; and improving media regulation to reduce the power of ideologically driven news corporations to provide cover for vested interests through propaganda and misinformation. Strategically, it might be possible to open a rift between (say) oil and gas companies and coal companies—holding out to oil and gas companies the promise that they, and not (dirtier) coal companies, can still access some of the remaining space in the atmosphere for carbon dioxide emissions, on condition that they help in fighting the coal industry. However, such a strategy would risk renewed lock-in to fossil fuels. Downie (2017) suggests that exploiting cleavages within the energy sector and entrenching new constituencies for renewables hold considerable potential for effecting a transition to more sustainable sources of energy.

AVOIDING RENEWED LOCK-IN

Many of the policies that others have proposed to address climate change would generate new forms of path dependency that are either high-risk or clearly pathological. Notably, technologies to capture emissions from coal-fired power stations (carbon capture and storage, or CCS) would prolong the age of coal if they were employed at a large scale, though so far effective commercialization of CCS technologies has proved elusive, not least because the fossil fuel industry has failed to invest meaningfully in research and development in this area (Martínez Arranz 2016). Now that the costs of renewable sources of energy are rapidly falling, large-scale public investment in fossil fuel CCS for electricity generation at the expense of renewable technologies may well entrench rather than alleviate carbon lock-in.

A still more clearly undesirable kind of lock-in would be caused by adopting solar geoengineering. As we pointed out in chapter 3, relying on technologies such as injecting sulfate aerosols or titanium dioxide particles into the upper atmosphere to reduce solar radiation would require governance institutions of unprecedented global power and permanence, because the machinery could never be allowed to fail. These requirements would lock the world in to a single path for an indefinite future, because falling off that path would mean immediate climate catastrophe.

INTRODUCING ELEMENTS OF REFLEXIVITY

We have located hints of reflexivity in existing governance. Our discussion of the Paris Agreement on climate change in chapter 3, for example, emphasized the climate regime's movement toward hybrid multilateralism (which joined traditionally opposed multilateral and polycentric approaches), and its reconsideration of the rigid divide between developed and developing countries. Other hints can be found in connection with existing practices such as:

- *Public inquiries*, though much depends on the terms on which they operate. At worst, narrow terms of reference and limited procedures for information-gathering and public engagement ensure there will be no challenge to dominant practices. At best, they can scrutinize the assumptions about the principles that existing policies, practices, or proposals are predicated upon. For example, the French government initiated a high-profile commission— whose chairs included Nobel economics laureates Joseph Stiglitz and Amartya Sen—that scrutinized different measures of prosperity and argued that "the time is ripe [...] to shift emphasis from measuring economic production to measuring people's well-being" in the context of sustainability (Stiglitz, Sen, and Fitoussi 2009: 12). And in 2016 the state government of Victoria in Australia conducted a public inquiry into the performance of its own Environmental Protection Agency, which recommended among other things taking a longer-term view, more assertiveness in holding polluters to account, an emphasis on environmental justice, and a more effective capacity to regulate greenhouse gas emissions (Victorian Government 2016). Inquiries could also be initiated by civil society. The Australian Panel of Experts on Environmental Law, for example, launched by a coalition of non-government organizations, produced a "blueprint" for Australian environmental law that included a combination of environmental democracy, flexible and responsive environmental governance, and environmental rights (APEEL 2017), thus complementing the idea of living frameworks outlined earlier in this chapter. To our knowledge there have been no public inquiries on the political or institutional implications of the Anthropocene: that will need to change.

- *Independent review bodies.* Independent statutory bodies in the UK, Australia and elsewhere have had an important role in thinking through the principles that should inform each country's share of the global carbon budget (Committee on Climate Change 2015; Climate Change Authority 2014). However, as the Australian government's subsequent efforts to abolish and (when that proved unsuccessful) undermine the Climate Change Authority show, challenges to dominant practices can trigger a punitive response. Likewise, the UK's Sustainable Development Commission, initiated by a Labour government in 2001, was abolished by a Conservative government in 2011, not long after it had published a widely discussed report on how societies could flourish without economic growth (Jackson 2009).[3]

- *Procedural environmental rights.* The ability to contest core values and practices is, as we saw in chapter 4, essential to ecological reflexivity and also a requirement of planetary justice. Some progress in this area has been achieved through the spread of procedural environmental rights, including rights to participate in environmental decision-making, to

---

[3] Australia's National Sustainability Council suffered an even swifter demise: it was abolished in 2013 by a new conservative government, only a year after it was established. Subsequently most of the Council's original members formed a non-governmental body to succeed it: the National Sustainable Development Council.

access environmental information, and to access mechanisms to remedy violations of environmental law. Of particular importance here is the Convention on Access to Information, Public Participation in Decision-Making and Access to Justice in Environmental Matters (commonly known as the Aarhus Convention; see Weaver 2018). At present the vast majority of parties to the Convention are European states, but with a coordinated diplomatic effort it could gain wider global acceptance.

- *Mandated attention to ecological concerns*, for example in environmental impact assessment, state of the environment reporting, and climate risk disclosure. These mandates can apply not just to government departments but also to private corporations reporting to their shareholders. Institutions need to attend not only to their local environmental impacts but also to their impacts on the Earth system, as well as the impacts of a changing Earth system (e.g. drought or sea level rise) that may affect the ability of those institutions to function properly.

- *Requirements for periodic review of legislation and institutions in light of performance.* Meadowcroft (2007: 161) sees periodic review of sustainable development strategies as a way to "embed reflexivity in governance routines." Seto et al. (2016: 437) see cyclical review as a key to cultivating the "institutional plasticity" needed to avoid undesirable new forms of lock-in arising from efforts to entrench environmental policies and behavior. An example here would be where periodic review reveals that tighter vehicle emission standards end up facilitating urban sprawl and fail to bring about cuts in overall emissions, because driving long distances becomes more environmentally benign than before (see Gonzalez 2005, on the United States). The solution need not require abandoning tighter emission standards, but could involve neutralizing the adverse side effects of regulation in other ways, for example by land use planning controls that discourage the further expansion of unsustainable transport infrastructure.

- *Sunset clauses for legislation and policies.* These could apply to all policies with a substantial environmental impact—especially economic ones. By putting an automatic expiry date on new policy initiatives, sunset clauses can temper the risk that societies will be stuck with policies that may have been well-intentioned at the time but turn out to be environmentally harmful. Think for example of the huge benefits that could be achieved if there were a sunset clause on government subsidies of fossil fuels. The danger is of course that the sun could set on environmentally benign policies too, suggesting the (constitutional) need for sunset clauses to be accompanied by a ratchet mechanism of the sort we see in the Paris Agreement on climate change, which would specify that there can be no retreat on core standards of environmental protection (as proposed by APEEL 2017 and pactenvironment.org 2017).

More innovative proposals might include:

- *Custodians for non-humans and future generations.* In chapter 4 we discussed examples where governments have appointed custodians for ecosystems and future generations.

- *Linking citizens with Earth system expertise.* As outlined in chapter 7, there is much to be gained by linking citizens and experts in a more productive exchange on addressing risks to the Earth system. Such an exchange could include greater uptake of the results of deliberative forums in scientific assessments such as IPCC or IPBES reports, or creating citizens' forums that directly inform the work of those bodies.

- *Learning from experimentation.* Decentralized experimentation, as we saw in chapter 7, can yield new ways of thinking about global environmental problems and innovative steps to solve them. However, decentralized approaches (such as local movements for food sustainability) often fail to add up to an effective whole, and insights generated by one initiative often fail to be adopted elsewhere. This points to the need for more extensive social learning that could engage activists, old and new media, universities, and governments.

- A *global dissent channel* to enable people who participate in or are affected by global environmental institutions to air dissenting opinions on policy questions.[4] Opinions submitted to the channel would require a timely response from power-holders. The channel could receive communications about bodies such as the UNFCCC or CBD, but its operations would be independent of those institutions. Approximations of a dissent channel can be found in some international institutions (such as the World Bank's Grievance Redress Service and the Green Climate Fund's Independent Redress Mechanism) but eligibility to submit complaints is generally limited to people adversely affected by specific projects funded by the institution, rather than including citizens or officials who wish to voice disagreement with the institution's overall priorities or practices.[5] The amount of traffic in the channel could be kept manageable by crowdsourcing dissent, enabling large numbers of affected people to submit a single complaint. To address the possibility of the channel being overwhelmed by organized campaigns or

---

[4] This idea takes its name from the US State Department's longstanding Dissent Channel. The Channel's effectiveness in prompting reform remains limited (Gurman 2011) but at times it has served as an important means for diplomats to express disagreement with government policy. A dissent cable signed by around 1,000 officials objecting to President Trump's ban on migration from several Muslim-majority countries, for example, became "one of the broadest protests by American officials against their president's policies" (Gettleman 2017).

[5] Numerous UN human rights treaties have channels for receiving individual complaints, but complaints can only be made against national governments that have joined the complaints mechanism for the treaty in question.

ill-founded but popular ideas, some kind of filter would be necessary; perhaps a body composed of randomly selected citizens of the kind we discussed at length in chapter 7. Precisely because it would be non-partisan, such a body would be in a good position to screen out implausible claims.

- *Electoral system reform.* Electoral systems in many countries are dominated by older people who vote in larger numbers than young people and when doing so tend to prioritize immediate concerns over the future. Weighting each individual's vote by the average life expectancy for their age would counteract this problem, and indeed reinforce rather than undermine political equality if equality is interpreted as equal consideration of all life chances.

- *Reflexivity units.* No government that we know of has a reflexivity policy. No government that we know of has an organizational unit devoted to building reflexive capacity. But if we can have a Behavioural Insights Team (or "nudge unit") in government—as in the UK, an idea copied by other governments—why not a reflexivity unit, charged with identifying the potential for introducing moments of reflexivity in government?[6] Such a unit might contemplate the hints of reflexivity already found in government, and think about ways of expanding them.

- *Educating for reflexivity.* Ecological reflexivity requires individuals to develop a capacity for critical thinking as well as an appreciation of the environmental conditions that enable them to flourish, and an ability to translate critical reflection into political action. Some schools and universities have standalone courses on critical thinking, environmental education and civics; these could be expanded and better integrated.

We introduce these suggestions not because they would jointly yield reflexive governance: they would not. The requisite state shift in thinking about institutions we have called for will not be constituted by incremental changes. But introducing these elements of reflexivity—and learning from them—might facilitate more effective rethinking of dominant institutions and their pathological path dependencies, and so at least provide the beginnings of more thoroughgoing reform pathways. These suggestions also show that even though what reflexivity requires of institutions is highly demanding, this need not be an excuse for paralysis, because it is possible to identify actions

---

[6] The "nudge" unit takes ideas from behavioral economics and psychology, and seeks to apply them in all areas of government (Thaler and Sunstein 2008; Halpern 2015). These ideas generally involve small "nudges" to get people to behave in desirable ways. Examples range from putting the healthy options first in a cafeteria line, to encouraging people to reduce their electricity consumption by showing on electricity bills how the billpayer's usage compares to that of other households in the area. For a critique of nudge theory, see Mols et al. (2015).

that can and (given the urgency of safeguarding the Earth system) must be taken now to build momentum for transformative change.

As we stressed in chapter 7, this kind of rethinking requires an effective formative sphere in which principles for collective action are created, questioned, and developed. This formative sphere needs to involve meaningful, inclusive, and ecologically grounded deliberation. Establishing ecological reflexivity as a core priority of governance at all levels is not going to be easy, and will not happen just by accumulating institutional and policy innovations, even those that yield demonstrably positive results. Established priorities for economic development, security, and welfare must be bent in more sustainable directions by recognizing that our ability to achieve these priorities beyond the short term depends on safeguarding the capacities of the Earth system to sustain life. It also requires overcoming path dependencies in thinking, and that will only happen with a more critical, inclusive, and consequential democratic public sphere.

We may not be able to escape the Anthropocene, but we can escape the path dependencies that threaten the pursuit of reflexive sustainability, planetary justice, and ecological democracy. While there are no guarantees, we do not have to end up like cyanobacteria.

REFERENCES

Abbott, Kenneth W. (2012). The Transnational Regime Complex for Climate Change. *Environment and Planning C: Government and Policy* 30 (4): 571–90.

Abbott, Kenneth W. (2017). Orchestrating Experimentation in Non-State Environmental Commitments. *Environmental Politics* 26 (4): 738–63.

Ackerman, Bruce A. (1991). *We the People*, I: *Foundations* (Cambridge, MA: Belknap Press).

Agyeman, Julian (2013). *Introducing Just Sustainabilities: Policy, Planning, and Practice* (London: Zed Books).

Agyeman, Julian, Robert D. Bullard, and Bob Evans (eds) (2003). *Just Sustainabilities: Development in an Unequal World* (Cambridge, MA: MIT Press).

Akenji, Lewis (2014). Consumer Scapegoatism and Limits to Green Consumerism. *Journal of Cleaner Production* 63: 13–23.

APEEL (2017). *Blueprint for the Next Generation of Australian Environmental Law* (Carlton, Victoria: Australian Panel of Experts on Environmental Law).

Arias-Maldonado, Manuel (2013). Rethinking Sustainability in the Anthropocene. *Environmental Politics* 22 (3): 428–46.

Ayling, Julie, and Neil Gunningham (2017). Non-State Governance and Climate Policy: The Fossil Fuel Divestment Movement. *Climate Policy* 17 (2): 131–49.

Baber, Walter F., and Robert V. Bartlett (2005). *Deliberative Environmental Politics: Democracy and Ecological Rationality* (Cambridge, MA: MIT Press).

Bäckstrand, Karin, and Jonathan W. Kuyper (2017). The Democratic Legitimacy of Orchestration: The UNFCCC, Non-State Actors, and Transnational Climate Governance. *Environmental Politics* 26 (4): 764–88.

Bäckstrand, Karin, Jonathan W. Kuyper, Björn-Ola Linnér, and Eva Lövbrand (2017). Non-State Actors in the New Landscape of International Climate Cooperation: From Copenhagen to Paris and Beyond. *Environmental Politics* 26 (4): 561–79.

Bai, Xuemei, Sander van der Leeuw, Karen O'Brien, Frans Berkhout, Frank Biermann, Eduardo S. Brondizio, Christophe Cudennec, John Dearing, Anantha Duraiappah, Marion Glaser, Andrew Revkin, Will Steffen, and James Syvitski (2016). Plausible and Desirable Futures in the Anthropocene: A New Research Agenda. *Global Environmental Change* 39: 351–62.

Baland, Jean-Marie, Pranab K. Bardhan, and Samuel Bowles (2007). *Inequality, Cooperation, and Environmental Sustainability* (Princeton, NJ: Princeton University Press).

Barber, Benjamin R. (2013). *If Mayors Ruled the World: Dysfunctional Nations, Rising Cities* (New Haven, CT: Yale University Press).

Barber, Benjamin R. (2017). *Cool Cities: Urban Sovereignty and the Fix for Global Warming* (New Haven, CT: Yale University Press).

Barnett, Anthony, and Peter Carty (1998). *The Athenian Option: Radical Reform for the House of Lords* (London: Demos).

Barnosky, Anthony D., Elizabeth A. Hadly, Jordi Bascompte, Eric L. Berlow, James H. Brown, Mikael Fortelius, Wayne M. Getz, John Harte, Alan Hastings, Pablo A. Marquet, Neo

D. Martinez, Arne Mooers, Peter Roopnarine, Geerat Vermeij, John W. Williams, Rosemary Gillespie, Justin Kitzes, Charles Marshall, Nicholas Matzke, David P. Mindell, Eloy Revilla, and Adam B. Smith (2012). Approaching a State Shift in Earth's Biosphere. *Nature* 486: 52–8.

Barrett, Scott (2014). Solar Geoengineering's Brave New World: Thoughts on the Governance of an Unprecedented Technology. *Review of Environmental Economics and Policy* 8 (2): 249–69.

Barry, Christian, and Luara Ferracioli (2013). Young on Responsibility and Structural Injustice. *Criminal Justice Ethics* 32 (3): 247.

Barry, Christian, and Gerhard Øverland (2016). *Responding to Global Poverty: Harm, Responsibility, and Agency* (Cambridge: Cambridge University Press).

Baskin, Jeremy (2015). Paradigm Dressed as Epoch: The Ideology of the Anthropocene. *Environmental Values* 24 (1): 9–29.

Beck, Silke, Maud Borie, Jason Chilvers, Alejandro Esguerra, Katja Heubach, Mike Hulme, Rolf Lidskog, Eva Lövbrand, Elisabeth Marquard, Clark Miller, Tahani Nadim, Carsten Neßhöver, Josef Settele, Esther Turnhout, Eleftheria Vasileiadou, and Christoph Görg (2014). Towards a Reflexive Turn in the Governance of Global Environmental Expertise: The Cases of the IPCC and the IPBES. *GAIA—Ecological Perspectives for Science and Society* 23 (2): 80–7.

Beck, Ulrich, Anthony Giddens, and Scott Lash (1994). *Reflexive Modernization: Politics, Tradition and Aesthetics in the Modern Social Order* (Cambridge: Polity).

Beckman, Ludvig (2008). Do Global Climate Change and the Interest of Future Generations Have Implications for Democracy? *Environmental Politics* 17 (4): 610–24.

Beeson, Mark (2010). The Coming of Environmental Authoritarianism. *Environmental Politics* 19 (2): 276–94.

Beitz, Charles R. (1999 [1979]). *Political Theory and International Relations* (Princeton, NJ: Princeton University Press).

Benedick, Richard Elliot (1991). *Ozone Diplomacy: New Directions in Safeguarding the Planet* (Cambridge, MA: Harvard University Press).

Bennett, E. M., G. D. Peterson, and E. A. Levitt (2005). Looking to the Future of Ecosystem Services. *Ecosystems* 8: 125–32.

Bennett, Jane (2010). *Vibrant Matter: A Political Ecology of Things* (Durham, NC: Duke University Press).

Benson, Melinda Harm, and Robin Kundis Craig (2014). The End of Sustainability. *Society and Natural Resources* 27 (7): 777–82.

Berke, Philip R., Jack Kartez, and Dennis Wenger (1993). Recovery after Disaster: Achieving Sustainable Development, Mitigation and Equity. *Disasters* 17 (2): 93–109.

Biermann, F., K. Abbott, S. Andresen, K. Bäckstrand, S. Bernstein, M. M. Betsill, H. Bulkeley, B. Cashore, J. Clapp, C. Folke, A. Gupta, J. Gupta, P. M. Haas, A. Jordan, N. Kanie, T. Kluvánková-Oravská, L. Lebel, D. Liverman, J. Meadowcroft, R. B. Mitchell, P. Newell, S. Oberthür, L. Olsson, P. Pattberg, R. Sánchez-Rodrguez, H. Schroeder, A. Underdal, S. Carmago Vieira, C. Vogel, O. R. Young, A. Brock, and R. Zondervan (2012). Navigating the Anthropocene: Improving Earth System Governance. *Science* 335 (6074): 1306–7.

Biermann, Frank (2014). *Earth System Governance: World Politics in the Anthropocene* (Cambridge, MA: MIT Press).

Biermann, Frank, Xuemei Bai, Ninad Bondre, Wendy Broadgate, Chen-Tung Arthur Chen, Opha Pauline Dube, Jan Willem Erisman, Marion Glaser, Sandra van der Hel, Maria Carmen Lemos, Sybil Seitzinger, and Karen C. Seto (2016). Down to Earth: Contextualizing the Anthropocene. *Global Environmental Change* 39: 341–50.

Biermann, Frank, Philipp Pattberg, Harro van Asselt, and Fariborz Zelli (2009). The Fragmentation of Global Governance Architecture: A Framework for Analysis. *Global Environmental Politics* 9 (4): 14–40.

Blake, Michael (2001). Distributive Justice, State Coercion, and Autonomy. *Philosophy and Public Affairs* 30 (3): 257–96.

Bodansky, Daniel, Jutta Brunnée, and Lavanya Rajamani (2017). *International Climate Change Law* (Oxford: Oxford University Press).

Bonneuil, Christophe, and Jean-Baptiste Fressoz (2016). *The Shock of the Anthropocene: The Earth, History and Us* (London: Verso).

Borie, Maud, and Mike Hulme (2015). Framing Global Biodiversity: IPBES between Mother Earth and Ecosystem Services. *Environmental Science and Policy* 54: 487–96.

Bowen, Frances (2014). *After Greenwashing: Symbolic Corporate Environmentalism and Society* (Cambridge: Cambridge University Press).

Brandi, Clara (2015). Safeguarding the Earth System as a Priority for Sustainable Development and Global Ethics: The Need for an Earth System SDG. *Journal of Global Ethics* 11 (1): 32–6.

Breakthrough Institute (2015). An Ecomodernist Manifesto. http://www.ecomodernism.org/.

Bridgewater, Peter, Rakhyun E. Kim, and Klaus Bosselmann (2014). Ecological Integrity: A Relevant Concept for International Environmental Law in the Anthropocene? *Yearbook of International Environmental Law* 25 (1): 61–78.

Brulle, Robert J. (2014). Institutionalizing Delay: Foundation Funding and the Creation of U.S. Climate Change Counter-Movement Organizations. *Climatic Change* 122 (4): 681–94.

Bryner, Gary C. (2000). The United States: "Sorry—Not our Problem." In *Implementing Sustainable Development: Strategies and Initiatives in High Consumption Societies*, ed. William M. Lafferty and James Meadowcroft (Oxford: Oxford University Press), pp. 273–302.

Bulkeley, Harriett (2011). Cities and Subnational Governments. In *The Oxford Handbook of Climate Change and Society*, ed. John S. Dryzek, Richard B. Norgaard, and David Schlosberg (Oxford: Oxford University Press), pp. 464–78.

Bulkeley, Harriet, Liliana Andonova, Karin Bäckstrand, Michele Betsill, Daniel Compagnon, Rosaleen Duffy, Ans Kolk, Matthew Hoffmann, David Levy, Peter Newell, Tori Milledge, Matthew Paterson, Philipp Pattberg, and Stacy VanDeveer (2012). Governing Climate Change Transnationally: Assessing the Evidence from a Database of Sixty Initiatives. *Environment and Planning C: Government and Policy* 30 (4): 591–612.

Bulkeley, Harriet, JoAnn Carmin, Vanesa Castán Broto, Gareth A. S. Edwards, and Sara Fuller (2013). Climate Justice and Global Cities: Mapping the Emerging Discourses. *Global Environmental Change* 23 (5): 914–25.

Bulkeley, Harriett, Vanessa Castán Broto, Mike Hodson, and Simon Marvin (eds) (2010). *Cities and Low-Carbon Transitions* (London: Routledge).

Bullard, Robert D., and Beverly Wright (eds) (2009). *Race, Place, and Environmental Justice After Hurricane Katrina* (Boulder, CO: Westview).

Büscher, Bram, Robert Fletcher, Dan Brockington, Chris Sandbrook, William M. Adams, Lisa Campbell, Catherine Corson, Wolfram Dressler, Rosaleen Duffy, Noella Gray, George Holmes, Alice Kelly, Elizabeth Lunstrum, Maano Ramutsindela, and Kartik Shanker (2017). Half-Earth or Whole Earth? Radical Ideas for Conservation, and Their Implications. *Oryx* 51 (3): 407–10.

Camacho, Alejandro J. (2009). Adapting Governance to Climate Change: Managing Uncertainty Through a Learning Infrastructure. *Emory Law Journal* 59 (1): 1–77.

Caney, Simon (2005). *Justice Beyond Borders: A Global Political Theory* (Oxford: Oxford University Press).

Caro, Tim, Jack Darwin, Tavis Forrester, Cynthia Ledoux-Bloom, and Caitlin Wells (2012). Conservation in the Anthropocene. *Conservation Biology* 26 (1): 185–8.

Carruthers, David (2001). From Opposition to Orthodoxy: The Remaking of Sustainable Development. *Journal of Third World Studies* 18 (2): 93–112.

Catney, Philip, and Timothy Doyle (2011). The Welfare of Now and the Green (Post) Politics of the Future. *Critical Social Policy* 31 (2): 174–93.

Ceva, Emanuela (2012). Beyond Legitimacy: Can Proceduralism Say Anything Relevant About Justice? *Critical Review of International Social and Political Philosophy* 15 (2): 183–200.

Chaffin, Brian C., Hannah Gosnell, and Barbara A. Cosens (2014). A Decade of Adaptive Governance Scholarship: Synthesis and Future Directions. *Ecology and Society* 19 (3): Article 56.

Chakrabarty, Dipesh (2009). The Climate of History: Four Theses. *Critical Inquiry* 35 (2): 197–222.

Chambers, Simone (2009). Rhetoric in the Public Sphere: Has Deliberative Democracy Abandoned Mass Democracy? *Political Theory* 37: 323–50.

Chancel, Lucas, and Thomas Piketty (2015). *Carbon and Inequality: From Kyoto to Paris* (Paris: Paris School of Economics).

Chasek, Pamela S., and Lynn M. Wagner (2016). Breaking the Mold: A New Type of Multilateral Sustainable Development Negotiation. *International Environmental Agreements: Politics, Law and Economics* 16 (3): 397–413.

Chasek, Pamela S., Lynn M. Wagner, Faye Leone, Ana-Maria Lebada, and Nathalie Risse (2016). Getting to 2030: Negotiating the Post-2015 Sustainable Development Agenda. *Review of European, Comparative and International Environmental Law* 25 (1): 5–14.

Ciplet, David, J. Timmons Roberts, and Mizan R. Khan (2015). *Power in a Warming World: The New Global Politics of Climate Change and the Remaking of Environmental Inequality* (Cambridge, MA: MIT Press).

Clémençon, Raymond (2012). Welcome to the Anthropocene: Rio+20 and the Meaning of Sustainable Development. *Journal of Environment and Development* 21 (3): 311–38.

Climate Change Authority (2014). Reducing Australia's Greenhouse Gas Emissions: Targets and Progress Review: Final Report. http://www.climatechangeauthority.gov.au/files/files/Target-Progress-Review/Targets%20and%20Progress%20Review%20Final%20Report.pdf.

Climate Citizen (2009). Bolivia Responds to US On Climate Debt: "If You Break It, You Buy It," 12 December 2009. https://takvera.blogspot.com/2009/12/bolivia-responds-to-us-on-climate-debt.html.

Committee on Climate Change (2015). The Fifth Carbon Budget: The Next Step Towards a Low-Carbon Economy. https://www.theccc.org.uk/wp-content/uploads/2015/11/Committee-on-Climate-Change-Fifth-Carbon-Budget-Report.pdf.

Cornell, Sarah, Frans Berkhout, Willemijn Tuinstra, J. David Tàbara, Jill Jäger, Ilan Chabay, Bert de Wit, Richard Langlais, David Mills, Peter Moll, Ilona M. Otto, Arthur Petersen, Christian Pohl, and Lorrae van Kerkhoff (2013). Opening up Knowledge Systems for Better Responses to Global Environmental Change. *Environmental Science and Policy* 28: 60–70.

Costanza, Robert, Rudolf de Groot, Paul Sutton, Sander van der Ploeg, Sharolyn J. Anderson, Ida Kubiszewski, Stephen Farber, and R. Kerry Turner (2014). Changes in the Global Value of Ecosystem Services. *Global Environmental Change* 26 (1): 152–8.

Costanza, Robert, Gar Alperovitz, Herman Daly, Joshua Farley, Carol Franco, Tim Jackson, Ida Kubiszewski, Juliet Schor, and Peter Victor (2013). Building a Sustainable and Desirable Economy-in-Society-in-Nature. In *State of the World 2013* (Washington, DC: Worldwatch Institute), pp. 126–42.

Crawford, Neta C. (2002). *Argument and Change in World Politics: Ethics, Decolonization, and Humanitarian Intervention* (Cambridge: Cambridge University Press).

Crist, Eileen (2013). On the Poverty of Our Nomenclature. *Environmental Humanities* 3: 129–47.

Crocker, David A. (2008). *Ethics of Global Development: Agency, Capability, and Deliberative Democracy* (Cambridge: Cambridge University Press).

Cronon, William (1996). The Trouble with Wilderness; or, Getting Back to the Wrong Nature. *Environmental History* 1 (1): 7–28.

Cronon, William (2013). Foreword. In Christopher W. Wells, *Car Country: An Environmental History* (Seattle, WA: University of Washington Press), pp. ix–xiv.

Crutzen, Paul, and Eugene F. Stoermer (2000). The "Anthropocene." *Global Change Newsletter* 41: 17–18.

Curato, Nicole (2019). *Democracy in a Time of Misery: From Spectacular Tragedy to Deliberative Action* (Oxford: Oxford University Press).

Dalby, Simon (2016). Framing the Anthropocene: The Good, the Bad and the Ugly. *Anthropocene Review*, 3 (1): 33–51.

Daly, Herman E. (1990). Toward Some Operational Principles of Sustainable Development. *Ecological Economics* 2 (1): 1–6.

Dauvergne, Peter (2016). The Sustainability Story: Exposing Truths, Half-Truths, and Illusions. In *New Earth Politics: Essays from the Anthropocene*, ed. Simon Nicholson and Sikina Jinnah (Cambridge, MA: MIT Press), pp. 387–404.

Davies, Robin, and Jonathan Pickering (2017). How Should Development Co-Operation Evolve? Views from Developing Countries. *Development Policy Review* 35 (S1): O10–O28.

de Búrca, Gráinne, Robert O. Keohane, and Charles Sabel (2013). New Modes of Pluralist Global Governance. *New York University Journal of International Law and Politics* 45 (3): 723–86.

de Búrca, Gráinne, Robert O. Keohane, and Charles Sabel (2014). Global Experimentalist Governance. *British Journal of Political Science* 44 (3): 477–86.

Deaton, Angus (2013). *The Great Escape: Health, Wealth, and the Origins of Inequality* (Princeton, NJ: Princeton University Press).

Depledge, Joanna (2006). The Opposite of Learning: Ossification in the Climate Change Regime. *Global Environmental Politics* 6 (1): 1–22.

Di Chiro, Giovanna (2016). Environmental Justice and the Anthropocene Meme. In *The Oxford Handbook of Environmental Political Theory*, ed. Teena Gabrielson, Cheryl Hall, John M. Meyer, and David Schlosberg (Oxford: Oxford University Press), pp. 362–81.

Di Chiro, Giovanna (2017). Welcome to the White (M)Anthropocene? A Feminist-Environmental Critique. In *Routledge Handbook of Gender and Environment*, ed. Sherilyn MacGregor (London: Routledge), pp. 487–505.

Di Paola, Marcello (2015). Virtues for the Anthropocene. *Environmental Values* 24 (2): 183–207.

Diamond, Jared (2005). *Collapse: How Societies Choose to Fail or Survive* (New York: Viking Penguin).

Dietz, Thomas (2013). Bringing Values and Deliberation to Science Communication. *Proceedings of the National Academy of Sciences* 110 (Supp. 3): 14081–7.

Dobson, Andrew (1990). *Green Political Thought: An Introduction* (London: Unwin Hyman).

Dobson, Andrew (1998). *Justice and the Environment: Conceptions of Environmental Sustainability and Dimensions of Social Justice* (Oxford: Oxford University Press).

Dobson, Andrew (2007). Social Justice and Environmental Sustainability: Ne'er the Twain Shall Meet? In *Just Sustainabilities: Development in an Unequal World*, ed. Julian Agyeman, Robert D. Bullard, and Bob Evans (Cambridge, MA: MIT Press), pp. 83–95.

Dobson, Andrew (2010). Democracy and Nature: Speaking and Listening. *Political Studies* 58 (4): 752–68.

Doelle, Meinhard (2014). The Birth of the Warsaw Loss & Damage Mechanism: Planting a Seed to Grow Ambition? *Carbon and Climate Law Review* 1: 35–45.

Downie, Christian (2017). Business Actors, Political Resistance, and Strategies for Policymakers. *Energy Policy* 108 (Supplement C): 583–92.

Dryzek, John S. (1987). *Rational Ecology: Environment and Political Economy* (Oxford: Blackwell).

Dryzek, John S. (1995). Political and Ecological Communication. *Environmental Politics* 4: 13–30.

Dryzek, John S. (2000). *Deliberative Democracy and Beyond: Liberals, Critics, Contestations* (Oxford: Oxford University Press).

Dryzek, John S. (2009). Democratization as Deliberative Capacity-Building. *Comparative Political Studies* 42 (11): 1379–402.

Dryzek, John S. (2010). Rhetoric in Democracy: A Systemic Appreciation. *Political Theory* 38 (3): 319–39.

Dryzek, John S. (2013a). The Deliberative Democrat's Idea of Justice. *European Journal of Political Theory* 12 (4): 329–46.

Dryzek, John S. (2013b). *The Politics of the Earth: Environmental Discourses* (3rd edn, Oxford: Oxford University Press).

Dryzek, John S. (2015). Democratic Agents of Justice. *Journal of Political Philosophy* 23 (4): 361–84.

Dryzek, John S. (2016a). Can There Be a Human Right to an Essentially Contested Concept? The Case of Democracy. *Journal of Politics* 78 (2): 357–67.

Dryzek, John S. (2016b). Institutions for the Anthropocene: Governance in a Changing Earth System. *British Journal of Political Science* 46 (4): 937–56.

Dryzek, John S. (2017). The Meanings of Life for Non-State Actors in Climate Politics. *Environmental Politics* 26 (4): 789–99.

Dryzek, John S, André Bächtiger, and Karolina Milewicz (2011). Toward a Deliberative Global Citizens' Assembly. *Global Policy* 2 (1): 33–42.

Dryzek, John S., David Downes, Christian Hunold, and David Schlosberg, with Hans-Kristian Hernes (2003). *Green States and Social Movements: Environmentalism in the United States, United Kingdom, Germany, and Norway* (Oxford: Oxford University Press).

Dryzek, John S., Robert E. Goodin, Aviezer Tucker, and Bernard Reber (2009). Promethean Elites Encounter Precautionary Publics: The Case of GM Foods. *Science, Technology and Human Values* 34 (3): 263–88.

Dryzek, John S., and Alex Y. Lo (2015). Reason and Rhetoric in Climate Communication. *Environmental Politics* 24: 1–16.

Dryzek, John S., and Simon Niemeyer (2006). Reconciling Pluralism and Consensus as Political Ideals. *American Journal of Political Science* 50 (3): 634–49.

Dryzek, John S., and Simon Niemeyer (2008). Discursive Representation. *American Political Science Review* 102 (4): 481–93.

Dryzek, John S., Richard B. Norgaard, and David Schlosberg (2013). *Climate-Challenged Society* (Oxford: Oxford University Press).

Dryzek, John S., and Jonathan Pickering (2017). Deliberation as a Catalyst for Reflexive Environmental Governance. *Ecological Economics* 131: 353–60.

Dryzek, John S., and David Schlosberg (1995). Disciplining Darwin: Biology in the History of Political Science. In *Political Science in History: Research Programs and Political Traditions*, ed. James Farr, John S. Dryzek, and Stephen T. Leonard (Cambridge: Cambridge University Press), pp. 123–44.

Dusenberry, James (1960). Comment on an Economic Analysis of Fertility. In National Bureau for Economic Research, *Demographic and Economic Change in Developed Countries* (Princeton, NJ: Princeton University Press), pp. 231–4.

Earth System Governance Project (2018). Taskforce on Planetary Justice Research. http://www.earthsystemgovernance.net/planetary-justice/.

Eckersley, Robyn (2004). *The Green State: Rethinking Democracy and Sovereignty* (Cambridge, MA: MIT Press).

Eckersley, Robyn (2012). Moving Forward in the Climate Negotiations: Multilateralism or Minilateralism? *Global Environmental Politics* 12 (2): 24–42.

Eckersley, Robyn (2017). Geopolitan Democracy in the Anthropocene. *Political Studies* 65 (4): 983–99.

Edenhofer, Ottmar, and Martin Kowarsch (2015). Cartography of Pathways: A New Model for Environmental Policy Assessments. *Environmental Science and Policy* 51: 56–64.

Eliasoph, Nina (1998). *Avoiding Politics: How Americans Produce Apathy in Everyday Life* (Cambridge: Cambridge University Press).

Ellis, Erle, Mark Maslin, Nicole Boivin, and Andrew Bauer (2016). Involve Social Scientists in Defining the Anthropocene. *Nature* 540: 192–3.

Erskine, Toni (2001). Assigning Responsibilities to Institutional Moral Agents: The Case of States and Quasi-States. *Ethics and International Affairs* 15 (2): 67–85.

Erskine, Toni (2003). Introduction: Making Sense of "Responsibility" in International Relations—Key Questions and Concepts. In *Can Institutions Have Responsibilities? Collective Moral Agency and International Relations*, ed. Toni Erskine (Basingstoke: Palgrave Macmillan), pp. 1–16.

Felicetti, Andrea (2016). *Deliberative Democracy and Social Movements: Transition Initiatives in the Public Sphere* (London: Rowman & Littlefield).

Finnemore, Martha, and Kathryn Sikkink (1998). International Norm Dynamics and Political Change. *International Organization* 52 (4): 887–917.

Folke, Carl (2006). Resilience: The Emergence of a Perspective for Social-Ecological Systems Analysis. *Global Environmental Change* 16 (3): 53–67.

Folke, Carl, Stephen R. Carpenter, Brian Walker, Martin Scheffer, Terry Chapin, and Johan Rockström (2010). Resilience Thinking: Integrating Resilience, Adaptability, and Transformability. *Ecology and Society* 15 (4): Article 20.

Folke, Carl, Thomas Hahn, Per Olsson, and Jon Norberg (2005). Adaptive Governance of Social-Ecological Systems. *Annual Review of Environment and Resources* 30: 441–73.

Fox, Oliver, and Peter Stoett (2016). Citizen Participation in the UN Sustainable Development Goals Consultation Process: Toward Global Democratic Governance? *Global Governance* 22 (4): 555–73.

Fricker, Miranda (2007). *Epistemic Injustice: Power and the Ethics of Knowing* (Oxford: Oxford University Press).

Fukuda-Parr, Sakiko, and David Hulme (2011). International Norm Dynamics and the "End of Poverty": Understanding the Millennium Development Goals. *Global Governance* 17 (1): 17–36.

Gagnon, Jean-Paul (2013). *Evolutionary Basic Democracy: A Critical Overture* (Dordrecht: Springer).

Galaz, Victor (2014). *Global Environmental Governance, Technology and Politics: The Anthropocene Gap* (Cheltenham: Edward Elgar).

Gambino, Lauren (2017). Pittsburgh Fires Back at Trump: We Stand with Paris, Not You. *The Guardian*, 2 June 2017. https://www.theguardian.com/us-news/2017/jun/01/pittsburgh-fires-back-trump-paris-agreement/.

Gammage, William (2011). *The Biggest Estate on Earth: How Aborigines Made Australia* (Sydney: Allen & Unwin).

Gardiner, Stephen (2011a). Is No One Responsible for Global Environmental Tragedy? Climate Change as a Challenge to Our Ethical Concepts. In *The Ethics of Global Climate Change*, ed. Denis G. Arnold (Cambridge: Cambridge University Press), pp. 38–59.

Gardiner, Stephen M. (2011b). Climate Justice. In *The Oxford Handbook of Climate Change and Society*, ed. John S. Dryzek, Richard B. Norgaard, and David Schlosberg (Oxford: Oxford University Press), pp. 309–22.

Gardiner, Stephen M. (2011c). *A Perfect Moral Storm: The Ethical Tragedy of Climate Change* (New York: Oxford University Press).

Gat, Azar (2013). Is War Declining—and Why? *Journal of Peace Research*, 50 (2): 149–57.

Gellers, Joshua C. (2016). Crowdsourcing Global Governance: Sustainable Development Goals, Civil Society, and the Pursuit of Democratic Legitimacy. *International Environmental Agreements: Politics, Law and Economics* 16 (3): 415–32.

Gellers, Joshua C. (2017). *The Global Emergence of Constitutional Environmental Rights* (London: Routledge).

Gettleman, Jeffrey (2017). State Dept. Dissent Cable on Trump's Ban Draws 1,000 Signatures. *New York Times*, 31 January 2017. https://www.nytimes.com/2017/01/31/world/americas/state-dept-dissent-cable-trump-immigration-order.html/.

Gilabert, Pablo, and Holly Lawford-Smith (2012). Political Feasibility: A Conceptual Exploration. *Political Studies* 60 (4): 809–25.

Global Carbon Project (2017). Global Carbon Atlas. http://www.globalcarbonatlas.org/en/CO2-emissions.

Godfrey-Smith, Peter (2016). *Other Minds: The Octopus and the Evolution of Intelligent Life* (London: HarperCollins).

Gonzalez, George A. (2005). Urban Sprawl, Global Warming, and the Limits of Ecological Modernisation. *Environmental Politics* 19 (4): 344–62.

Goodin, Robert E. (1985). *Protecting the Vulnerable: A Re-Analysis of Our Social Responsibilities* (Chicago, IL: University of Chicago Press).

Goodin, Robert E. (1992). *Green Political Theory* (Cambridge: Polity).

Goodin, Robert E. (1996a). Institutions and their Design. In *Theories of Institutional Design*, ed. Robert E. Goodin (Cambridge: Cambridge University Press), pp. 1–53.

Goodin, Robert E. (1996b). Enfranchising the Earth, and its Alternatives. *Political Studies* 44 (5): 835–49.

Goodin, Robert E., and Simon J. Niemeyer (2003). When Does Deliberation Begin? Internal Reflection Versus Public Discussion in Deliberative Democracy. *Political Studies* 51 (4): 627–49.

Gottlieb, Robert (1993). *Forcing the Spring: The Transformation of the American Environmental Movement* (Washington, DC: Island Press).

Gough, Ian, and James Meadowcroft (2011). Decarbonizing the Welfare State. In *The Oxford Handbook of Climate Change and Society*, ed. John S. Dryzek, Richard B. Norgaard, and David Schlosberg (Oxford: Oxford University Press), pp. 490–503.

Griffin, Donald R. (2001). *Animal Minds: Beyond Cognition to Consciousness* (Chicago, IL: University of Chicago Press).

Griggs, David, Mark Stafford-Smith, Owen Gaffney, Johan Rockstrom, Marcus C. Ohman, Priya Shyamsundar, Will Steffen, Gisbert Glaser, Norichika Kanie, and Ian Noble (2013). Sustainable Development Goals for People and Planet. *Nature* 495 (7441): 305–7.

Grönlund, Kimmo, André Bächtiger, and Maija Setälä (eds) (2014). *Deliberative Mini-Publics: Involving Citizens in the Democratic Process* (Colchester: ECPR Press).

Gunderson, Lance H., and C. S. Holling (eds) (2002). *Panarchy: Understanding Transformations in Human and Natural Systems* (Washington, DC: Island Press).

Gunnarsson-Östling, Ulrika, and Åsa Svenfelt (2018). Sustainability Discourses and Justice: Towards Social-Ecological Justice. In *Routledge Handbook of Environmental Justice*, ed. Ryan Holifield, Jayajit Chakraborty, and Gordon Walker (London: Routledge), pp. 160–71.

Gurman, Hannah (2011). The Other Plumbers Unit: The Dissent Channel of the U.S. State Department. *Diplomatic History* 35 (2): 321–49.

Haas, Peter M. (1992). Banning Chlorofluorocarbons: Epistemic Community Efforts to Protect Stratospheric Ozone. *International Organization* 46 (1): 187–224.

Hajer, Maarten, Måns Nilsson, Kate Raworth, Peter Bakker, Frans Berkhout, Yvo de Boer, Johan Rockström, Kathrin Ludwig, and Marcel Kok (2015). Beyond Cockpit-ism: Four Insights to Enhance the Transformative Potential of the Sustainable Development Goals. *Sustainability* 7 (2): 1651–60.

Hajer, Maarten A. (1995). *The Politics of Environmental Discourse: Ecological Modernization and the Policy Process* (Oxford: Clarendon Press).

Halpern, David (2015). *Inside the Nudge Unit: How Small Changes Can Make a Big Difference* (London: W.H. Allen).

Hamilton, Clive (2016). The Anthropocene as Rupture. *Anthropocene Review* 3 (2): 93–106.

Hamilton, Clive (2017). *Defiant Earth: The Fate of Humans in the Anthropocene* (Cambridge: Polity).

Hamilton, Clive, François Gemenne, and Christophe Bonneuil (2015). *The Anthropocene and the Global Environmental Crisis: Rethinking Modernity in a New Epoch* (London: Routledge).

Haraway, Donna (2015). Anthropocene, Capitalocene, Plantationocene, Chthulucene: Making Kin. *Environmental Humanities* 6 (1): 159–65.

Hay, Colin (2006). Constructive Institutionalism. In *The Oxford Handbook of Political Institutions*, ed. R. A. W. Rhodes, Sarah A. Binder, and Bert A. Rockman (Oxford: Oxford University Press), pp. 56–74.

Hay, Colin, and Ben Rosamond (2002). Globalisation, European Integration, and the Discursive Construction of Economic Imperatives. *Journal of European Public Policy* 9 (2): 147–67.

Hayward, Tim (2006). Global Justice and the Distribution of Natural Resources. *Political Studies* 54 (2): 349–69.

Hayward, Tim (2012). Climate Change and Ethics. *Nature Climate Change* 2 (12): 843–8.

Heede, Richard (2014). Tracing Anthropogenic Carbon Dioxide and Methane Emissions to Fossil Fuel and Cement Producers, 1854–2010. *Climatic Change* 122 (1–2): 229–41.

Heyward, Clare (2015). Is There Anything New under the Sun?: Exceptionalism, Novelty and Debating Geoengineering Governance. In *The Ethics of Climate Governance*, ed. Aaron Maltais and Catriona McKinnon (London: Rowman & Littlefield), pp. 135–54.

Heyward, Clare, and Dominic Roser (2016). Introduction. In *Climate Justice in a Non-Ideal World*, ed. Clare Heyward and Dominic Roser (Oxford: Oxford University Press), pp. 1–17.

Higgs, Eric (2012). History, Novelty, and Virtue in Ecological Restoration. In *Ethical Adaptation to Climate Change: Human Virtues of the Future*, ed. Allen Thompson and Jeremy Bendik-Keymer (Cambridge, MA: MIT Press), pp. 81–102.

Hoff, Holger, and Ivonne Lobos Alva (2017). *How the Planetary Boundaries Framework Can Support National Implementation of the 2030 Agenda*. Policy Brief (Stockholm: Stockholm Environment Institute).

Hoffmann, Matthew J. (2011). *Climate Governance at the Crossroads: Experimenting with a Global Response after Kyoto* (New York: Oxford University Press).

Höhne, Niklas, Helcio Blum, Jan Fuglestvedt, Ragnhild Skeie, Atsushi Kurosawa, Guoquan Hu, Jason Lowe, Laila Gohar, Ben Matthews, Ana Nioac de Salles, and Christian Ellermann (2011). Contributions of Individual Countries' Emissions to Climate Change and Their Uncertainty. *Climatic Change* 106 (3): 359–91.

Holland, Breena (2008). Justice and the Environment in Nussbaum's "Capabilities Approach": Why Sustainable Ecological Capacity is a Meta-Capability. *Political Research Quarterly* 61 (2): 319–32.

Holland, Breena (2017). Procedural Justice in Local Climate Adaptation: Political Capabilities and Transformational Change. *Environmental Politics* 26 (3): 391–412.

Hourdequin, Marion (2013). Restoration and History in a Changing World. *Ethics and the Environment* 18 (2): 115–34.

Howard, Jo, and Joanna Wheeler (2015). What Community Development and Citizen Participation Should Contribute to the New Global Framework for Sustainable Development. *Community Development Journal* 50 (4): 552–70.

Hume, David (1739). *A Treatise of Human Nature* (London: John Noon).

Hunt, Terry L. (2006). Rethinking the Fall of Easter Island. *American Scientist* 94 (5): 412.

Inglehart, Ronald (1977). *The Silent Revolution: Changing Values and Political Styles Among Western Publics* (Princeton, NJ: Princeton University Press).

Jackson, Tim (2009). Prosperity without Growth? The Transition to a Sustainable Economy ([London]: Sustainable Development Commission).

Jamieson, Dale (2014). *Reason in a Dark Time: Why the Struggle Against Climate Change Failed—and What It Means for Our Future* (New York: Oxford University Press).

Jamieson, Dale W., and Marcello Di Paola (2016). Political Theory for the Anthropocene. In *Global Political Theory*, ed. David Held and Pietro Maffettone (Cambridge: Polity), pp. 254–80.

Jasanoff, Sheila (2004). The Idea of Co-Production. In *States of Knowledge: The Co-Production of Science and Social Order*, ed. Sheila Jasanoff (London: Routledge), pp. 1–12.

Jeffries, Michael J. (2006). *Biodiversity and Conservation* (2nd edn, London: Routledge).

Jetñil-Kijiner, Kathy (2014). United Nations Climate Summit Opening Ceremony—a Poem to My Daughter. 23 September 2014. https://www.kathyjetnilkijiner.com/united-nations-climate-summit-opening-ceremony-my-poem-to-my-daughter/.

Jiang, Jiani, Wentao Wang, Can Wang, and Yanhua Liu (2017). Combating Climate Change Calls for a Global Technological Cooperation System Built on the Concept of Ecological Civilization. *Chinese Journal of Population Resources and Environment* 15 (1): 21–31.

Kahneman, Daniel (2011). *Thinking, Fast and Slow* (New York: Farrar, Straus & Giroux).

Kamau, Macharia, Pamela Chasek, and David O'Connor (2018). *Transforming Multilateral Diplomacy: The Inside Story of the Sustainable Development Goals* (London: Routledge).

Kates, Robert W., Thomas M. Parris, and Anthony A. Leiserowitz (2005). What Is Sustainable Development? Goals, Indicators, Values, and Practice. *Environment* 47 (3): 8.

Kay, Adrian (2005). A Critique of the Use of Path Dependency in Policy Studies. *Public Administration* 83 (3): 553–71.

Keen, David (2008). *Complex Emergencies* (Cambridge: Polity).

Keohane, Robert O., and David G. Victor (2011). The Regime Complex for Climate Change. *Perspectives on Politics* 9 (1): 7–23.

Khan, Mizan R., and J. Timmons Roberts (2013). Adaptation and International Climate Policy. *Wiley Interdisciplinary Reviews: Climate Change* 4 (3): 171–89.

Kim, Rakhyun E., and Klaus Bosselmann (2015). Operationalizing Sustainable Development: Ecological Integrity as a Grundnorm of International Law. *Review of European, Comparative and International Environmental Law* 24 (2): 194–208.

Klein, Naomi (2014). *This Changes Everything: Capitalism vs. the Climate* (New York: Simon & Schuster).

Kolstad, Charles, Kevin Urama, John Broome, Annegrete Bruvoll, Micheline Cariño Olvera, Don Fullerton, Christian Gollier, William Michael Hanemann, Rashid Hassan, Frank Jotzo, Mizan R. Khan, Lukas Meyer, and Luis Mundaca (2014). Social, Economic, and Ethical Concepts and Methods. In *Climate Change 2014, Mitigation of Climate Change*. Contribution of Working Group III to the Fifth Assessment Report of the Intergovernmental Panel on Climate Change (IPCC) (New York: Cambridge University Press).

Kopnina, Helen (2016). Half the Earth for People (or More)? Addressing Ethical Questions in Conservation. *Biological Conservation* 203 (Supplement C): 176–85.

Kothari, Ashish, Federico Demaria, and Alberto Acosta (2014). Buen Vivir, Degrowth and Ecological Swaraj: Alternatives to Sustainable Development and the Green Economy. *Development* 57 (3–4): 362–75.

Kotzé, Louis J., and Paola Villavicencio Calzadilla (2017). Somewhere between Rhetoric and Reality: Environmental Constitutionalism and the Rights of Nature in Ecuador. *Transnational Environmental Law* 6 (3): 401–33.

Kuyper, Jonathan (2013). Historical Institutionalism in World Politics: Prospects for Democratisation. PhD thesis, Australian National University, Canberra.

Lafferty, William M. (1996). The Politics of Sustainable Development: Global Norms for National Implementation. *Environmental Politics* 5 (2): 185–208.

Langford, Malcolm (2016). Lost in Transformation? The Politics of the Sustainable Development Goals. *Ethics and International Affairs* 30 (2): 167–76.

Latour, Bruno (2014). Agency at the Time of the Anthropocene. *New Literary History* 45 (1): 1–18.

Le Blanc, David (2015). Towards Integration at Last? The Sustainable Development Goals as a Network of Targets. *Sustainable Development* 23 (3): 176–87.

Leach, Melissa (2013). Democracy in the Anthropocene? Science and Sustainable Development Goals at the UN. *Huffington Post*, 28 March 2013. http://www.huffingtonpost.co.uk/Melissa-Leach/democracy-in-the-anthropocene_b_2966341.html.

Leach, Melissa, Ian Scoones, and Andy Stirling (2010). *Dynamic Sustainabilities: Technology, Environment, Social Justice* (London: Routledge).

Lélé, Sharachchandra M. (1991). Sustainable Development: A Critical Review. *World Development* 19 (6): 607–21.

Lenton, Timothy M., Herman Held, Elmar Kriegler, Jim W. Hall, Wolfgang Lucht, Stefan Rahmstorf, and Hans Joachim Schellnhuber (2008). Tipping Elements in the Earth's Climate System. *Proceedings of the National Academy of Sciences* 105 (6): 1786–93.

Li, Nan, Joseph Hilgard, Dietram A. Scheufele, Kenneth M. Winneg, and Kathleen Hall Jamieson (2016). Cross-Pressuring Conservative Catholics? Effects of Pope Francis' Encyclical on the U.S. Public Opinion on Climate Change. *Climatic Change* 139 (3): 367–80.

Li, Quan, and Rafael Reuveny (2006). Democracy and Environmental Degradation. *International Studies Quarterly* 50 (4): 935–56.

Liao, S. Matthew, Anders Sandberg, and Rebecca Roache (2012). Human Engineering and Climate Change. *Ethics, Policy, and the Environment* 15 (2): 206–21.

Lichtenberg, Judith (2010). Negative Duties, Positive Duties, and the "New Harms." *Ethics* 120 (3): 557–78.

Lindblom, Charles E. (1982). The Market as Prison. *Journal of Politics* 44: 324–36.

List, Christian (2004). Democracy in Animal Groups: A Political Science Perspective. *Trends in Ecology and Evolution* 19 (4): 168–9.

List, Christian, and Philip Pettit (2011). *Group Agency: The Possibility, Design, and Status of Corporate Agents* (Oxford: Oxford University Press).

Litfin, Karen T. (1994). *Ozone Discourses: Science and Politics in Global Environmental Cooperation* (New York: Columbia University Press).

Lo, Alex Y. (2013). Agreeing to Pay under Value Disagreement: Reconceptualizing Preference Transformation in Terms of Pluralism with Evidence from Small-Group Deliberations on Climate Change. *Ecological Economics* 87: 84–94.

Locke, John (1988 [1690]). *Two Treatises of Government*, ed. P. Laslett (Cambridge: Cambridge University Press).

Lomborg, Bjørn (ed.) (2010). *Smart Solutions to Climate Change: Comparing Costs and Benefits* (Cambridge: Cambridge University Press).

Lorimer, Jamie (2017). The Anthropo-Scene: A Guide for the Perplexed. *Social Studies of Science* 47 (1): 117–42.

Lövbrand, Eva, Silke Beck, Jason Chilvers, Tim Forsyth, Johan Hedrén, Mike Hulme, Rolf Lidskog, and Eleftheria Vasileiadou (2015). Who Speaks for the Future of Earth? How Critical Social Science Can Extend the Conversation on the Anthropocene. *Global Environmental Change* 32: 211–18.

Lukacs, Martin (2014). New, Privatized African City Heralds Climate Apartheid. *The Guardian*, 21 January 2014. https://www.theguardian.com/environment/true-north/2014/jan/21/new-privatized-african-city-heralds-climate-apartheid/.

Mace, Georgina M., Belinda Reyers, Rob Alkemade, Reinette Biggs, F. Stuart Chapin Iii, Sarah E. Cornell, Sandra Díaz, Simon Jennings, Paul Leadley, Peter J. Mumby, Andy Purvis, Robert J. Scholes, Alistair W. R. Seddon, Martin Solan, Will Steffen, and Guy Woodward (2014). Approaches to Defining a Planetary Boundary for Biodiversity. *Global Environmental Change* 28: 289–97.

MacNeil, Robert, and Matthew Paterson (2012). Neoliberal Climate Policy: From Market Fetishism to the Developmental State. *Environmental Politics* 21 (2): 230–47.

Malm, Andreas, and Alf Hornborg (2014). The Geology of Mankind? A Critique of the Anthropocene Narrative. *Anthropocene Review* 1 (1): 62–9.

Mangat, Rupinder, Simon Dalby, and Matthew Paterson (2018). Divestment Discourse: War, Justice, Morality and Money. *Environmental Politics* 27 (2): 187–208.

Mann, Michael E., Raymond S. Bradley, and Malcolm K. Hughes (1998). Global-Scale Temperature Patterns and Climate Forcing over the Past Six Centuries. *Nature* 392 (6678): 779.

Mansbridge, Jane, James Bohman, Simone Chambers, Thomas Christiano, Archon Fung, John Parkinson, Dennis F. Thompson, and Mark E. Warren (2012). A Systemic Approach to Deliberative Democracy. In *Deliberative Systems*, ed. John Parkinson and Jane Mansbridge (Oxford: Oxford University Press), pp. 1–26.

Marion Suiseeya, Kimberly R. (2014). Negotiating the Nagoya Protocol: Indigenous Demands for Justice. *Global Environmental Politics* 14 (3): 102–24.

Marris, Emma (2011). *Rambunctious Garden: Saving Nature in a Post-Wild World* (New York: Bloomsbury).

Marsh, David (2010). Stability and Change: The Last Dualism? *Critical Policy Studies* 4 (1): 86–101.

Martin, Adrian, Shawn McGuire, and Sian Sullivan (2013). Global Environmental Justice and Biodiversity Conservation. *Geographical Journal* 179 (2): 122–31.

Martínez Arranz, Alfonso (2016). Hype among Low-Carbon Technologies: Carbon Capture and Storage in Comparison. *Global Environmental Change* 41 (Supplement C): 124–41.

Martinez-Alier, Joan (2002). *The Environmentalism of the Poor: A Study of Ecological Conflicts and Valuation* (Cheltenham: Edward Elgar).

Masson-Delmotte, Valérie, Michael Schulz, Ayako Abe-Ouchi, Jürg Beer, Andrey Ganopolski, Jesus Fidel González Rouco, Eystein Jansen, Kurt Lambeck, Jürg Luterbacher, and Tim Naish (2013). Information from Paleoclimate Archives. In *Climate Change 2013: The Physical Science Basis*. Contribution of Working Group I to the Fifth Assessment Report of the Intergovernmental Panel on Climate Change (New York: Cambridge University Press).

McCright, Aaron, and Riley Dunlap (2011). The Politicization of Climate Change and Polarization in the American Public's Views of Global Warming, 2001–2010. *Sociological Quarterly* 52 (2): 155–94.

McKibben, Bill (1989). *The End of Nature* (New York: Random House).

McKinnon, Catriona (2009). Runaway Climate Change: A Justice-Based Case for Precautions. *Journal of Social Philosophy* 40 (2): 187–203.

McNeill, John Robert, and Peter Engelke (2016). *The Great Acceleration: An Environmental History of the Anthropocene since 1945* (Cambridge, MA: Harvard University Press).

Meadowcroft, James (2007). National Sustainable Development Strategies: Features, Challenges and Reflexivity. *European Environment* 17 (3): 152–63.

Meadows, Donella H. (2008). *Thinking in Systems: A Primer* (White River Junction, VT: Chelsea Green).

Meadows, Donella H., Dennis L. Meadows, Jørgen Randers, and William H. Behrens III (1972). *The Limits to Growth* (New York: Universe Books).

Meinshausen, Malte, Nicolai Meinshausen, William Hare, Sarah C. B. Raper, Katja Frieler, Reto Knutti, David J. Frame, and Myles R. Allen (2009). Greenhouse Gas Emission Targets for Limiting Global Warming to 2°C. *Nature* 458: 1158–62.

Milanovic, Branko (2016). *Global Inequality: A New Approach for the Age of Globalization* (Cambridge, MA: Harvard University Press).

Miller, Brian, Michael E. Soulé, and John Terborgh (2014). "New Conservation" or Surrender to Development? *Animal Conservation* 17 (6): 509–15.

Miller, David (2007). *National Responsibility and Global Justice* (Oxford: Oxford University Press).

Mitchell, Timothy (2011). *Carbon Democracy: Political Power in the Age of Oil* (London: Verso Books).

Moellendorf, Darrel (2012). Climate Change and Global Justice. *Wiley Interdisciplinary Reviews: Climate Change* 3 (2): 131–43.

Molina, Mario, Durwood Zaelke, K. Madhava Sarma, Stephen O. Andersen, Veerabhadran Ramanathan, and Donald Kaniaru (2009). Reducing Abrupt Climate Change Risk Using the Montreal Protocol and Other Regulatory Actions to Complement Cuts in CO_2 Emissions. *Proceedings of the National Academy of Sciences* 106 (49): 20616–21.

Mols, Frank, S. Alexander Haslam, Jolanda Jetten, and Niklas K. Steffens (2015). Why a Nudge Is Not Enough: A Social Identity Critique of Governance by Stealth. *European Journal of Political Research* 54 (1): 81–98.

Montanaro, Laura (2018). *Who Elected Oxfam? A Democratic Defense of Self-Appointed Representatives* (Cambridge: Cambridge University Press).

Moore, Jason W. (ed.) (2016). *Anthropocene or Capitalocene? Nature, History, and the Crisis of Capitalism* (Oakland, CA: PM Press).

Moser, Susanne C., and Lisa Dilling (2011). Communicating Climate Change: Closing the Science-Action Gap. In *The Oxford Handbook of Climate Change and Society*, ed. John S. Dryzek, Richard B. Norgaard, and David Schlosberg (Oxford: Oxford University Press), pp. 161–74.

Mulgan, Tim (2011). *Ethics for a Broken World: Imagining Philosophy after Catastrophe* (London: Routledge).

Muller, Adrian, and Markus Huppenbauer (2016). Sufficiency, Liberal Societies and Environmental Policy in the Face of Planetary Boundaries. *GAIA—Ecological Perspectives for Science and Society* 25 (2): 105–9.

Nagel, Thomas (2005). The Problem of Global Justice. *Philosophy and Public Affairs* 33 (2): 113–47.

National Research Council (2010). *Adapting to the Impacts of Climate Change* (Washington, DC: National Academies Press).

Neuhäuser, Christian (2014). Structural Injustice and the Distribution of Forward-Looking Responsibility. *Midwest Studies in Philosophy* 38 (1): 232–51.

Neumayer, Eric (2003). *Weak versus Strong Sustainability: Exploring the Limits of Two Opposing Paradigms* (Cheltenham: Edward Elgar).

Newell, Peter, and Matthew Paterson (2010). *Climate Capitalism: Global Warming and the Transformation of the Global Economy* (Cambridge: Cambridge University Press).

Niemeyer, Simon (2002). Deliberation in the Wilderness: Transforming Policy Preferences through Discourse. PhD thesis, Australian National University.

Niemeyer, Simon (2013). Democracy and Climate Change: What Can Deliberative Democracy Contribute? *Australian Journal of Politics and History* 59 (3): 429–48.

Niemeyer, Simon (2014a). A Defence of (Deliberative) Democracy in the Anthropocene. *Ethical Perspectives* 21 (1): 15–45.

Niemeyer, Simon (2014b). Scaling up Deliberation to Mass Publics: Harnessing Mini-Publics in a Deliberative System. In *Deliberative Mini-Publics: Involving Citizens in the Democratic Process*, ed. Kimmo Grönlund, André Bächtiger, and Maija Setälä (Colchester: ECPR Press), pp. 177–202.

Nisbet, Matthew C. (2014). Disruptive Ideas: Public Intellectuals and Their Arguments for Action on Climate Change. *Wiley Interdisciplinary Reviews: Climate Change* 5 (6): 809–23.

Nolt, John (2011). Nonanthropocentric Climate Ethics. *Wiley Interdisciplinary Reviews: Climate Change* 2 (5): 701–11.

Norgaard, Richard B. (1988). Sustainable Development: A Co-Evolutionary View. *Futures* 20 (6): 606–20.

Norgaard, Richard B. (2007). Deliberative Economics. *Ecological Economics* 63 (2–3): 375–82.

Norgaard, Richard B. (2008). Finding Hope in the Millennium Ecosystem Assessment. *Conservation Biology* 22 (4): 862–9.

Norgaard, Richard B. (2013). The Econocene and the California Delta. *San Francisco Estuary and Watershed Science* 11 (3): 1–5.

Norström, Albert V., Astrid Dannenberg, Geoff McCarney, Manjana Milkoreit, Florian Diekert, Gustav Engström, Ram Fishman, Johan Gars, Efthymia Kyriakopoolou, Vassiliki Manoussi, Kyle Meng, Marc Metian, Mark Sanctuary, Maja Schlüter, Michael Schoon, Lisen Schultz, and Martin Sjöstedt (2014). Three Necessary Conditions for Establishing Effective Sustainable Development Goals in the Anthropocene. *Ecology and Society* 19 (3): Article 8.

North, Douglass (1990). *Institutions, Institutional Change and Economic Performance* (Cambridge: Cambridge University Press).

Noss, Reed F., Andrew P. Dobson, Robert Baldwin, Paul Beier, Cory R. Davis, Dominick A. Dellasala, John Francis, Harvey Locke, Katarzyna Nowak, Roel Lopez, Conrad Reining, Stephen C. Trombulak, and Gary Tabor (2012). Bolder Thinking for Conservation. *Conservation Biology* 26 (1): 1–4.

Nussbaum, Martha (2006). *Frontiers of Justice: Disability, Nationality, Species Membership* (Cambridge, MA: Belknap Press).

O'Neill, Onora (2001). Agents of Justice. *Metaphilosophy* 32 (1/2): 180–95.

Oldfield, Frank (2016). Paradigms, Projections and People. *Anthropocene Review* 3 (2): 163–72.

Olsson, Lennart, Anne Jerneck, Henrik Thoren, Johannes Persson, and David O'Byrne (2015). Why Resilience is Unappealing to Social Science: Theoretical and Empirical Investigations of the Scientific Use of Resilience. *Science Advances* 1 (4): e1400217.

Olsson, Per, Victor Galaz, and Wiebren J. Boonstra (2014). Sustainability Transformations: A Resilience Perspective. *Ecology and Society* 19 (4): Article 1.

Ophuls, William (1977). *Ecology and the Politics of Scarcity* (San Francisco, CA: W.H. Freeman).

Oreskes, Naomi (2007). The Scientific Consensus on Climate Change: How Do We Know We're Not Wrong? In *Climate Change: What It Means for Us, Our Children, and Our Grandchildren*, ed. Jospeh F. C. DiMento and Pamela Doughman (Cambridge, MA: MIT Press), pp. 65–99.

Oreskes, Naomi, and Erik M Conway (2011). *Merchants of Doubt: How a Handful of Scientists Obscured the Truth on Issues from Tobacco Smoke to Global Warming* (New York: Bloomsbury).

Orsini, Amandine, and Daniel Compagnon (2013). From Logics to Procedures: Arguing within International Environmental Negotiations. *Critical Policy Studies* 7 (3): 273–91.

Ostrom, Elinor (1990). *Governing the Commons: The Evolution of Institutions for Collective Action* (Cambridge: Cambridge University Press).

Ostrom, Elinor (2009). A Polycentric Approach for Coping with Climate Change. World Bank Policy Research Working Paper 5095 (Washington, DC: World Bank).

Ostrom, Elinor, and Marco A. Janssen (2004). Multi-Level Governance and Resilience of Social-Ecological Systems. In *Globalisation, Poverty and Conflict*, ed. Max Spoor (Dordrecht: Kluwer), pp. 239–59.

pactenvironment.org (2017). Draft Global Pact for the Environment. http://pactenvironment.emediaweb.fr/wp-content/uploads/2017/07/Global-Pact-for-the-Environment-project-24-June-2017.pdf.

Paehlke, Robert, and Douglas Torgerson (eds) (2005). *Managing Leviathan: Environmental Politics and the Administrative State* (2nd edn, Peterborough, ON: Broadview).

Page, Edward A. (2006). *Climate Change, Justice and Future Generations* (Cheltenham: Edward Elgar).

Page, Edward A. (2007). Intergenerational Justice of What: Welfare, Resources or Capabilities? *Environmental Politics* 16 (3): 453–69.

Palmer, Clare (2011). Does Nature Matter? The Place of the Nonhuman in the Ethics of Climate Change. In *The Ethics of Global Climate Change*, ed. Denis G. Arnold (Cambridge: Cambridge University Press), pp. 272–91.

Parr, Adrian (2009). *Hijacking Sustainability* (Cambridge, MA: MIT Press).

Participate (2013). Response to the High Level Panel on the Post-2015 Development Agenda Report. http://participatesdgs.org/publications/participate-response-to-the-high-level-panel-on-the-post-2015-development-agenda-report/.

Pascual, Unai, Patricia Balvanera, Sandra Díaz, György Pataki, Eva Roth, Marie Stenseke, Robert T. Watson, Esra Başak Dessane, Mine Islar, and Eszter Kelemen (2017). Valuing Nature's Contributions to People: The IPBES Approach. *Current Opinion in Environmental Sustainability* 26: 7–16.

Paterson, Matthew (2007). *Automobile Politics: Ecology and Cultural Political Economy* (Cambridge: Cambridge University Press).

PBL (2015). Climate Action Outside the UNFCCC: Assessment of the Impact of International Cooperative Initiatives on Greenhouse Gas Emissions. PBL Netherlands Environmental Assessment Agency. http://www.pbl.nl/sites/default/files/cms/pbl-2015-climate-action-outside-the-unfccc_01188.pdf.

Petsko, Gregory A. (2011). The Blue Marble. *Genome Biology* 12 (4): 112.

Pickering, Jonathan (2015). Top-Down Proposals for Sharing the Global Climate Policy Effort Fairly: Lost in Translation in a Bottom-up World? In *Ethical Values and the Integrity of the Climate Change Regime*, ed. Hugh Breakey, Vesselin Popovski, and Rowena Maguire (Aldershot: Ashgate), pp. 89–104.

Pickering, Jonathan (2016). Moral Language in Climate Politics. In *Climate Justice in a Non-Ideal World*, ed. Clare Heyward and Dominic Roser (Oxford: Oxford University Press), pp. 255–76.

Pickering, Jonathan (2017). Deliberating About Justice in the Convention on Biological Diversity. Unpublished working paper.

Pickering, Jonathan (2018). Ecological Reflexivity: Characterising an Elusive Virtue for Environmental Governance in the Anthropocene. *Environmental Politics*, 1–22.

Pickering, Jonathan, and Christian Barry (2012). On the Concept of Climate Debt: Its Moral and Political Value. *Critical Review of International Social and Political Philosophy* 15 (5): 667–85.

Pickering, Jonathan, Jeffrey S. McGee, Sylvia I. Karlsson-Vinkhuyzen, and Joseph Wenta (2018). Global Climate Governance between Hard and Soft Law: Can the Paris Agreement's "Crème Brûlée" Approach Enhance Ecological Reflexivity? *Journal of Environmental Law*, 1–28.

Pickering, Jonathan, and Åsa Persson (2018). Democratising Planetary Boundaries. Unpublished working paper.

Pickering, Jonathan, Steve Vanderheiden, and Seumas Miller (2012). "If Equity's In, We're Out": Scope for Fairness in the Next Global Climate Agreement. *Ethics and International Affairs* 26 (4): 423–43.

Pielke Jr., Roger A. (2007). *The Honest Broker: Making Sense of Science in Policy and Politics* (Cambridge: Cambridge University Press).

Pierson, Paul (2000). Increasing Returns, Path Dependence, and the Study of Politics. *American Political Science Review* 94 (2): 251–67.

Pierson, Paul (2004). *Politics in Time: History, Institutions and Social Analysis* (Princeton, NJ: Princeton University Press).

Pinker, Stephen (2011). *The Better Angels of Our Nature: Why Violence Has Declined* (New York: Viking).

Plumwood, Val (2002). *Environmental Culture: The Ecological Crisis of Reason* (London: Routledge).

Pogge, Thomas (2008). *World Poverty and Human Rights: Cosmopolitan Responsibilities and Reforms* (2nd edn, Cambridge: Polity).

Pope Francis (2015). *Encyclical Letter: Laudato Sí of the Holy Father Francis: On Care for Our Common Home* (Rome: Vatican Press).

Purdy, Jedediah (2015). *After Nature: A Politics for the Anthropocene* (Cambridge, MA: Harvard University Press).

Putnam, Robert D., with Robert Leonardi and Raffaella Y. Nanetti (1993). *Making Democracy Work: Civic Traditions in Modern Italy* (Princeton, NJ: Princeton University Press).

Quiggin, John (2012). *Zombie Economics: How Dead Ideas Still Walk among Us* (Princeton, NJ: Princeton University Press).

Rajamani, Lavanya (2016). Ambition and Differentiation in the 2015 Paris Agreement: Interpretative Possibilities and Underlying Politics. *International and Comparative Law Quarterly* 65 (2): 493–514.

Rao, Vijayendra, and Paromita Sanyal (2010). Dignity through Discourse: Poverty and the Culture of Deliberation in Indian Village Democracies. *Annals of the American Academy of Political and Social Science* 629 (1): 146–72.

Rask, Mikko, and Richard Worthington (eds) (2015). *Governing Biodiversity through Democratic Deliberation* (London: Routledge).

Rask, Mikko, Richard Worthington, and Minna Lammi (eds) (2012). *Citizen Participation in Global Environmental Governance* (London: Earthscan).

Rawls, John (1999a). *The Law of Peoples* (Cambridge, MA: Harvard University Press).

Rawls, John (1999b). *A Theory of Justice* (rev. edn, Cambridge, MA: Belknap Press; orig. edn, 1971).

Rawls, John (2005). *Political Liberalism* (expanded edn, New York: Columbia University Press; orig. edn 1993).

Raworth, Kate (2012). A Safe and Just Space for Humanity: Can We Live within the Doughnut? *Oxfam Policy and Practice: Climate Change and Resilience* 8 (1): 1–26.

Raworth, Kate (2017). *Doughnut Economics: Seven Ways to Think Like a 21st-Century Economist* (London: Random House).

Resilience Alliance (2018). Key Concepts. https://www.resalliance.org/key-concepts.

Ripberger, Joseph T., Hank C. Jenkins-Smith, Carol L. Silva, Deven E. Carlson, Kuhika Gupta, Nina Carlson, and Riley E. Dunlap (2017). Bayesian versus Politically Motivated Reasoning in Human Perception of Climate Anomalies. *Environmental Research Letters* 12 (11): 114004.

Robinson, John (2004). Squaring the Circle? Some Thoughts on the Idea of Sustainable Development. *Ecological Economics* 48 (4): 369–84.

Rockström, Johan, Will Steffen, Kevin Noone, Åsa Persson, F. Stuart Chapin, Eric F. Lambin, Timothy M. Lenton, Marten Scheffer, Carl Folke, Hans Joachim Schellnhuber, Björn Nykvist, Cynthia A. de Wit, Terry Hughes, Sander van der Leeuw, Henning Rodhe, Sverker Sörlin, Peter K. Snyder, Robert Costanza, Uno Svedin, Malin Falkenmark, Louise Karlberg, Robert W. Corell, Victoria J. Fabry, James Hansen, Brian Walker, Diana Liverman, Katherine Richardson, Paul Crutzen, and Jonathan A. Foley (2009). A Safe Operating Space for Humanity. *Nature* 461 (7263): 472–5.

Rogers, Adam (2017). Los Angeles Says It'll Stay in the Paris Climate Agreement It Isn't In. *Wired*, 18 May 2017. https://www.wired.com/2017/05/cities-cant-sign-treaties-can-still-fight-climate-change/.

Roy, Eleanor Ainge (2017). New Zealand River Granted Same Legal Rights as Human Being. *The Guardian*, 16 March 2017. https://www.theguardian.com/world/2017/mar/16/new-zealand-river-granted-same-legal-rights-as-human-being.

Rubenstein, Jennifer (2014). The Misuse of Power, Not Bad Representation: Why it is Beside the Point that Nobody Elected Oxfam. *Journal of Political Philosophy* 22 (2): 204–30.

Rull, Valentí, Núria Cañellas-Boltà, Alberto Saez, Olga Margalef, Roberto Bao, Sergi Pla-Rabes, Blas Valero-Garcés, and Santiago Giralt (2013). Challenging Easter Island's Collapse: The Need for Interdisciplinary Synergies. *Frontiers in Ecology and Evolution* 1 (3): 1–5.

Russell-Smith, Jeremy, Catherine Monagle, Margaret Jacobsohn, Robin L. Beatty, Bibiana Bilbao, Adriana Millán, Hebe Vessuri, and Isabelle Sánchez-Rose (2017). Can Savanna Burning Projects Deliver Measurable Greenhouse Emissions Reductions and Sustainable Livelihood Opportunities in Fire-Prone Settings? *Climatic Change* 140 (1): 47–61.

Safi, Michael (2017). Ganges and Yamuna Rivers Granted Same Legal Rights as Human Beings. *The Guardian*, 21 March 2017. https://www.theguardian.com/world/2017/mar/21/ganges-and-yamuna-rivers-granted-same-legal-rights-as-human-beings/.

Samuelsohn, Darren (2009). No "Pass" for Developing Countries in Next Climate Treaty, Says U.S. Envoy. *New York Times*, 9 December 2009. http://www.nytimes.com/gwire/2009/12/09/09greenwire-no-pass-for-developing-countries-in-next-clima-98557.html?pagewanted=all/.

Sanders, Elizabeth (2006). Historical Institutionalism. In *The Oxford Handbook of Political Institutions*, ed. R. A. W. Rhodes, Sarah A. Binder, and Bert A. Rockman (Oxford: Oxford University Press), pp. 39–55.

Sanklecha, Pranay (2017). Should There Be Future People? A Fundamental Question for Climate Change and Intergenerational Justice. *Wiley Interdisciplinary Reviews: Climate Change* 8 (3): e453.

Schlosberg, David (2004). Reconceiving Environmental Justice: Global Movements and Political Theories. *Environmental Politics* 13 (3): 517–40.

Schlosberg, David (2007). *Defining Environmental Justice: Theories, Movements, and Nature* (Oxford: Oxford University Press).

Schlosberg, David (2013). Theorising Environmental Justice: The Expanding Sphere of a Discourse. *Environmental Politics* 22 (1): 37–55.

Schlosberg, David, and David Carruthers (2010). Indigenous Struggles, Environmental Justice, and Community Capabilities. *Global Environmental Politics* 10 (4): 12–35.

Schlosberg, David, and Romand Coles (2016). The New Environmentalism of Everyday Life: Sustainability, Material Flows and Movements. *Contemporary Political Theory* 15 (2): 160–81.

Schlosberg, David, and Lisette B. Collins (2014). From Environmental to Climate Justice: Climate Change and the Discourse of Environmental Justice. *Wiley Interdisciplinary Reviews: Climate Change* 5 (3): 359–74.

Schmidt, Jeremy J., Peter G. Brown, and Christopher J. Orr (2016). Ethics in the Anthropocene: A Research Agenda. *Anthropocene Review* 3 (3): 188–200.

Schmidt, Vivien A. (2008). Discursive Institutionalism: The Explanatory Power of Ideas and Discourse. *Annual Review of Political Science* 11: 303–26.

Scripps CO_2 Program (2018). Atmospheric CO_2 Data: Ice-Core Merged Products. http://scrippsco2.ucsd.edu/data/atmospheric_co2/icecore_merged_products.

Seeley, Thomas D. (2010). *Honeybee Democracy* (Princeton, NJ: Princeton University Press).

Sen, Amartya (1999). *Development as Freedom* (Oxford: Oxford University Press).

Sen, Amartya (2009). *The Idea of Justice* (London: Allen Lane).

Sénit, Carole-Anne, Frank Biermann, and Agni Kalfagianni (2017). The Representativeness of Global Deliberation: A Critical Assessment of Civil Society Consultations for Sustainable Development. *Global Policy* 8 (1): 62–72.

Seto, Karen C., Steven J. Davis, Ronald B. Mitchell, Eleanor C. Stokes, Gregory Unruh, and Diana Ürge-Vorsatz (2016). Carbon Lock-In: Types, Causes, and Policy Implications. *Annual Review of Environment and Resources* 41 (1): 425–52.

Shearman, David, and Joseph Wayne Smith (2007). *The Climate Change Challenge and the Failure of Democracy* (Westport, CT: Praeger).

Shue, Henry (2014). *Climate Justice: Vulnerability and Protection* (Oxford: Oxford University Press).

Sikkink, Kathryn (2011). *The Justice Cascade: How Human Rights Prosecutions are Changing World Politics* (New York: W.W. Norton).

Singer, Peter (2009). A Day for Planetary Justice. *Project Syndicate*, 14 October 2009. https://www.project-syndicate.org/commentary/a-day-for-planetary-justice.

Skocpol, Theda (1979). *States and Social Revolutions: A Comparative Analysis of France, Russia and China* (Cambridge: Cambridge University Press).

Smith, Adrian, and Andy Stirling (2007). Moving Outside or Inside? Objectification and Reflexivity in the Governance of Socio-Technical Systems. *Journal of Environmental Policy and Planning* 9 (3–4): 351–73.

Smith, Graham (2003). *Deliberative Democracy and the Environment* (London: Routledge).

Spash, Clive L. (2010). The Brave New World of Carbon Trading. *New Political Economy* 15 (2): 169–95.

Spijkers, Otto, and Arron Honniball (2015). Developing Global Public Participation (2): Shaping the Sustainable Development Goals. *International Community Law Review* 17 (3): 251–96.

Steffen, Will, Wendy Broadgate, Lisa Deutsch, Owen Gaffney, and Cornelia Ludwig (2015). The Trajectory of the Anthropocene: The Great Acceleration. *Anthropocene Review* 2 (1): 81–98.

Steffen, Will, Paul J. Crutzen, and John R. McNeill (2007). The Anthropocene: Are Humans Now Overwhelming the Great Forces of Nature? *Ambio* 36 (8): 614–21.

Steffen, Will, Åsa Persson, Lisa Deutsch, Jan Zalasiewicz, Mark Williams, Katherine Richardson, Carole Crumley, Paul Crutzen, Carl Folke, Line Gordon, Mario Molina, Veerabhadran Ramanathan, Johan Rockström, Martin Scheffer, Hans Joachim Schellnhuber, and Uno Svedin (2011). The Anthropocene: From Global Change to Planetary Stewardship. *Ambio* 40 (7): 739–61.

Steffen, Will, Katherine Richardson, Johan Rockström, Sarah E. Cornell, Ingo Fetzer, Elena M. Bennett, Reinette Biggs, Stephen R. Carpenter, Wim de Vries, Cynthia A. de Wit, Carl Folke, Dieter Gerten, Jens Heinke, Georgina M. Mace, Linn M. Persson, Veerabhadran Ramanathan, Belinda Reyers, and Sverker Sörlin (2015). Planetary Boundaries: Guiding Human Development on a Changing Planet. *Science* 347 (6223): 1259855.

Steffen, Will, Johan Rockström, and Robert Costanza (2011). How Defining Planetary Boundaries Can Transform Our Approach to Growth. *Solutions* 2 (3): 59–65.

Stephens, Tim (2017). Reimagining International Environmental Law in the Anthropocene. In *Environmental Law and Governance for the Anthropocene*, ed. Louis Kotzé (Oxford: Hart), pp. 31–54.

Stern, David I. (2004). The Rise and Fall of the Environmental Kuznets Curve. *World Development* 32 (8): 1419–39.

Stevens, Caleb, Robert Winterbottom, Jenny Springer, and Katie Reytar (2014). *Securing Rights, Combating Climate Change: How Strengthening Community Forest Rights Mitigates Climate Change* (Washington, DC: World Resources Institute).

Stevenson, Hayley (2013). *Institutionalizing Unsustainability: The Paradox of Global Climate Governance* (Berkeley, CA: University of California Press).

Stevenson, Hayley, and John S. Dryzek (2014). *Democratizing Global Climate Governance* (Cambridge: Cambridge University Press).

Stiglitz, Joseph E. (2002). *Globalization and its Discontents* (New York: W.W. Norton).

Stiglitz, Joseph E., Amartya Sen, and Jean-Paul Fitoussi (2009). *Report by the Commission on the Measurement of Economic Performance and Social Progress* (Paris: Commission on the Measurement of Economic Performance and Social Progress).

Susskind, Lawrence, Sarah McKearnan, and Jennifer Thomas-Larmer (eds) (1999). *The Consensus-Building Handbook: A Comprehensive Guide to Reaching Agreement* (Thousand Oaks, CA: Sage).

Takacs, David (1996). *The Idea of Biodiversity: Philosophies of Paradise* (Baltimore, MD: Johns Hopkins University Press).

Täuber, Susanne, Martijn van Zomeren, and Maja Kutlaca (2015). Should the Moral Core of Climate Issues Be Emphasized or Downplayed in Public Discourse? Three Ways to Successfully Manage the Double-Edged Sword of Moral Communication. *Climatic Change* 130 (3): 453–64.

Tengö, Maria, Eduardo S. Brondizio, Thomas Elmqvist, Pernilla Malmer, and Marja Spierenburg (2014). Connecting Diverse Knowledge Systems for Enhanced Ecosystem Governance: The Multiple Evidence Base Approach. *Ambio* 43 (5): 579–91.

Terman, Rochelle, and Erik Voeten (2018). The Relational Politics of Shame: Evidence from the Universal Periodic Review. *Review of International Organizations* 13 (1): 1–23.

Thaler, Richard H., and Cass R. Sunstein (2008). *Nudge: Improving Decisions About Health, Wealth, and Happiness* (New Haven, CT: Yale University Press).

Thompson, Jennifer (2014). A History of Climate Justice. *Solutions* 5 (2): 89–92.

Torgerson, Douglas (1994). Strategy and Ideology in Environmentalism: A De-Centered Approach to Sustainability. *Industrial and Environmental Crisis Quarterly* 8: 295–321.

Torgerson, Douglas (1999). *The Promise of Green Politics: Environmentalism and the Public Sphere* (Durham, NC: Duke University Press).

Tutu, Desmond (2007). We Do Not Need Climate Change Apartheid in Adaptation. *UNDP Human Development Report blog.* http://hdr.undp.org/en/content/we-do-not-need-climate-change-apartheid-adaptation.

UN (2012). The Future We Want. A/RES/66/288 (11 September 2012).

UN (2015a). Secretary General's Remarks to Press Conference on the Outcome Document of the Post-2015 Development Agenda. 3 August 2015. http://www.un.org/sg/statements/index.asp?nid=8879.

UN (2015b). Transforming Our World: The 2030 Agenda for Sustainable Development. United Nations General Assembly Resolution A/RES/70/1 (21 October 2015).

UN (2017). My World Survey. https://myworld2030.org/.

UN Development Group (2013). *A Million Voices: The World We Want: A Sustainable Future with Dignity for All* (New York: United Nations).

UNDP and UNEP (2013). *Breaking Down the Silos: Integrating Environmental Sustainability in the Post-2015 Agenda.* Report of the Thematic Consultation on Environmental Sustainability in the Post-2015 Agenda (United Nations Development Programme and United Nations Environment Programme).

UNEP (2016a). *The Emissions Gap Report 2016* (Nairobi: United Nations Environment Programme).

UNEP (2016b). Amendment to the Montreal Protocol on Substances That Deplete the Ozone Layer ["Kigali Amendment"]. United Nations Environment Programme. http://conf.montreal-protocol.org/meeting/mop/mop-28/final-report/English/Kigali_Amendment-English.pdf.

UNFCCC (1992). United Nations Framework Convention on Climate Change. FCCC/INFOR-MAL/84 - GE.05-62220.

UNFCCC (2016). Adoption of the Paris Agreement. FCCC/CP/2015/10/Add.1 (29 January 2016).

UNFCCC (2017). Global Climate Action. http://climateaction.unfccc.int/.

Valentini, Laura (2011). *Justice in a Globalized World: A Normative Framework* (Oxford: Oxford University Press).

van Asselt, Harro (2016). The Role of Non-State Actors in Reviewing Ambition, Implementation, and Compliance under the Paris Agreement. *Climate Law* 6 (1–2): 91–108.

van Zeben, Josephine (2015). Establishing a Governmental Duty of Care for Climate Change Mitigation: Will Urgenda Turn the Tide? *Transnational Environmental Law* 4 (2): 339–57.

Vanderheiden, Steve (2008). Radical Environmentalism in an Age of Antiterrorism. *Environmental Politics* 17 (2): 299–318.

Vanderheiden, Steve (2015). Informational Approaches to Climate Justice. In *The Ethics of Climate Governance*, ed. Aaron Maltais and Catriona McKinnon (New York: Rowman & Littlefield), pp. 111–32.

Victorian Government (2016). Independent Inquiry into the Environmental Protection Authority. http://epa-inquiry.vic.gov.au/__data/assets/file/0008/336698/Inquiry-report-EPA_June.pdf.

Vogel, Steven (2015). *Thinking Like a Mall: Environmental Philosophy After the End of Nature* (Cambridge, MA: MIT Press).

Voigt, Christina, and Felipe Ferreira (2016). Differentiation in the Paris Agreement. *Climate Law* 6 (1–2): 58–74.

Waas, Tom, Jean Hugé, Aviel Verbruggen, and Tarah Wright (2011). Sustainable Development: A Bird's Eye View. *Sustainability* 3 (10): 1637–61.

Walker, Gordon (2012). *Environmental Justice: Concepts, Evidence and Politics* (London: Routledge).

Walzer, Michael (1983). *Spheres of Justice: A Defense of Pluralism and Equality* (New York: Basic Books).

Wapner, Paul (2014). The Changing Nature of Nature: Environmental Politics in the Anthropocene. *Global Environmental Politics* 14 (4): 36–54.

We Are Still In (2017). http://wearestillin.com/.

Weaver, Duncan (2018). The Aarhus Convention and Process Cosmopolitanism. *International Environmental Agreements: Politics, Law and Economics* 18 (2): 199–213.

WEF (2018). *The Global Risks Report 2018* (13th edn, Geneva: World Economic Forum).

Westley, Frances, Per Olsson, Carl Folke, Thomas Homer-Dixon, Harrie Vredenburg, Derk Loorbach, John Thompson, Måns Nilsson, Eric Lambin, Jan Sendzimir, Banny Banerjee, Victor Galaz, and Sander van der Leeuw (2011). Tipping toward Sustainability: Emerging Pathways of Transformation. *Ambio* 40 (7): 762–80.

Widerberg, Oscar (2017). The "Black Box" Problem of Orchestration: How to Evaluate the Performance of the Lima-Paris Action Agenda. *Environmental Politics* 26 (4): 715–37.

Wienhues, Anna (2017). Sharing the Earth: A Biocentric Account of Ecological Justice. *Journal of Agricultural and Environmental Ethics* 30 (3): 367–85.

Williston, Byron (2015). *The Anthropocene Project: Virtue in the Age of Climate Change* (Oxford: Oxford University Press).

Wilson, Edward O. (2016). *Half-Earth: Our Planet's Fight for Life* (New York: W.W. Norton).

Winkler, Harald, Niklas Höhne, Guy Cunliffe, Takeshi Kuramochi, Amanda April, and Maria Jose de Villafranca Casas (2017). Countries Start to Explain How Their Climate Contributions Are Fair: More Rigour Needed. *International Environmental Agreements: Politics, Law and Economics* 18 (1): 99–115.

Wisor, Scott (2012). After the MDGs: Citizen Deliberation and the Post-2015 Development Framework. *Ethics and International Affairs* 26 (1): 113–33.

Wohlleben, Peter (2016). *The Hidden Life of Trees: What they Feel, How They Communicate* (Carlton, Victoria: Black Inc.).

Wolf, Clark (1995). Contemporary Property Rights, Lockean Provisos, and the Interests of Future Generations. *Ethics* 105 (4): 791–818.

Wong, James K. (2016). A Dilemma of Green Democracy. *Political Studies* 64 (1 suppl.): 136–55.

World Bank (2017). World Development Indicators. https://data.worldbank.org/products/wdi.

World Commission on Environment and Development (1987). *Our Common Future* (Oxford: Oxford University Press).

WWF (2016). *Living Planet Report 2016: Risk and Resilience in a New Era* (Gland, Switzerland: WWF International).

Young, Iris Marion (2006). Responsibility and Global Justice: A Social Connection Model. *Social Philosophy and Policy* 23: 102–30.

Young, Iris Marion (2013). *Responsibility for Justice* (New York: Oxford University Press).

Young, Oran R. (2010). Institutional Dynamics: Resilience, Vulnerability and Adaptation in Environmental and Resource Regimes. *Global Environmental Change* 20 (3): 378–85.

Young, Oran R. (2017). *Governing Complex Systems: Social Capital for the Anthropocene* (Cambridge, MA: MIT Press).

Young, Oran R., Arild Underdal, Norichika Kanie, and Rakhyun E. Kim (2017). Goal Setting in the Anthropocene: The Ultimate Challenge of Planetary Stewardship. In *Governing through Goals: Sustainable Development Goals as Governance Innovation*, ed. Norichika Kanie and Frank Biermann (Cambridge, MA: MIT Press), pp. 53–74.

Ypi, Lea (2012). *Global Justice and Avant-Garde Political Agency* (Oxford: Oxford University Press).

Zalasiewicz, Jan, Colin N. Waters, Juliana A. Ivar do Sul, Patricia L. Corcoran, Anthony D. Barnosky, Alejandro Cearreta, Matt Edgeworth, Agnieszka Gałuszka, Catherine Jeandel, Reinhold Leinfelder, J. R. McNeill, Will Steffen, Colin Summerhayes, Michael Wagreich, Mark Williams, Alexander P. Wolfe, and Yasmin Yonan (2016). The Geological Cycle of Plastics and Their Use as a Stratigraphic Indicator of the Anthropocene. *Anthropocene* 13: 4–17.

Zalasiewicz, Jan, Colin N. Waters, Colin P. Summerhayes, Alexander P. Wolfe, Anthony D. Barnosky, Alejandro Cearreta, Paul Crutzen, Erle Ellis, Ian J. Fairchild, Agnieszka Gałuszka, Peter Haff, Irka Hajdas, Martin J. Head, Juliana A. Ivar do Sul, Catherine Jeandel, Reinhold Leinfelder, John R. McNeill, Cath Neal, Eric Odada, Naomi Oreskes, Will Steffen, James Syvitski, Davor Vidas, Michael Wagreich, and Mark Williams (2017). The Working Group on the Anthropocene: Summary of Evidence and Interim Recommendations. *Anthropocene* 19: 55–60.

INDEX

CPSIA information can be obtained
at www.ICGtesting.com
Printed in the USA
LVHW051927100123
736865LV00004B/232

9 780198 809623